BUILDING CHESTER

BY

PHILLIP E JONES

PAGE NO:	TITLE:
PAGE 3	CHAPTER ONE - INTRODUCTION
PAGE 10	CHAPTER TWO – BUILDERS AND ARCHITECTS
PAGE 20	CHAPTER THREE – CREATING THE CHESTER LOOK
PAGE 45	CHAPTER FOUR – THE HIGH CROSS
PAGE 49	CHAPTER FIVE – NORTHGATE STREET
PAGE 72	CHAPTER SIX – NORTHGATE AND BEYOND
PAGE 79	CHAPTER SEVEN – CHESTER CATHEDRAL AND ITS PRECINCTS
PAGE 87	CHAPTER EIGHT – WATERGATE STREET
PAGE 99	LOWER WATERGATE STREET
PAGE 106	NUNS ROAD AND CASTLE ESPLANADE
PAGE 111	CHESTER'S CASTLE AND COURT BUILDINGS
PAGE 123	CASTLE LANE AND GLOVERSTONE
PAGE 131	BRIDGE STREET
PAGE 145	LOWER BRIDGE STREET
PAGE 161	GROSVENOR STREET AND PEPPER STREET
PAGE 176	THE AMPHITHEATRE AND SAINT JOHN'S
PAGE 184	EASTGATE STREET
PAGE 197	FOREGATE STREET

THE AUTHOR

PHILLIP E JONES

CHAPTER ONE

INTRODUCTION

For a stranger to Chester, the opportunity to explore the streets and buildings of such an ancient city, with its near two millennia of continuous occupation, must promise much to the first time visitor. The presence of the city's almost intact circuit of defensive walls, its many early churches, world famous shopping Rows and its overtly historical character, all suggest a city that has its foundations in earlier times and with a few exceptions one that is totally bereft of the ugly utilitarian architecture, common in most modern English city's. However, it is precisely because of its great age, that the city has in fact been constantly subjected to regular periods of development, destruction and renovation throughout its history, a process that continues to reshape the precincts of the former Roman fortress even through to the present day.

Starting with the impressive sandstone buildings of the Romans, Chester has successively been inhabited by the dwellings and structures of the post-Roman Britons, the Anglo-Saxons and the Normans. Later still, there were those of the medieval subjects of the Plantagenet kings, the inhabitants of Tudor Chester, then the Stuarts, the Georgians, Victorians; and finally, those of the modern age, with all of these periods and their people's adding their distinctive character to the city that stands today.

Following the restoration of British rule in the late 4th or early 5th centuries most of the land is thought to have returned to the ownership of the individual monarchs or tribal leaders who held power within their own particular regions and that would certainly have included the inner precincts of the former Roman fortress at Chester. Although large scale reuse of this land is thought to have been impossible, given the presence of the many still standing larger Roman buildings which may or may not have been reoccupied, the smaller, less robust structures, such as the rows of legionary barracks, storerooms and workshops were speculated to have been swept away, so that the site could then be used for other more peaceful purposes, such as settlement and agricultural.

However, for hundreds of years the vitally important sea port of Chester was reported to have been fought over and successively occupied by the Britons of Wales and the newly emerging Anglo Saxon peoples who had first settled in Britain during the 5th century. These ongoing disputes, which ultimately would have prevented long term settlement of the land, both inside and outside of the fortress' defensive walls was only thought to have finally been resolved in the 7th century, around the time that Aethelred, the king of Mercia was said to have ordered the construction of the first Anglo Saxon church of St John the Baptist at Chester around 689 AD.

Where definitive evidence of Anglo Saxon habitation has been found, both inside and outside of the fortress' defences, it suggests a relatively modest level of occupation and cultivation. A small number of sites have been discovered, all of which indicate isolated pockets of ploughed land and meagre buildings constructed with simple timbers and covered with thatched roofs. One of these sites, located behind the modern western frontages of today's Lower Bridge Street and close to the river, suggested that there had been limited use of the land, followed by a period of abandonment and then a further period of use.

Typically, Anglo Saxon lands of the time, especially those in a settlement and bordering its earlier Roman streets or roads would have been portioned out into long individual strips, approximately ten metres wide and 30 metres deep, which would have ran backwards from the main thoroughfare. As a major regional sea port, trade centre and stopping-off point for those travelling between the north and south of Britain, Chester with its already well established Roman street plan was entirely different from the numbers of new settlements, which were beginning to spring up elsewhere during the same period and which often allowed for an entirely different street layout.

It has been suggested that where these early individual plots were occupied by merchants, tradesmen and manufacturers, then their street frontages would have contained the stalls and booths from which they sold their wares. Initially, these would have been simple timber built structures that could be secured at night and behind which the merchant and his family would have lived. His workshops, stores and animals would have been housed at the rear of the property, possibly separated from the living area by wooden or wattle and daub hurdles, with yet another part of the site given over to food production or possibly fuel storage.

Records suggest that many of the substantial buildings built, employed and then subsequently abandoned by the Roman's were later "robbed out" by successive generations of British or Anglo Saxon inhabitants of Chester, no doubt to be used in the construction of the extended city defences, or the foundations of the city's newly arriving religious houses, with only the most formidable architectural elements left in place for future generations to find. The western and southern walls of the former Roman fortress were both thought to have become victims of this largely medieval practice, having become obsolete following the Anglo Saxon extension of the city's defences in the late 9th and early 10th centuries. A similar fate was thought to have befallen the Roman Principia and Praetorium buildings, both of which stood at the centre of the military fortress, in the area of the modern day Town Hall and its indoor market. The little of these two impressive structures that does remain in situ is mainly buried beneath later Anglo Saxon churches, or has been swept away entirely during the modern day redevelopment of the area.

During the Anglo Saxon occupation of Chester, from the late 7th century through to the 11th century, when the city finally fell to the Norman forces of Duke William, Chester's inner precincts were thought to have been far more sparsely populated than they are today. Large sections of this inner ground was thought to have been given over to both industrial and agricultural purposes, including the city's famed leather industries and the individual share-croppers that were reported to have been granted land in return for protecting the city from its many potential enemies. Once again, in the area of today's Lower Bridge Street, archaeologists have uncovered evidence of later Anglo Saxon occupation and activity, notably the discovery of sunken tanning pits which were thought to have been used by the city's leather tanners who occupied this section of the city, but were then displaced by the forces of William the Conqueror who arrived in the second half of the 11th century. It is perhaps worth noting that such discoveries are always likely to be fairly fragmentary, given that much of Chester's inner city fabric remains occupied by historic buildings and their even earlier substructures, some of which can have timbers and beams dating from the 13th century.

The advent of the Norman occupation of Chester is said to have witnessed the arrival of much larger scale buildings, particularly the religious houses which settled in the city with the approval and under the protection of the Earls of Chester, who were first appointed by

William the Conqueror in around 1070. It was during the following 167 year period that a series of new stone-built structures were raised in the city, including the numerous Churches, Convents, Chapel's and of course the great Halls of the noble lords who attended the Earl at Chester. Today, very few if any of these grand buildings survive above street level and those that do have been modified or restructured to meet later housing styles, tastes or needs and much of what does remain, is often hidden behind much later building structures.

As time passed, construction techniques improved and as the merchant classes became more successful and of course wealthier, their early booths and stalls would have given way to much more substantial multi-layered buildings which occupied a greater part of the individual plot. First formally recorded in around 1331, it is thought that the elevated shopping Rows in Chester have actually been in existence from the middle of the 13th century. Their construction was thought to have been brought about by the accumulation of debris and rubbish left by earlier periods of occupation, most notably by the Roman's and their large military buildings, which caused a height differential between street level and the land which lay beyond the main thoroughfares. As a consequence, supporting under-crofts or cellars were built to provide a level platform on which to build the first floor stores and medieval halls, where the merchants could conduct their business and accommodate their families.

The raised buildings themselves were reported to be similar in style to their ground level contemporaries, being large covered halls which incorporated a first floor shop front, that sat directly beneath the private chambers or solar which accommodated the owner and his family. To the rear of the shop front and often as high as both shop and private chamber was the main hall of the property where the family ate their meals and entertained their visitors, as well as being used to accommodate a number of their staff or servants during the night. Before the advent of the brick built chimney in the 15th or 16th centuries, most of these halls would have had a central hearth, standing on a substantial earthen or sandstone floor that reduced the likelihood of fire which occasionally got out of control and engulfed the timber building that surrounded it. Once brick and stone built fireplaces became more readily available and commonplace, they tended to be located at a central point of the property or at the rear gable end of the building, their construction helping to reduce the potential for accidental blazes.

The street level under-crofts or cellars which underpinned these elevated halls generally had sandstone walls or stone-built arches which supported the great weight of the rooms constructed above them, often with massive timbers helping to carry the immense loads. This newly created space would often have been used as a shop, storeroom or workshop, but was not always owned by the same person who lived above. A number of the 13th and 14th century under-crofts that continue to exist in Chester today, were undoubtedly formed in this manner; and most are of such good quality and construction, that they were obviously undertaken on behalf the very wealthiest individuals who could afford the extremely high cost of building them. Bearing that in mind, it seems likely that most, if not all, such under-crofts would have been covered by great medieval halls or houses which is not always the case in modern day Chester, suggesting that a good number of these grand properties have been subsequently destroyed or demolished in later times. These same cellars are also commonly associated with Chester's vital and vibrant medieval sea port, where exotic spices, foreign wines and continental fabrics were first landed in England, before being stored in the rock cut or stone built under-crofts which sat below the specific merchant's property.

Rather than the extensive single terrace of elevated shops that we know today, the early versions of these raised walkways were thought to have been separated by intersecting banks and ditches which marked the boundary of each individual plot of land. In some cases these gaps later developed into the passageways and city thoroughfares which were later added into the medieval street plan, but in most cases were simply absorbed into the adjoining buildings as they were subsequently rebuilt over time. The very presence of these early boundary markers might in fact account for the inevitable emergence of the interlinked elevated rows for which Chester has become world renowned, with neighbouring merchants linking their adjoining properties by way of wooden planks or timber bridges, thus saving their clients from having to climb individual stairwell's to each and every property that they wished to visit. Today's Leen Lane, Godstall Lane and Feathers Lane are perhaps remnants of these early property boundaries, which have subsequently developed into narrow thoroughfares that have been added into the city's ancient fabric. Early records also suggest that both Leen Lane and its neighbour, Godstall Lane, both of which now exist at an elevated position on the north side of Eastgate Street, in fact began their lives as narrow, street level passageways that ran northward on a steep incline towards the churchyard of St Oswald's within Chester's Norman Abbey precincts.

On the western flank of modern day Bridge Street, at its junction with White Friars, there is a stone façade comprised of three arches, which today proclaims a date of 1274, although it is known to have been refaced and renovated since that time. Nevertheless, given its stated construction date and the original materials employed, both of which would be contemporary with many of the city's stone built under-crofts, clearly this was the site of an important building erected by an extremely wealthy and influential person within the city; and perhaps suggests what a large number of Chester's 13th century buildings might well have looked like in the 13th and 14th centuries. However, this particular buildings close proximity to the former sites of St Bridget's Church and the city's Carmelite Friary, which were both said to have been in existence during the property's stated construction period, might equally suggest that the façade owes as much to a religious connection, as it does to a more secular one.

An additional feature of these elevated shops and first floor town houses were the street level covered arcades which were undoubtedly a greater feature in early Chester than they are today. Thought to have started off as weight supporting beams for the piers or overhangs which formed part of the city's medieval buildings they inadvertently became a covered walkway for those that were walking along or working at street level. Later still, such porches and arcades were added to buildings, not as a necessary support, but purely as an architectural feature which might add to the comfort and experience of the shoppers that visited the individual business premises, rather like the Sedan Chair porches which were added to the houses of some of the city's most wealthy inhabitants during the 18th century. At a time when most of Chester's main shopping streets were thought to have been little better than open sewers, it was commonplace for all sorts of effluent to be cast out of the upper storey shops and apartments and it was perhaps gratifying for the shopper in the city centre to have both covered rows and arcades to shelter beneath, rather than risk being drenched by something unspeakably vile. It also seems apparent that over time Chester's main shopping streets became much narrower and more crowded as both buildings and store fronts continued to encroach further forward into the main thoroughfares, leaving little room for the hawkers and shoppers who were all jostling for the same limited space. Even up till the late 18th and early 19th centuries most of Chester's main shopping streets, but more notably the city's High Cross and Market Square, were known to have been much more cramped and far narrower than their present day counterparts, simply because of the levels of unregulated encroachment by the city's various business communities.

The next great period of change in land ownership came during the 16th century, following the nationwide Dissolution of the Monasteries by Henry VIII during the 1540's, which saw the great Norman Abbey's, Churches and Monasteries stripped of their historic status and authority, their often substantial financial assets and their generally extensive property holdings. Chester's 500 year old Norman Abbey was far more fortunate than a number of the city's other religious houses however, being re-founded as the Cathedral of Christ and The Blessed Virgin, although in a much more reduced and far poorer state. This was a better fate though, than that which faced the Franciscan, Dominican and Carmelite Friars and the Benedictine Nuns of St Mary's in Chester, all of whom were dispossessed of their houses and properties by the Crown. Within the modern day city the lands which had previously been owned by these religious communities included the area to the west of the city stretching from the River Dee northward to the city walls, incorporating today's Grey Friars, Black Friars, Nuns Road, Stanley Place, City Walls Road and Linenhall Place. The Carmelite's former home had included much of the area now enclosed by Grosvenor Street in the south, Watergate Street to the north, Bridge Street to the east and Nicholas Street to the west. Having seized the lands of the city's religious orders, the King and his agents, were then reported to have either granted or sold the properties to members of the local aristocracy, leased them to local merchants and landowners or simply put them in the hands of the corporation who subsequently sold them or rented them out to raise local revenues.

Prior to the 17th century and the highly divisive and destructive English Civil War in which Chester played such a pivotal role, much of the centre of the city would have been occupied by large numbers of great medieval buildings, commonly owned by the landed Royalist family's of the age or the more successful city merchants. In complete contrast to these ornate and wealthy buildings however, the city would also have played host to large swathes of poor quality housing, specifically built to accommodate the many traders, labourers and workmen who made their living within the city walls, serving Chester's thriving mercantile community or their more aristocratic neighbours.

In fact, many of the city's current landmark buildings that continually draw admiration from both resident and visitor alike, are in fact, simply modern day facsimiles for much earlier structures which had been systematically removed during periods of redevelopment or which were known to have been destroyed during military engagements, particularly during the 17th century when the city was besieged by the forces of the English Parliament. Many ancient Chester houses were deliberately demolished by the Royalist defenders of the city, in order to prevent them providing cover or sustenance for their enemies who lay outside the historic battlements; and many more within the walls were thought to have been destroyed by Parliamentary cannon fire, which was employed to undermine the defensive will of Chester's Royalist garrison, by essentially destroying the city around their ears.

An incalculable amount of damage was done to the city's historic buildings and civic infrastructure during the period September 1645 to February 1646, when the city was subjected to regular bombardment and a very close siege, instigated by the Parliamentary commander Sir William Brereton, who owned property in the city. Eastgate Street and Watergate Street were both said to have been particularly hard hit by the Parliamentary cannon fire and most of the outlying properties in Northgate Street, Foregate Street and the outlying suburb of Handbridge were reported to have been deliberately razed from the ground by the Royalist defenders of the city, thus preventing them being used by the Parliamentarians as firing points or as accommodations.

Apart from the city's circuit of defensive walls, its great Norman Abbey, its collection of ancient churches and Chester's then still hidden Roman amphitheatre; very little has remained untouched by this notable military confrontation, or the subsequent 300 years of relative peace and diminishing national importance, which has seen the former fortress deliberately shift its civic identity from that of ancient military base and international trading port, to one of regional tourist attraction and retail shopping centre. Consequently, much of Chester's modern day architecture owes much more to the noted architects of the 18th, 19th and 20th centuries, rather than to any of those now forgotten and generally obscure medieval builders who preceded them.

Much of Chester's medieval architecture was thought to have been swept away over the period of 250 years, beginning in the reign of Henry VIII and finishing in the Georgian period, when fairly large scale redevelopments were taking place throughout the city. Although extensive building work took place during the late 18th century, much of this was on land that 200 years earlier had been owned by the city's medieval religious centres and therefore had little impact on the look of central Chester and its historic main streets. Where rebuilding did take place, architects, builders and local authorities tried to ensure that earlier styles were replicated where possible and where frontages had to be replaced or altered, then the inner timbers of the property, often dating from the 15th, 16th and 17th centuries were retained where possible. Few relatively complete buildings from these periods continue to stand in the city today though, save for the Blue Bell Inn and the previously noted Three Arches, although a large number of 13th, 14th and 15th cellars or under-crofts continue to underpin today's modern buildings.

Perhaps because of its historic character and a failure to redevelop anything other than the main streets of the city, by the middle of the 19th century, Chester was reported to have had over 150 housing "courts" within the city, all of which were typically poor quality, high density units, which were little better than medieval "hovels". Often centred round small plots of land that had been formally owned by Chester's dissolved religious houses, many of these buildings were said to have been raised by unscrupulous builders and landlords eager to make money from the very poorest inhabitants of the city. The worst of these "courts" were thought to be located at the rear of the city's famous shopping streets, out of sight of the visiting tourists and shoppers, but close enough to be a nuisance and health hazard for Chester's relatively affluent traders, shopkeepers and property owners.

The worst of this housing was said to be at the rear of the city's Watergate Street, Lower Bridge Street, Shoemaker's Row and adjoining Commonhall, Castle, Goss, Crook and Trinity Streets, all of which lay just behind the main street frontages which played host to the thousands of tourists and visitors to the city. At the rear of the finely constructed buildings of Watergate Street stood Posnett's Court and Chapel Court, the latter being associated with a Baptist Chapel that had been established there in 1806, but which in a little over a century had been demolished to make way for the photographic laboratories of Will R Rose. In the same area of the city and being equally dire and perilous was Cathcart's Square, which had previously been known as Herbert's Yard, before becoming Herbert's Court and finally Cathcart's Square. Although any further construction of such housing courts were reported to have been prohibited under the terms of the 1845 Improvement Act, those that did remain in the city, along with other later equally poor high density housing, continued to be one of the less favourable features of the city right through to the first half of the 20th century.

Standing above the site of much earlier Roman archaeology, including the much discussed and as yet still unidentified "elliptical building" discovered during the 1960's excavation of the Market Hall site, this area of slum housing stretched from Watergate Street in the south to Princess Street in the north and was bounded by St Martin's Way and Northgate Street to the west and east respectively. Many of these courts were generally constructed around former stables, yards, industrial buildings and back gardens which had existed for hundreds of years and which were often completely unsuitable for domestic occupation. Despite this, local landlords and builders simply converted older standing properties or raised rudimentary brick and slate, up and down terraces, piped in communal water sources, laid down basic drainage and then rented their improvised housing to the city's most needy and poorest inhabitants.

Although the streets to the rear of Chester's impressive Town Hall and Market Hall were said to have played host to the largest area of slum housing within the city, equally poor housing was reported to have existed throughout the wider area. Shepherd's Court near Newgate Street and Victoria Buildings off Lower Bridge Street, were just two further examples of these "courts", where a back to back, two up and two down terraced cottage could cost its tenants up to ten shillings per week, a substantial amount for a poorly paid manual worker. Gough's Court was located just off Upper Northgate Street, Parke's Court was situated near Love Street, whilst Davies' Court, which was sited off Steam Mill Street was renowned for being infested with rats, no doubt caused by the great amounts of cereal crops being transported and stored along the length of the city's canal system.

Fortunately though, over the past 50 years or so many of these poor quality courts and tenements have been consigned to history, demolished as part of the wider modernisation of the city centre, with their former and future tenants being re-housed in the then newly built suburban housing estates of Newton, Blacon, Handbridge and Saltney. However, along with the welcomed demise of these sites, Chester was also thought to have lost a large number of archaeological treasures, most notably those that were destroyed during the construction of the city's inner ring road system, as well as the accompanying Forum and Grosvenor Shopping Centre developments.

The purpose of this book is to try and investigate the development of Chester, in terms of the city's historic streets and landmark buildings, as well as identifying the individual masons, builders and architects who are responsible for creating the city that stands today.

CHAPTER TWO

BUILDERS AND ARCHITECTS

Builders as such, are known to have existed for thousands of years, ever since mankind first decided to construct shelters from the native materials that existed around him, as opposed to living in naturally occurring caves and hollows. However, it was probably only with the dawn of permanent settlement, as opposed to the temporary camps of itinerant hunter gatherers, that the skills of what we would now recognise as a builder began to be developed and appreciated, although in all likelihood, basic construction skills would have been shared amongst the men of the village, who would have worked together to build their community.

Although Chester's extensive history generally begins with the legions of Rome, there is ample evidence to indicate that the site of our modern city, at one time played host to a pre-Roman Iron Age community, who occupied and farmed the land for hundreds of years, before finally being driven off or destroyed by the incoming legionary forces. However, unlike their military successors who left their immense defensive walls, great communal buildings and occasional works of art, as evidence of their extensive occupation, their Iron Age predecessors left little more than post holes and pits, many of which were swept away or simply hidden by the later grandiose architecture of the Roman builders of Chester.

Even where evidence of pre-Roman occupation remains intact though, its very nature prevents identification of the individual builder, bearing in mind that most Iron Age houses would have been made of timber, mud and thatch, which usually would have been built by an individual settler or possibly by members of that particular community. Even assuming that such people had been inclined to mark their work, which was most certainly not the case, the very nature of the building materials themselves would have assured anonymity, as it rotted away, leaving only indentations and soil discolouration to actually identify its very existence.

Although the succeeding Roman builders of Chester were known to be far more skilled than their British counterparts, in terms of constructing buildings of a far greater scale and from a greater variety of materials, they too seem to have built their military fortresses and great civic buildings in a communal fashion, rather than having to employ individually skilled builders. Along the length of Chester's still standing Roman walls, there are stone cut records recalling the efforts of individual legionary units, who were assigned the task of erecting a particular section of the fortress' defensive wall, suggesting that all members of the resident legion were well enough trained to build their camp to a given standard.

The arrival of Rome's legions during the first half of the 1st century probably also saw the dawn of the specialist craftsmen, the masons, smiths and the carpenters who brought with them the tools of their trades, enabling them to produce work of a standard previously unimagined by their British counterparts. It is also likely that the 2nd Legion that first occupied the site at Chester had amongst its ranks a military engineer who was entirely responsible for the structure and layout of the fortress, as well as the many buildings that lay within its walled precincts.

Prior to the Romans, British building projects were thought to have been entirely limited by both knowledge and generally inadequate skill levels, which saw building sizes and weights limited by the almost sole use of timber posts and lintels. The arrival of the Roman military builders, surveyors and engineers however, with their much more efficient load bearing pillars and arches, coupled with their ability to employ a variety of materials, including concrete and sandstone allowed them to construct buildings of a much greater size and with a far greater life span.

By the late 4th and early 5th centuries though, the Romans were reported to have abandoned Britain, as well as the many thousands of buildings that they had constructed during their 300 year occupation of the province. Along with the soldiers themselves, the skills and techniques used to design and build these impressive Roman facades also seems to have left the country at the same time; and it would be another 500 years before the next stage of Chester's building development would begin, with the builders and engineers who came to Britain with the forces of Duke William of Normandy.

Although a number of substantial Anglo Saxon buildings were thought to have been constructed throughout Britain between the 5th and 11th centuries, mostly by native Kings, the vast majority of dwellings, including Royal Halls were still constructed of timber, mud, thatch, as well as wattle and daub. The main exception to these basic and often temporary buildings were Britain's growing number of religious houses, but even these were fairly rudimentary constructions, sometimes built using recycled stonework that had been taken from much earlier, but by then abandoned Roman buildings.

According to local records, prior to Duke William's capture of the city in 1070, there were reported to be at least five such religious houses in Chester, four lying within the precincts of the extended Anglo Saxon fortress and the final one, located close to the site of the Roman's abandoned amphitheatre. Dating from before its rededication to St Werburgh in around 875 AD by the Anglo Saxon leader Aethelflaeda, the first of these early Anglo Saxon churches was reported to have previously been dedicated to Saint's Peter and Paul and has been speculated to have a late Roman foundation, following the adoption of Christianity as the official religion of the Empire by the Emperor Constantine. Earlier still, this same site, now marked by Chester's magnificent Cathedral, was reputed to have housed a temple dedicated to the Roman deity Apollo, replacing an even earlier native British shrine which was said to have pre-dated the invasion of Britain in the 1st century AD.

Today's St Peter's church, at Chester's High Cross is reported to have been re-founded by Aethelflaeda towards the end of the 9th or beginning of the 10th century, following the Anglo Saxon leaders use of its former home as the site for St Werbugh's new Abbey church, which was dedicated sometime around 875 AD. The third city church that was said to pre-date the Norman conquest of Chester was the one dedicated to St Bridget, which was otherwise known as St Brides. Formerly occupying a site at the junction of Bridge Street and Lower Bridge Street, this ancient church was reported to stand on, or close to the site of the Porta Praetoria, the long since extinct southern gate of the Roman fortress.

Supposedly dating from the 8th century and having been founded on the orders of the monarch, King Offa, this historic church, along with the nearby St Michael's, was said to have formed the "two churches" that became a notable city landmark for hundreds of years. Sadly though, unlike its religious partner, St Bridget's became a victim of the city's redevelopment during the 19th century and eventually passed into history.

The fourth and final city church that is said to have preceded Duke William's capture of Chester in 1070 is the generally small former parish church of St Olave's, which stands on the eastern flank of today's Lower Bridge Street. Dedicated to a canonised monarch who was reported to have died in 1030, there is a suggestion that this church had existed well before the death of King Olaf and that its dedication to his memory is of a much later date, possibly sometime after Chester had fallen to the Norman invaders. The fifth of these Anglo Saxon churches; and the only one lying outside of the city's defences, was known to have been dedicated to St John the Baptist and was said to have been founded by King Aethelred of Mercia in around 689 AD, as the result of a dream regarding a white hart attributed to that particular monarch. It has been suggested that the first church was built by its religious community re-using the huge sandstone blocks from the abandoned Roman amphitheatre that stood close by.

In common with the invading Romans who conquered Britain some 1000 years earlier, the forces of William the Conqueror were thought to have been accompanied by the skilled military engineers, architects and builders who had helped him to build his continental kingdom, including its many castles, towns and cities. The greatest building developments generally credited to King William I and his new Norman administration in Britain was the multitude of new Christian Churches and Abbey's, alongside that particularly continental military invention, the motte and bailey castle.

Although many of these individual Norman castles, Abbey's, Monasteries and Churches are commonly ascribed to the particular nobleman who founded or funded them, in reality they were almost certainly designed and built by other more qualified, but largely unknown military engineers and architects acting on behalf of the monarch or church authorities. Within specific religious houses, the will of the presiding Abbot generally determined the layout, scale and timetable for the development of the building, with experienced church architects preparing the plans in conjunction with the head of the house, local nobles supplying the finance and members of the religious community supplying the labour and materials.

The same was thought to be true in the construction of Britain's numerous castles and keeps, raised in the years following William's successful conquest of the native British forces. Although most of these fortress' are attributed to the nobleman or landowner who bore the financial cost of building them, their construction, design and physical layout was generally determined by a small number of military engineers whose expertise was in this particular field and who would travel the country to advise and watch over the construction of these individual fortresses. As with the Churches, Abbey's and Monasteries that were being built around the same time, these new defensive positions were thought to have been constructed by members of the local military garrison, whose numbers were supplemented by hired labourers, or perhaps more commonly by members of the local civilian population who were forced or coerced into helping to build the new military base.

It was also largely thanks to the new Norman administration that permanent records of both national and local building work and perhaps more importantly, those responsible for overseeing them began to be kept. However, one of the earliest and most notable architects cum engineers in Chester was not recorded until the late 13th and early 14th centuries.

Richard L'enginour has been attributed with the title of "Engineer", when in reality he was thought to be a Master Mason, who was said to have been employed by Edward I to help construct his castles at Chester, Flint, Rhuddlan and Conwy following the king's bitter wars with the native Princes of North Wales. Notably, Edward was reported to have granted the Dee Mills to his master mason and provided him with allowances for the grinding of corn during a "time of war". Despite his efforts in helping to secure Edward's hold on the Principality though, much of the credit for building these impressive Plantagenet fortresses has largely been credited to a much better known foreign military engineer and architect, Master James St George, who was reported to have been employed by the king directly.

Around the same time that he was involved with Edward's grand castle building campaign, Richard was also said to have been directly responsible for the reconstruction of the ancient Weir at Chester, as well as some of the first of the long extinct Dee Mills which used to grind the city's corn. L'enginour was reported to have held the office of Mayor of Chester between 1304 and 1305 and was said to have died in 1315. By the time of his death though, Richard was known to have acquired substantial grants at both Pulford and Eccleston and his extensive lands at Eaton were said to have been settled on his daughter when she married.

By 1310, Richard was also thought to have demolished the Abbey's early Presbytery to make way for additional piers within the still comparatively new church building. A shrine dedicated to St Werburgh was also reported to have been built between the High Altar and the Lady Chapel around the same time, but this was later said to have been severely damaged during the Dissolution instigated by King Henry VIII. Three years before his death the "Engineer" was also known to have completed the construction of St Werburgh's Choir at the city's medieval Abbey in around 1312.

Richard's contemporaries and successors in Chester included the likes of Robert de Paris or otherwise recorded as Parisius, John de Helpeston and Robert Fagan, all of whom were recorded as having been employed in and around the city in the early part of the 14th century. De Paris was thought to be a master mason in his own right who was reported to have been employed by the much notable L'enginour to undertake work on King Edward's castles, specifically those at Chester and at Flint. Following the death of L'enginour in 1315 Paris was recorded to have purchased the late engineer's home, which lay close to the ancient church of St Olave's in Chester's Lower Bridge Street. This property was later known as "Praer's Hall" or "Hawarden Hall", the former title thought to reflect a variation of de Paris' family name.

John de Helpeston is perhaps best remembered in the city, as the builder of Chester's Water Tower which was also called the New Tower and was primarily built to protect the city's ancient port, although with the subsequent silting and "canalisation" of the River Dee it now stands apart from the waters that it was built to defend. This tower is commonly thought to date from 1331, although different records suggest separate dates, with one stating 1322 and another 1336, although the stated building cost of £100 remains the same in most historical records. Another member of this family, William de Helpeston who was also reported as a Master Mason in the second half of the 14th century, was recorded to have undertaken building work on the eastern choir at Chester's Norman Abbey, having earlier signed a contract with the Abbot.

Robert Fagan was reported to be a master mason in the northwest of England around the end of the 14th century and like his contemporaries Robert de Paris and John de Helpeston was thought to have helped construct many of the major buildings and defensive structures within Chester. In 1391 he was reported to have constructed the Bell Tower at St Asaph cathedral and the following year agreed a contract with the agent of the Earl of Arundel to build a bridge over the River Dee near Chirk. In 1396 Fagan was appointed as the Master Mason of Cheshire and North Wales for life and two years later was contracted to repair the various castles of North Wales by the king's agents. As part of this contract, Fagan was given permission to employ as many stone-masons and workmen he felt were needed to complete the task.

Although there were undoubtedly many more masons and master masons living and working in Chester around the same period, they often remain largely unrecorded, save for their individual marks which were etched into the physical fabric of the buildings that they created. However a number of the medieval crypts dating from between the 13th and 15th centuries which still exist in Chester through to the modern day might well owe their original construction to the likes of Fagan, de Paris, de Helpeston or their predecessor L'enginour.

Over the next two centuries building trends were thought to have remained relatively unchanged in Chester, with most city properties being constructed of timber, apart from those owned by the crown or the church, both of whom could afford to build in the more expensive stone. However, by the beginning of the 16th century the manufacturing and use of bricks, largely ignored in Britain since the time of the Roman occupation, was actively encouraged by local authorities and most notably by the crown. Although clearly expensive materials to begin with, as brick making was still in its infancy, landed aristocrats and wealthy merchants initially built their new properties in a half timbered style, thereby reducing the cost of building, but benefiting greatly from the advantages of these new construction materials, not least because of its fire retarding properties.

Although the house brick itself would have been a major innovation of the Tudor age, the likelihood is that their use as a construction material would have held few fears for the skilled masons and stoneworkers of the period, who were used to handling much larger and heavier blocks of quarried stone. As bricks began to replace stonework as the preferred building materials for new houses, no doubt a shortage of skilled workman soon made itself apparent and ultimately led to the development of the specialist brick layer, who then took his place alongside the city's masons, slaters, carpenters and paviors.

In Chester, city records for the 17th and 18th centuries note an ever increasing number of young men who were being apprenticed to local bricklayers; such was the demand for these workmen's services. Generally contracted for a period of some seven years, having completed their apprenticeship, many of these young men would then be employed on a full time basis by their former teacher or would find work as "jobbing" bricklayers, travelling around the region from one job to another.

A 17th century Chester builder who was particularly noteworthy was one William Hughes, who was said to have become embroiled in a civil case with a member of the Randal Holme family in 1671, in a dispute relating to the construction and cost of Holmes' "Old Lamb's Row" building which at that time stood at the southern end of Bridge Street. Hughes had been elected a Freeman of the city in 1664 and appears to have been a highly successful builder and brick manufacturer in Chester, with records suggesting that in 1682 his kiln at Hough Green was producing around 40,000 bricks a year, many of which were no doubt used to help rebuild the city following the devastation caused by the English Civil War. Between 1679 and 1680 he was reported to have built a property close to the Cow Lane cockpit and bowling green in the city, which is thought to be marked by the modern day Catholic Club in Brook Street. Another Hughes, called John, a brother to William was also known to have worked in the building trade around the same time, only this time as a Slater. One Thomas Yates was reported to have been employed by William Hughes as a bricklayer in 1671 and yet another Chester builder was Thomas Morris, who is recorded to have built a house in Newgate Street for a local barrister called Andrew Kenrick.

Morris appears to have been notable for his inability to manage his finances however, borrowing heavily against his assets and ultimately leaving his family with numerous debts that were only finally settled some years after the builder himself had died. Born the son of a city Linen Draper and Bricklayer, Thomas was admitted as a Freeman of Chester in 1688 by right of being the son of a city Freeman and although his trade was not reported at the time, it has subsequently been assumed that he was a "jobbing" builder, making his living by undertaking his own individual construction projects or by sub-contracting his labour to other city builders of the time.

Sometime around 1703/4, Morris was said to have made an agreement with a local Barrister called Kenrick to construct a new mansion house that the lawyer would then rent from the builder. The site of the proposed new property was thought to have been located close to the historic "Wolf Gate" and lay below the level of the city's defensive walls, an area now occupied by the Bridgewater Arms, a multi-storey office building and the entrance to the Grosvenor Precincts car park and delivery bays. Having purchased the site and received the necessary permission from the city Corporation to demolish the existing cottages and outbuildings, as well as to build his new property, Morris then seems to have faced an almost immediate financial problem. Being a man of little means, he was forced to borrow money from a number of sources in order to complete the project and it was this lack of finance and the servicing of these debts that would ultimately prove to be his undoing.

Although it was reported that Morris had borrowed several hundred pounds to build the new city mansion in the first place, by the end of 1704 the property was still incomplete and although he was said to have finished the stables and coach houses, the mansion itself had only been raised to its second floor and still required further work and investment. Forced to borrow even more money from city lenders, including the parish of St Bridget's which loaned him the sum of £25, Thomas was thought to be finding it increasingly difficult to meet the interest payments on his outstanding loans, let alone the principal amount borrowed.

Eventually however, Morris was thought to have completed work on the property and his new tenant, Andrew Kenrick and his family were finally able to take up the tenancy of their new home, although the rent agreed between the two men failed to fully cover the outstanding debts that Morris had accrued in actually building the house. Consequently, Morris' creditors were reported to have pursued the unfortunate builder for their outstanding monies, including the unpaid interest and sought to recover their loans from the sale of Morris' assets, including presumably, the Kenrick's mansion.

Almost inevitably the matter became embroiled in extensive legal wrangling which seems to have only been finalised in 1718, when Kenrick himself purchased the property and in doing so, helping to settle most of the outstanding debts that Morris' surviving family members had been burdened with. As for the hapless builder himself, he was reported to have later found employment as a shoe-maker in the city and spent the remainder of his life trying to service the debts that his speculative property venture had left him with.

Despite the development of the brick building industry throughout the country and the occasional practice of re-facing ancient stone walls with much newer brickwork, the sheer numbers of historic Churches, Chapels, Castles, Abbey's and Cathedrals ensured that the skills of the medieval master mason would remain very much in demand. One John Shaw was reported to be a Master Mason in Chester who was asked by the Constable of the castle, Thomas Lount, to undertake repairs on parts of the fortress that formerly housed prisoners, notably the gatehouse of the outer bailey, as well as the Exchequer building.

Shaw reported that the castle buildings were in a fairly ruinous condition and that parts of the gatehouse had already fallen down, much to the danger of the soldiers on guard and passers-by. He also reported that the remaining part of the gatehouse, that part still standing, was so seriously decayed that if it was not taken down, then it would surely fall down of its own accord. Within the wider castle complex, the Prothonotary's lodgings, the Constables lodgings and the Grand Jury room, the Judges lodging and the ancient Flag Tower were all reported to be in poor condition and all required urgent remedial work which would cost several hundreds of pounds to complete.

Another noted city mason of the early 18th century was John Tilston who was responsible for rebuilding the fairly ruinous Pemberton's Parlour on the city walls around 1709 and was also thought to be involved in helping to reconstruct other parts of the still badly damaged city fabric, much of which still bore the scars of the Civil War siege that had taken place some 60-odd years earlier. Tilston was also remembered for his ornate statue of Queen Anne dressed in her coronation robes, which at one time graced the city's new Exchange Building, the predecessor of today's Victorian Town Hall, which had first been raised in 1698 but was then destroyed by fire in 1862.

The 100 years marking the end of the Civil War hostilities in 1645 through to the middle of the 18th century seems to have been the period when Chester was fundamentally altered, changing it from a vitally important military outpost and embarkation point, to a quaint residential backwater that might make a living from its many archaeological treasures and retail outlets. Together with its geographical position which guaranteed its use as a staging post to Ireland, or to the emerging industrial giants of Liverpool and Manchester, Chester's civic and financial fortunes now depended on the modernisation and expansion of its historic precincts.

As early as the late 18th century, individual architects, builders and investors were also beginning to develop particular areas of the city, many of which lay behind the existing shop front premises which ran the length of the city's main thoroughfares. In the Queen Street area of Chester, which lay just off the northern side of the city's Foregate Street, two men, John Chamberlain and Roger Rogerson were reported to be building a number of properties sometime around 1778. Sadly, in the past 50 years or so, much of this area has been subjected to major redevelopment and very few of these elegant late 18th century properties have survived, save for a small number which have now become completely isolated at Queens Place, which is located close to the Shropshire Union Canal and now totally obscured by the monolithic Tesco supermarket and Housing Association properties. It has also been reported that during this same period, as houses were being rebuilt by their owners, that a number of residents took the opportunity to build beyond the limits of their properties or to change the layout, look or style of the building, despite this contravening civic statutes and were subsequently fined by the local authorities as a consequence.

Around the same time that Chamberlain and Rogerson were developing parts of Queen Street, yet another Chester builder was reported to be constructing properties within the ancient precincts of the city's Cathedral. Thomas Boswell was successively recorded as a Barber, a Cheese Factor and a city Alderman in Chester during the mid 1700's, who also dabbled as a part-time builder in the city. The son of one George Boswell, a tradesman in Chester, between 1768 and 1770, Thomas was said to have built several houses on a piece of land which lay between the Abbey Court and the city's walls, today reportedly marked as numbers 1 and 2 Abbey Green. At the same time that he was building these properties, Boswell was also thought to be seeking permission to erect a footway from these new houses to the city's walls, which he was subsequently granted. The new footpath is thought to be marked by a doorway which opened onto steps that led from the city walls directly to Abbey Green. His final building project was reported to be the rebuilding of the property close to the modern day Northgate, until recently occupied by a branch of Sayers the bakers. During the 18th century the premises were said to have housed a city tavern called the "Hen and Chicken", which was reportedly rebuilt by Thomas Boswell in 1782, the same year that the builder died.

The two most notable architects of the period from 1788 to 1829 were Thomas Harrison and Joseph Turner, the latter best known for his two stone archways, at the city's Watergate and Bridgegate, which replaced their much earlier and by then generally ruinous medieval predecessors. Acquiring the designation "Of Chester" Thomas Harrison is famed for his numerous, but elegant buildings many of which were designed in the Greek revival style for which he was so renowned and which was celebrated by many subsequent architects who employed their talents in the city. The buildings and careers of both of these individual architects are featured in later pages of this book, but they were, needless to say, pivotal figures in the modernisation and development of the old city of Chester.

Some 50 or 60 years after Harrison and Turner had begun modernising ancient Chester; the likes of John Douglas, Thomas Meakin Lockwood and Thomas Mainwaring Penson were the most influential Chester architects of the Victorian period, with others such as H W Beswick and James Strong also contributing to both the layout and look of the city. Douglas and Lockwood are still generally recognised as the most important and influential architects of their age, not least because of the numbers of properties that they designed and built in and around Chester, often for the Grosvenor family, but also, occasionally for themselves. Details on these men, Douglas, Lockwood, Penson, etc., as well as the likes of James Harrison are featured separately in the next chapter.

Although the individual architects and their designs have helped to create the Chester "look" for which the city is celebrated, beyond the main streets of the city a large number of local builders, wealthy employers and the occasional philanthropist were all helping to expand and modernise the suburbs of Chester. William Boden, William Vernon and Thomas Edwards were perhaps the most noted city builders of the age and no doubt helped to construct many of the landmark projects, designed by their architectural contemporaries. During the 1830's two local builders were reported to have been occupying the Stanley Palace in Chester, yet despite the presence of a Mr Boden and a Mr Hodkinson, the building itself was reported to be in a relatively poor state of repair. Hodkinson's son was also thought to have been a pupil of the architect Thomas Harrison, so no doubt the family generally were instrumental in redesigning and rebuilding the historic fabric of Chester. Around the same time a local builder and investor from Oulton Place, Thomas Clare, has been reported to have been involved in the construction of over 500 houses on the outskirts of the city, in the suburb now called Newtown. Records suggest that Clare set about the building program around the same time that he was elected to Chester City Council in 1831.

It is perhaps worth noting that the Boden family appear to have played a fairly extensive part in the rebuilding of Chester, certainly from the middle of the 18th century and perhaps much earlier than that. In 1748, a John Boden was recorded as a bricklayer and plasterer in the city, whilst in 1754 one Edward Boden was reported to have been employed as a bricklayer, working on the old Bishop's Palace, which formerly occupied the site of the modern day Barclay's Bank building in Northgate Street. This is probably the same Edward Boden who would later train a number of Chester's 18th century builders, including John Evans, whose name was immortalised on a plaque in the city's cathedral. As previously mentioned, a builder called William Boden was working in Chester during the early 19th century and a Mr Walter M Boden was described as an architect living at Saighton on the outskirts of the city.

George Austin was another Chester citizen thought to have been largely responsible for building Stocks Lane in Boughton, whilst Enoch Kennerly along with Thomas Gorst and Sons was involved with erecting houses in both the Blacon area of Chester and along Sealand Road. At the time of his death, Kennerly was reported to have held several properties in Bouverie Street, Watergate Street, Filkins Lane and in Cambrian View.

William Seller was a prominent city Alderman and the owner of a local Brewery who has been credited with building the houses in the city street which still carries his name, albeit that virtually all of these properties have now been replaced by modern housing units. An associated local building contractor was a man called Thomas Kelly, who was reported to have built Christ Church in Newtown lived in the nearby Seller Street. The architect George Williams has been credited with designing the Dixon & Wardell's Chester Bank building in 1860, a classical stone building at the junction of the city's Eastgate Street and St Werburgh Street, now housing the National Westminster Bank. His designs were thought to be just one of many that were inspired by the classical architecture first brought into the city by Thomas Harrison of Chester.

The notable Brassey family are reported to have a similar connection with Chester, with Robert being credited with building both No 1 Hillside and Richmond Bank in the Boughton

area of the city. His brother Thomas, the famed railway engineer is also thought to have been involved with constructing Abbots Field in the Liverpool Road area of Chester, whilst another local man William Seaville is reported to have built Seaville Street in Boughton. The Abbots Field property, built by Thomas Brassey was ultimately gifted to Mr Wardell of Chester's Dixon and Wardell Bank, supposedly as a "thank you" from the engineer for the banker's efforts in helping Brassey to find finance for one of his landmark projects.

Between the two World Wars, a good deal of Chester's architecture was said to have been designed by the likes of John H Davies and Sons, Richard and Arthur Keane, as well as Arthur J Hayton. Francis Jones was the man responsible for designing the Manchester & District Bank Building, which is located at the junction of today's Foregate Street and Frodsham Street and dates from around 1921. Two Manchester based architects, Norman Jones and Leonard Rigby, were reported to be responsible for the designs of neo-Georgian building that houses the modern day Marks & Spencer store in Foregate Street, which is thought to date from 1932.

The Leeds based architect, Harry Wilson, designed the Burton Menswear building, located beneath the city's historic clock on the south side of Foregate Street, whilst Harry Weedon, designed the Art-Deco "Odeon" Cinema close to Chester's market square, which was completed by 1936. A year earlier, the architect Maxwell Ayrton, had seen his designs for St Werburgh's Row come to fruition, close to the city's ancient Cathedral precincts.

Born in 1874 and apprenticed to the architect H Beswick in Chester around 1890, Maxwell Ayrton remained in the city until 1897 before moving south to set up practice in London. In 1905 he went into partnership with J W Simpson, the Scottish born architect and as a result of their collaboration both men achieved a great deal of professional success. Ayrton was generally seen to be responsible for the design work of the partnership, which culminated in their work on Wembley Stadium for the British Empire Exhibition held in 1924-5.

Although there were undoubtedly any number of less celebrated architects, designers, engineers and builders involved with the development and modernisation of Chester during the 300 year period from 1645 to 1945, it was during this time that much of the city was fundamentally rebuilt from the ground up. The following chapter attempts to look at the buildings and careers of those leading builders and architects who history would possibly regard as being at the forefront of these changes.

CHAPTER THREE

CREATING THE CHESTER LOOK

Chester's modern streets are littered with numerous buildings that offer visitor's a wide variety of history, style and construction materials, ranging from 13th century cellars to brand new city buildings that are only a few years old. However, the type of property most commonly associated with Chester is the Black and White half-timbered, Tudor style building which often appears to suggest great age and history, even where little if any exists. The city can also boast a plentiful supply of classically elegant Georgian houses, along with revivals of the much more ancient styles of architecture, including Roman, Greek and Gothic.

Despite the fact that Chester can probably offer an example of any sort of architecture that has been employed in England over the past 2000 years, much of what actually captures the eye and the imagination of the visitor today is probably new in terms of the city's great age. And the reason for that is simple; it is because the central core of the city has been designed by a relatively small number of architects and designer's who have either been artistically and stylistically sympathetic to their predecessors, guided by current trends or perhaps even influenced by a wealthy employer who had very clear ideas of how he wanted the particular building to look.

This particular section offers a brief overview of the careers and works of that relatively small number of men who most people would agree have been at the forefront of creating modern day Chester and whose work continues to draw inspiration and admiration from the hundreds of thousands of people who visit the city every year. Before beginning with the career of the Georgian architect, Joseph Turner, it is perhaps worth remembering that the city was still recovering from the devastating effects of the English Civil War siege in 1645 and that Chester was no longer a viable trading port, or indeed a strategically important military base, any and all of which might account for the sudden and expansive rounds of modernisation which took place in the city over the following 150-200 years.

Joseph Turner (1729 - 1807)

Although Joseph Turner is commonly associated with the city of Chester and two of its most notable Georgian landmark structures, the Bridgegate and Watergate, he also has equally strong connections with the adjoining Welsh counties of Flintshire and Denbighshire, where he was reported to have been employed on a variety of important civic projects. It is also worth noting though that there seems to have been several generations of related architects, all of whom were called Joseph Turner, which has tended to confuse the issue of exactly which projects were undertaken by the different individuals.

An architect of some repute, the Joseph Turner in question, has been credited with designing the House of Correction at Hawarden, as well as the gaols at both Flint and Ruthin, although the first of these project was thought to date from around 1740 which would have made the architect about 11 years old when he undertook the design, which clearly cannot be the case. It seems likely therefore that the House of Correction at Hawarden was actually undertaken by an earlier Joseph Turner, possibly the father, rather than the son who worked in Chester and who is the subject of this particular history. He was said to have been involved with the repair of Hawarden Parish Church, as well as the Cathedral at St Asaph and designed the brick and stone house at Hawarden Castle for the local landowner Sir John Glynn. This building was later said to have been added to and enhanced by the renowned architect John Nash, the man credited with designing Buckingham Castle.

There is a suggestion that Turner may have been living or working in Whitchurch around 1756; as it is recorded that a Mr Turner, architect, was sent for from there to survey the old Exchange building at Chester, possibly as part of one of the series of alterations which were undertaken on this building throughout its lifetime. Eleven years later, in 1767, a Mr Turner of Hawarden was reportedly asked to survey Chester's medieval East Gate, its adjoining buildings and to design a new arch with a passageway above it. No record of his designs are thought to have survived, but evidently they were not accepted by the city's corporation, as another architect, a Mr Hayden, was eventually contracted to produce the gateway which stands in Chester today.

Regardless of this particular rejection of his work, Joseph Turner continued to operate in and around the city and in 1774 was recorded to have been formally admitted as a Freeman of Chester. In the same year he was known to have submitted his designs for the new Ruthin Gaol, which was reported to have been built in 1775. Some three years later, in 1778, he was recorded to have been the under-tenant of Further Bayley's Croft at Overleigh in the outlying township of Handbridge, although whether or not he was actually living there is unclear.

In 1780, the architect was reported to have been residing in Chester itself, notably in the area of Paradise Row, a relatively new and exclusive suburb of the city which lay to the west of the ancient city walls and adjacent to the River Dee. According to records of the time, Turner was involved in purchasing plots of land in the area from a Mr Chamberlain, although the reason for the new land acquisitions is not particularly stated, but presumably the land was being bought for residential development. The Crane Street area of Chester was reported to have been laid out sometime after 1769 and by 1831 was being described as one of the most pleasant streets in the whole of the city.

As his property holdings in the city increased, so too did his involvement in property and rental disputes which were commonly brought before the corporation and the courts. In 1780, he was reported to be in dispute over the rental of premises in both Queen Street and Crane Street, although full details of the disagreement are unclear. However, these cases failed to harm his architectural career, as in the following year he was asked to produce designs for a replacement for the city's medieval Bridgegate, which was thought to be in a fairly perilous condition at that time.

With his designs accepted by the corporation, Chester's medieval Bridgegate, including its flanking towers, drawbridge and portcullis' was thought to have been demolished around

1780/1 and Turners replacement gateway substantially completed by 1782. In the same period he was reported to have been elected as one of the city's Sheriffs in the autumn of that year.

In March 1785, Turner once again found himself in trouble with the local courts, when a local stonemason called John Broad prepared to sue the architect for £19 which he claimed he was owed for work done for the architect. However, the matter was finally settled when the stonemason's brother, who was also Mr Turner's foreman, promised to settle the debt on behalf of his employer, who at the time was reported to be "out of town".

The Chester Watergate was completed circa 1788/9 and replaced a much more ancient gateway which by the middle of the 18th century was recorded to have fallen into a fairly ruinous state. Historically held by members of the Stanley family, the Earls of Derby, this old medieval entrance was eventually bought by the city's corporation and demolished almost immediately, being replaced by Turner's archway which remains with us today.

During the 1780's, Turner was reported to have been employed to design a terrace of houses in the Black Friars area of the city, possibly including the notable Soughton House and was the reported architect for the former County Jail which was built on City Walls Road around 1807, but which was subsequently demolished and replaced by the Queens School building, designed by another local architect E A Ould.

The row of fine Georgian houses on the northern side of today's Lower Watergate Street are suggested as being designed by Turner and are thought to have been constructed around 1779, following the sale of building plots in the area the previous year. It was during the construction of these particular houses that a Roman Altar and the remains of a Roman Hypocaust were found, although many of these historic artefacts were said to have been simply disposed of by the local workmen employed to erect the buildings. Further north and adjoining these properties, the modern day Stanley Street and Stanley Place are also thought to date from around the same period, so it is possible that Turner would have been involved in designing a number of these stately buildings as well.

Nearby, on the western flank of modern day Nicholas Street the extensive terrace of elegant Georgian properties, previously known as "Pill Box Terrace" are largely attributed to the same architect. Commonly thought to have been occupied by Chester's professional classes, including a large number of doctors, from where it derived its locally held title, this whole area was thought to have been owned and inhabited by members of the local aristocracy and wealthy city merchants. Later architectural students however, have suggested that this particular terrace appears to have been built in a rather piecemeal fashion, which might imply that Turner was not the only designer involved in its overall construction.

Although not forgotten, perhaps one of Turner's most commonly overlooked designs is the narrow footbridge which spans the imposing canal gorge outside of Chester's Northgate. Known locally as the "Bridge of Sigh's" this now defunct footway which dates from around 1793 replaced an earlier, much more temporary bridge, that was said to have been erected sometime after this section of the canal was completed in 1775 and linked the city's still standing medieval Northgate Gaol with the Chapel of St John the Baptist within the Bluecoat School, where condemned felons received their final religious rites. Although the derivation of its name, Bridge of Sigh's, is lost in time, one suggestion is that it recalls the sighs of relief by the prisoner as they were finally released from their incarceration in the gaol's dark and damp confines, even though it was generally for their own execution. Alternatively, it has also been speculated that the name originates from the condemned prisoner's habit of sighing heavily as they were led to their ultimate doom, or occasionally saving the executioner the trouble of hanging them, by leaping into the canal gorge of their own volition and ending their own personal misery. To prevent this, Turner's bridge was originally designed with iron railings on either side, but these were thought to have been removed in later centuries as part of the nations need for scrap metals during times of war. By 1807 though, the bridge had become obsolete anyway, following the construction of Turner's new County Gaol in City Walls Road and the later demolition of Chester's infamous Northgate Gaol which was subsequently replaced by Thomas Harrison's gateway which continues to stand today.

Thomas Harrison (1744 – 1829)

Architect Thomas Harrison is now synonymous with the city and is unique in having been given the epithet "Of Chester" which no other building designer has since achieved. In 1785 the city's corporation was recorded to have run a competition to find a suitable replacement for the County gaol which was housed within the precincts of the medieval castle and offered a prize of 50 guineas to the winning entry. Typhus or more commonly "gaol fever" was known to be rife at Chester's historic castle prison and over the years hundreds of prisoners had succumbed to cold and disease while being held in its enclosed and airless conditions. The celebrated prison reformer John Howard had likened it to 'the black hole of Calcutta' and called for the city authorities to do away with the prison.

From the entries that they received the city authorities chose the plans of a relatively obscure 40-year-old architect called Thomas Harrison, who did not even live in Chester, but although unaware of it at the time, the adoption of his proposals would mark the start of a lifetimes work in the ancient city for the Yorkshire-born designer that would only end with his death in 1829.

The son of a local joiner from Richmond in Yorkshire, Thomas Harrison was born in 1744 and as a young man was said to have showed an early talent for both mathematics and mechanics. Given his natural aptitude it was not long before his abilities attracted the attention of an aristocratic benefactor, Sir Lawrence Dundas, who was keen to develop the young man's talents. He arranged for the young Harrison to receive an extensive education and the "Grand Tour", including an extended visit to Rome beginning in 1769 which allowed him to study the great architectural buildings of the "eternal" city. It was thought to be during this period that Harrison began to develop the architectural skills that he would later employ in many of his future commissions. In Rome his architectural drawings were said to have been so appreciated and admired by the Pontiff, Pope Ganganelli, that he was reported to have rewarded the young architect with a gold and silver papal medal.

Returning to England in 1776, Harrison was reported to have received a commission to design the new Skerton Bridge across the River Lune, reportedly the first level bridge in the country and soon followed this up with work on Lancaster's Shire Hall, both of which projects were reported to have been substantially completed by 1783. He continued to undertake several projects in Lancashire, even while he was employed at Chester and was said to have received the commission to rebuild the precincts of Lancaster's historic castle, a project which was thought to have lasted right through until 1802.

Almost immediately Harrison's proposals for the old gaol at Chester were extended to include the entire medieval castle complex, including the great Shire Hall and the many other medieval structures that had degraded so badly over the previous decades. Beginning in 1788 these ancient buildings were systematically demolished and swept away to be replaced with the modern castle development which inhabits the site today. Harrison's new castle would ultimately include a magnificent Shire Hall, Crown Courts, Armoury, Prison and Military Barracks, all of which would take him the next 35 years to complete. Housed within three great sections, fronted by a central courtyard, the architects new castle buildings were described as being the finest County buildings in the Greek Revival style anywhere in the country and helping to establish him as one of the most pre-eminent regional architects of the age.

By 1792 the new gaol had been completed, its dirty disease-ridden communal chambers replaced by new individual cells for the prisoners, offering light and space to those that were incarcerated. Inmates that were being held for minor civil offences like debt were now kept separate from the more serious felons that were incarcerated for murder, theft, etc. At the time of its completion this new gaol was regarded by most as a real step forward in penal reform and yet it was later demolished to make way for the new County Hall which stands over the site today. However, it is also worth noting that there were some reports that large sections of the new gaol had to be rebuilt at a later date, due to the fact that much of this modern "humanitarian" prison had in fact been built by the inmates themselves, which led to an extremely poor level of construction throughout.

Between 1791 and 1801 the centrepiece of the new castle complex was constructed, the magnificently colonnaded portico incorporating the county's Shire Hall and judicial Courts. To the east and west of this central building, new wings were added, which would subsequently accommodate the castle's Armoury and Military Barracks. Now extending well beyond the limits of the original medieval walls Harrison designed a new gateway for the castle in the form of a 'Propylaeum' built on large stone columns. It was also during the reconstruction of the castle complex that Harrison was reported to have designed and built St Martin's Lodge, one of his homes in the city, which is dated from around 1796.

Although the problem was not obvious during Harrison's time, the decision to build the Shire Hall and its Courts directly above the former medieval castle's moat would later prove to be a costly decision. In the 1920s large cracks began to appear in the court buildings which were attributed to the inadequate foundations that lay below them. Remedial work was undertaken almost immediately and by 1922 the building and its supporting columns had been fully restored. To this day Chester Crown Court regularly hears a number of high profile criminal cases, but is most commonly linked with the 1960s trial of Myra Hindley and Ian Brady who were tried and found guilty of the infamous Moors Murders.

The Yorkshire-born architect was also said to have undertaken a partial restoration of the city's historic Cathedral, which had suffered much over the previous centuries and continued to be visited by a number of the nations leading architects in an effort to maintain its fabric, even after Harrison had completed his work. Visitors and commentators alike had been moved to highlight the dreadfully poor condition of its magnificent stonework and to call for action to save the historic structure. Between 1818 and 1820 extensive renovations were undertaken by the architect to preserve the building's inner and outer fabric and to ensure that it would survive intact in the coming decades.

Harrison was also responsible for the overall design of Chester's second river crossing, the Grosvenor Bridge, but sadly did not live to see its completion as he died on 29th March 1829, aged 85. Opened by the then 13-year-old Princess Victoria in 1833 the bridge project was reported to have been completed by William Cole, a pupil of Harrison's. Up until 1864 the Grosvenor Bridge was thought to be the world's greatest single span stone bridge, standing 200 feet wide and 60 feet high.

Although Harrison is still generally credited with the design of the new second crossing of the River Dee, the Grosvenor Bridge; it was largely constructed under the supervision of William Cole, one of Harrison's most notable pupils, simply because Harrison himself had resigned from the post of architect some years before the bridge was actually completed.

Plans for the proposed second crossing were thought to have originally been put in place as early as 1818, with a suggested location at Handbridge and much closer to the historic Old Dee Bridge which had served as the only permanent crossing for hundreds of years. However, problems regarding the foundations for the new river crossing and the need for Parliamentary permissions in order to construct the new bridge caused a delay of several years, during which time the likes of Brunel and Telford were thought to have become involved with the engineering aspects of the scheme, causing dissent amongst the various parties. By 1827 the plans had received all necessary permissions, but clearly Harrison, its designer, was thought to have become so exasperated by the unexpected and possibly unwelcome interference by these other equally notable and qualified engineers that he was said to have simply withdrawn from the project.

Another less well known engineer who was also reported to have been involved with the construction of Harrison's new Bridge crossing was James Trubshaw, the son of a local stonemason who had been born in Staffordshire in 1777. Trubshaw was reported to have left school at 11 years of age to work in his father's business and to learn his trade. In 1808, following his father's death, James was said to have set up his own building company and eventually progressed to become the Chief Engineer of the Trent and Mersey Canal Company. This post enabled him to gain both experience and recognition in the building of reservoirs and railway lines for the company, which he would carry with him throughout his life. Trubshaw gained note for his pioneering work in the technique of under excavation, which helped to stabilize leaning towers and steeples which seemed to be in danger of toppling over. The talented builder was also recorded to have worked on Fonthill Abbey, Buckingham Palace and Windsor Castle.

Before his death Thomas Harrison was also said to have rebuilt the ancient St Bridget's church around 1825 after it had been removed from its original home in Bridge Street to make way for the laying out of Grosvenor Road and relocating it close to the castle complex. Sadly the rebuilt church failed to survive later city developments and finally disappeared forever at the end of the 19th century along with a number of other historic buildings. As with the still standing Grosvenor Bridge though, the rebuilt church of St Bridget's was probably constructed under the watchful eye of William Cole, rather than the great architect Harrison.

Folliot House in Northgate Street which was built as his private residence dates from around 1788 is yet another Harrison building that has managed to last the test of time, albeit in a much reduced form, but is now largely hidden behind the 'Odeon' cinema and converted into offices. Further along Northgate Street Chester's northern gate was also designed by the same architect and erected between 1808 and 1810. This important civic project was later followed by a series of other commissions in the city including the Commercial Newsrooms, which later became the Barclay's City Club, the Wesleyan Chapel in St John Street which was completed in 1811, Dee Hills House, later the Ursuline Convent, which was completed in 1814, Richmond Terrace, built by Harrison for Robert Baxter in the same year and Watergate House which he built for his friend Henry Potts, the Clerk of the Peace and completed in 1820.

Although many of his landmark buildings were built in Chester and he made the city his adopted home, Harrison's reputation was reported to have travelled way beyond the limits of the city and the northwest region of Britain. Following his rebuilding of both Chester's and Lancaster's castle precincts and notably the formers infamous gaol, it was reported that a deputation was sent from London to request that Harrison visit the capital's worst prisons and recommend what work was needed to improve them. He was also recorded to have designed a number of celebratory columns around the region, including those at Shrewsbury, the Menai Straits and at Holyhead.

He was also known to have accepted and completed a number of commissions for wealthy landowners and aristocrats, including restoring the Elgin Marbles for their titled owner, as well as undertaking a number of works for various Scottish nobles at their ancestral seats. Closer to home he has been credited with designing the Lyceum in Liverpool, along with the Exchange Building in Manchester.

In 1843 a noted northwest architect wrote of Harrison that *"it was to be regretted that he (Harrison) had buried his fine talents in the obscure city of Chester, instead of settling in London and correcting the bad taste of Nash, Sloane and others"*

When he died in March 1829 Harrison was laid to rest in the family vault which was located in the churchyard of the newly raised St Bridget's which lay close to his home at St Martin's Lodge. Despite this church later being demolished, it was thought that the burial grounds were later absorbed into the parish of St Mary's which lay close to Harrison's new castle complex. However, when Chester's new inner ring road system was being laid out during the 1960's these grounds were reported to have been cleared to make way for the new roadway. Along with many other burials and family crypts, Thomas Harrison's vault was thought to have been rediscovered and a closer inspection revealed the presence of three separate coffins within the vault, although there was no clear indication of which one was Harrison's. All of the burials recovered at that time were reported to have been re-interred at the city's municipal Blacon cemetery on the outskirts of Chester.

Thomas Lunt (1770 - 1851)

One of the most notable local builders and altruistic businessmen of the later Georgian and early Victorian periods in Chester, who is often overlooked by history, was Thomas Lunt, who was reported to have been born in Tattenhall on the outskirts of Chester sometime during 1770.

A builder and iron founder who lived in the St John Street area of the city he was said to have laid out plans for the Bold Square area of the city as early as 1814, the name deriving from a Madam Bold who was thought to have lived there at the time. His small "Union" bridge which spanned the city's new Chester and Nantwich canal linked the newly emerging Egerton Street with Bold Square and Seller Street both of which stood on the southern bank of the waterway and is thought to date from around 1820. Seller Street itself was thought to have been built at the expense of a Mr William Seller, a noted local brewery owner and city politician who was said to have raised the rows of terraced housing for those that he employed in his various businesses. Today, only a fraction of Bold Square continues to stand in the city and virtually all of William Seller's properties have since been razed from the ground to make way for more modern housing developments.

Lunt has also been largely credited with the construction and layout of Egerton Street in the Newtown area of Chester, where he was thought to have established an Iron Foundry, supplying the much needed building material to the city's emerging industries and commercial interests. As well as Chester's long gone Commercial Hall, which once occupied a site close to today's British Home Stores and former Littlewood's store in Foregate Street, this historic character was also thought to be responsible for constructing Chester's

Union Hall in 1809 which stood on the opposite side of the same city thoroughfare, on the site now marked by the 1920's Mark's and Spencer's storefront.

Demolished during the early 1950's, Lunt's Commercial Hall, which was said to have been a forerunner of today's modern shopping centres, was constructed around 1815 and during its 135 year history had served as a second market hall in Chester, being occupied by a large number of both single and double shop units, located over two floors. During the city fairs which were held in both July and October of each year, tradesmen from all over the country, including London, Glasgow, Birmingham and Sheffield would converge on the Commercial Hall and sell their much needed wares to Chester's traders and shoppers.

As well as being a noted businessman within the city, Thomas was also said to be a member of the city's Quaker community who attended the Society of Friend's meeting house in Frodsham Street and was a renowned philanthropist and by repute, a man of high integrity and honour.

In the later part of his life, Thomas was reported to have found his financial circumstances much reduced, possibly as a result of his altruism and his suggested project for a vital canal scheme designed to reinvigorate the historic port of Chester. Designed to help the city to compete effectively with the commercial threat then being posed by both the Liverpool and Manchester inland waterway systems, his proposed plan to build a new ship canal from Dawpool or Mostyn direct to the city of Chester would have protected and expanded the diminishing inshore trade that operated into the city. However as with all such schemes that were suggested within the city, there seems to have been little public appetite or indeed financial assistance for such a scheme and so the plan was shelved, possibly much to Thomas Lunt's own personal financial cost.

Prior to his death, such were his financial difficulties, that a number of his friends within the local business community were said to have offered him financial aid, all of which were thought to have been politely refused by the extremely proud entrepreneur. He was then reported to have relocated himself and his family to Liverpool, where on the 7th November 1851 he was said to have passed away.

Rather than be buried away from his family roots however, later reports suggest that his body was subsequently removed to Tattenhall in Cheshire where he was interred along with his son John who had died in 1804, at the tender age of ten years and his daughter Martha who had died in 1798, aged twenty-two years old.

James Harrison (1814 - 1866)

Reportedly a relative of the much more famous architect Thomas Harrison of Chester, James was actually thought to be the son of one David or James Harrison, depending on which historical source is accepted as being accurate, who was said to be a noted mason and monument maker working in the Linen Hall Street area of the city. Like his father, James was also said to be a talented mason and is known to have produced a number of stone tablets for various Chester Churches, including that of William Currie at St Mary's on the hill which he was thought to have designed in 1834. His building designs were said to be heavily influenced by the Gothic architectural style and his work at both St Michael's and Holy Trinity Churches are thought to be some of his finest commissions in the city.

Although today Harrison is generally remembered for his rebuilding of religious buildings, in and around the Chester area, he along with his better known contemporaries were known to have undertaken a variety of commissions, both for the church authorities, as well as for a number of wealthy individuals who lived within Cheshire.

Between 1849 and 1850 St Michael's Church, which now serves as Chester's Heritage Centre, was largely rebuilt by Harrison, principally because much of its ancient fabric was in such a ruinous condition and its early steeple appears to have been in danger of falling down. Reportedly demolished during the winter months of 1848, using cranes borrowed from Chester's new castle complex, the foundation stone for the restored St Michael's church was reported to have been laid in May 1849 and the whole building completed by the early months of 1850.

Queens Park, which lies on the southern bank of the River Dee, was developed as a private residential estate by the businessman Enoch Gerrard who was thought to have employed a number of Chester's leading architects to design and build the affluent estate. James was reported to have begun his association with the landowner around 1850, about the same time that he was finalising his rebuilding of St Michael's church in the city.

Another of his earliest commissions in Chester was thought to be for the design of the Chester (later the Trustee's) Savings Bank building which is reported to date from the period between 1851 and 1853. Although the site now operates as a restaurant, the Chester Savings Bank was reported to have been founded around 1817 and was initially located in the city's Exchange building which was in the same general area of today's Victorian Town Hall. It was thought to have remained around the Market Square until 1846 when the bank premises were temporarily relocated to Goss Street, which is just off Watergate Street. In 1851 the owners were said to have purchased the land in Grosvenor Street for the specific purpose of erecting their brand new premises, which were designed by Harrison in a largely Tudor Gothic style.

Shortly after starting the Chester Savings Bank commission, Harrison was fortunate enough to be offered yet another church building project by the religious authorities. The church of the Holy Ascension at Upton-by-Chester was designed and built by the architect between 1852 and 1854, requiring him to switch between this project and the still to be completed bank building in Grosvenor Street.

St Nicholas' Chapel was reported to have been converted into a theatre around 1773, but the city's Mayor had issued a proclamation in 1777 prohibiting any further performances until such time as a licence was granted for that specific purpose, which given the nature of the building, required an Act of Parliament. It's later conversion into a Music Hall by Harrison between the years 1854 and 1855 simply marked one particular phase of the building's extensively mixed history, as it has later been used as a cinema, a clothes store and then a retail supermarket. The adjoining Music Hall Passage, leading from St Werburgh Street to Northgate Street, recalls this historic buildings previous existence as a place of entertainment, designed by Harrison. At the eastern end of the passage, large sandstone blocks from the Chapels very earliest foundation are still evident today.

Around the same time that Harrison was finalizing the work on St Nicholas' chapel, the brand new Christ Church located at Hough Green on the outskirts of Chester was in the process of being designed and constructed by the architect, with a reported completion date of 1855 assigned to the building.

Number 40 Bridge Street, Chester was rebuilt by Harrison in 1858 and in the same year, both numbers 51 and 53 in the same city thoroughfare were reported to have been rebuilt to the designs of the same architect, with both properties thought to originate from 1700.

The ancient St Olave's Church in Chester, which is reported to have been founded prior to the Norman Conquest of the city in 1070, was yet another restoration projects undertaken by Harrison, with the work reportedly being largely completed by 1859. Close by, the church of St Mary's within-the-walls, which today operates as an educational centre, was restored by Harrison around 1861.

The following year, God's Providence House, was rebuilt by Harrison in 1862 and is inscribed with the words "God's Providence is Mine Inheritance", a clear reference to the householders belief that God had spared him and his family from an outbreak of plague in the city. Carrying a date of 1652, the building was likely to have been rebuilt following the end of the Civil War siege of Chester, a time when poor sanitation and the influx of thousands of soldiers was thought to have caused several instances of the dreaded disease.

The Old Custom's House in Watergate Street was thought to have originally been built around 1633, the offices having been moved from Chester's medieval castle buildings around that time and was then rebuilt to Harrison's designs in around 1868, two years after the architects untimely death. The adjoining church of the Holy and Undivided Trinity, which now operates as the city's Guildhall, was also restored to Harrison's designs around the same time, but once again was only completed after his death, probably by his former pupils and later successors, Edwards and Kelly who were reported to have taken over his practice which was located in St Werburgh's Street, Chester.

The Volunteer Drill Hall in Chester was built by Public Subscription in 1869 and at the time of its construction ran from just off Pepper Street southward to Duke Street near the River Dee. This particular area of the city, including Albion Street and Albion Place had earlier replaced two of Chester's infamous housing "courts", namely Roberts and Wilkinson's which had formerly stood on part of the site. Despite having died at least three years before the Drill Hall was actually built, its accreditation to Harrison is thought to indicate that it was his plans that were used to construct the complex, even though its was his successors Kelly and Edwards who actually oversaw its building.

Despite being one of the city's most prominent architects and having left his mark on a number of Chester's landmark buildings, there is a suggestion that Harrison was a fairly solitary, perhaps even slightly tragic figure who continued to live with his parents, at their home in St Martin's-in-the-field right up until his comparatively early death at the age of 52.

Thomas Mainwaring Penson (1818 – 1864)

Thomas Mainwaring Penson was born into a family of regional architects, with his father also called Thomas, reportedly having studied under the renowned Thomas Harrison of Chester. His older brother Richard Kyrke Penson was also a noted architect in the family's home town of Oswestry, but Thomas Mainwaring Junior decided to pursue his career in the historic city of Chester.

He was responsible for the design of Overleigh Cemetery's Bridges & Gates between 1848 and 1850, although the actual layout of the cemetery grounds themselves was thought to have been the work of another landscape designer, a Mr Lister. Penson was reported to have designed a bridge within the grounds, which has long since disappeared, along with the gates and piers which continue to adorn the main entrances to the city's suburban graveyard. In a curious twist perhaps, this cemetery is still said to hold the mortal remains of Penson's architectural contemporaries, John Douglas, Thomas Meakin Lockwood, along with a number of other notable individuals, who were responsible for building the city we know today. Some seven years after completing his designs for the cemetery, Penson was reported to have returned to the same site, this time as the architect responsible for the design of the Henry Raikes tomb and monument, which was said to have been sculpted by one Thomas Earp. Raike, who lived between 1782 and 1854, was reported to have been the Chancellor of the Chester Diocese, as well as being an active politician within the city and his grand tomb, designed by Penson, continues to reflect both the wealth and importance of this particular individual.

Thomas has often been categorized as a student of the Gothic Revivalist style, who has been accused by some critics of over-embellishing his works with heavy ornamentation and irregular features. Penson's first architectural commission, in which he was said to have first employed the Black & White Revival style for which he and other Chester architects have become noted, was on the restoration of 22-24 Eastgate Street in around 1852, with one of the gables of the restored building still carrying a date of 1640, the year that it was originally built. In 1856 he was recorded to have undertaken another project at numbers 34-36 in the same street, having just completed an earlier project at the city's racecourse, rebuilding the grandstand which was thought to have been destroyed by fire during 1855. The Eastgate Street building designed by Penson is generally described as being classically revival in style and was perhaps influenced by or a tribute to the works of Thomas Harrison, who had reintroduced this style of architecture to Chester some 50-odd years earlier.

His next major undertaking in Chester was reported to be the "Browns" crypt building which is said to date from 1857/8 and built in a High Victorian Gothic style for the Brown family, who were reported to have been milliners and haberdashers in the city since 1828, when the business was first founded by Susannah Brown. As part of the commission, Penson's new department store building incorporated the medieval under-croft which had stood on the same site for hundreds of years and is used today as part of the modern shop premises. In 1858 and between this new Gothic building and his earlier restoration project of 1852 Penson then undertook a second Black and White restoration commission at no 26 Eastgate Street, which is described as a mid 17th century house that contains a number of early Jacobean features, including a ceiling, staircase and mantelpiece.

Penson has also been credited with designing Chester's long since demolished Militia Building, which he was thought to have completed sometime around 1858 and previously occupying the site of the 20th century Cheshire Police Headquarters which itself has recently been demolished to make way for a new multi-million pound hotel complex. Designed and built to house the soldiers and their families garrisoned at the nearby Chester Castle, this uniform and robust looking building was said to be reminiscent of a much earlier defensive structure, complete with castellated walls, but was thought by some to have been heavily influenced by the relatively modern fortress at Peckforton.

The Queen's Hotel in Chester's City Road, which still faces the Victorian General Railway Station it was built to serve, was rebuilt by Penson and Cornelius Sherlock from Liverpool in 1862 following a fire which had destroyed a large part of the earlier building, save for a brand new wing which had just been built and somehow managed to survive the inferno.

The modern day Grosvenor Hotel stands on the site of two former city hotels, the White Talbot and the Golden Talbot, which were, in their turn succeeded by the Royal Hotel. Its construction was thought to have caused the loss of a number of properties in the city's then still existent Fleshmongers Row, which later became known as Newgate Street. Although the modern hotel was thought to have been built to Thomas' designs, it has been suggested that the building itself was actually raised under the control of his older brother Richard, after the hostelry was first commissioned by the 2nd Duke of Westminster.

As with his equally notable fellow architect, James Harrison, Thomas died a comparatively young man, being 46 years of age at the time of his death. Just a year or so before his untimely demise, he was reported to have undertaken his final commission at Chester, the design of the east window of St John's church in the city, with the glass being supplied by Clayton and Bell.

John Douglas (1830 – 1911)

Douglas was the son of a local building contractor and surveyor from Sandiway in Cheshire who trained under Edward G Paley of Lancaster and was known to have travelled widely throughout Northern Europe and North West England, developing his own particular architectural style which mixed stone, brick and timber into a buildings construction. Having settled down to practice in the historic city of Chester around 1860, his emerging and highly individual style helped to further develop the "Black and White" revivalist look that has become synonymous with the city and which was said to have first been reintroduced by T M Penson some years earlier. Some of Douglas' best work is thought to be in St Werburgh Street in Chester.

Around the same time that he started in practice, Douglas was reported to have married Elizabeth Edmunds with whom he would have five children, although only two sons were reported to have survived to their majority. Initially living in the Abbey Square area of the city, where the architect had both his home and office, by 1869 Douglas was said to have removed his family home to Dee Hills on the outskirts of Chester, occupying one of two houses that he himself had designed and built at his own expense. However, although his professional life was thriving during the period, his family life was not so fortunate and in 1878 he was reported to have lost his beloved wife, Elizabeth, and 9 years later buried his eldest surviving son, Colin, who died of Tuberculosis at the surprisingly young age of 23.

By the mid 1890's, Douglas along with his single surviving son, Sholto, was thought to have moved to the new Walmoor Hill property that he had once again designed and built at his own expense, an impressive Tudor style buildings which was ridiculed by some and admired by many others. Despite the problems of his personal life, professionally, Douglas remained as one of the most pre-eminent and sought after regional architects of his age and counted amongst his clientele the great and the good of both northern England and the Welsh borders. His client list included the Duke of Westminster, Lord's Delamere and Leverhulme, various city and church authorities from around the region, as well as a plethora of individually wealthy landowners including the Egertons and the Frosts, etc.

Throughout his renowned career, the sheer breadth and variety of building designed by Douglas and his associated partners is not only surprising, but should perhaps be more aptly described as staggering. He undertook public and private commissions for churches, chapels, farm buildings and cottages, grand halls and mansions, hotels, as well as stables and even found time to design at least two hospitals within the northwest region. But his most famous and photographed design is undoubtedly Chester's world famous Eastgate Clock, reportedly the second most photographed clock in the world, behind Big Ben in London.

From 1885 Douglas was known to be in partnership with a Daniel Porter Fordham, a draughtsman who had previously been employed in the architect's offices, but from around 1889 onwards and following Fordham's retirement due to illness, he was reported to be practicing under the company name of Douglas and Minshall. Charles Howard Minshall had formerly been articled to Douglas during the 1870's, though remaining with the architect following the end of his apprenticeship and ultimately becoming a junior partner to his former employer. It was during this period that the firm was thought to have designed a number of buildings at Port Sunlight, including the Dell Bridge, the Lyceum, the Collegium and several other properties on the new estate, as well as collaborating with Minshall on houses that were constructed on the new Chester Road, Pool Bank and Primrose Hill. In 1909 however, the partnership was reported to have been dissolved, for what particular reason is unknown, although Douglas' personal circumstances, including

his alcoholic son Sholto, may have played a part in causing dissent between the partners. Minshall was later said to have established another practice in the city with an individual called E J Muspratt, although this business failed to achieve anything like the recognition of Douglas' firm.

Such was Douglas' reputation that examples of his work were illustrated throughout Europe including those of his buildings on the Eaton estate, the home of the Grosvenor family who were by far his most important and influential clients.

One of his first commissions for the Grosvenor family was for the design of the buildings at the newly opened Grosvenor Park complex which was undertaken sometime between 1865 and 1867 and included the half-timbered Park Lodge Building, featuring figures of a number of the city's early Norman rulers. This particular commission also included the designs for the canopy for the reportedly ancient "Billy Hobby's" well, as well as the elaborate gates and piers which adorned the entrance to the new leisure park complex.

Around the same time Douglas was commissioned to design St Bartholomew's Church at Sealand which was reported to have been built in around 1867. Today, the building serves as the parish church for worshippers from both the Sealand Road area of the city and for the nearby village of Saughall, but attracts little attention from fans of the architect, due to its semi-rural location.

As previously mentioned, in 1869 Douglas was reported to have acquired a plot of land on the outskirts of the city, in the Boughton area, on which he designed and built a pair of new properties, later known as 31 and 33 Dee Banks. The following year, he was thought to have undertaken the first phase of the buildings which now stand in the Bath Street area of the city, although the completed project is thought to be a mix of both Douglas and his contemporary Lockwood and taking until 1903 to fully complete.

Around 1874 Douglas designed and built numbers 15-27 on the east side of St Werburgh's Street in Chester for Mr George Hodkinson and two years later, in 1876, he was reported to have begun the initial phases of the new Christ Church in Newtown which he was thought to have completed in stages, between the years 1876 and 1900. The Baptist Chapel, in the newly laid out Grosvenor Park Road, now housing the Zion Chapel, was built by the architect around 1879 and at the same he began construction of the adjoining terrace of properties at numbers 6-11 Grosvenor Park Road. These were said to have been built at Douglas' own expense and later, along with his buildings in Bath Street formed part of the area which commonly became known as "Douglasville".

St Oswald's Vicarage, which later served as the English department of Chester College, was built by Douglas in 1880 and the following year he began the Grosvenor Club building in Eastgate Street, which later became the home of the N and S Wales Bank and today continues to serve a similar purpose for the HSBC. Completed in 1883, the property was thought to have been further extended by Douglas, sometime around 1908. The now often overlooked County Police Building at the corner of Grosvenor Park Road was built by the architect in 1884 and is similar in look to his earlier commission, the Grosvenor Club building, being faced with a highly attractive red brick.

The north Porch of the church of St John the Baptist was said to have been rebuilt by the architect in 1882 following the collapse of the nearby tower and 4 years later he was said to have also undertaken the rebuilding of the north-east Belfry. This was not the first time that the architect had completed work at St John's, as some reports suggest that Douglas had first completed work there around 1876, although the nature or scale of this earlier commission is unclear.

Parkers Buildings in Foregate Street, Chester were designed by Douglas around 1890 as accommodation for retired workers from the city's Grosvenor Estates and were erected by the Northern Counties Housing Association. This association with the Dukes of Westminster continued with the restoration of the historic Falcon Inn, the one time home of the Grosvenor family in the city, which was thought to have been restored by Douglas around 1894. Another of the architect's personal building projects, at numbers 2-18 St Werburgh's Street, on the eastern side of the thoroughfare, was thought to have been constructed between 1895 and 1899, with the then Duke reportedly influencing Douglas' choice of style for the new terrace of buildings.

As noted previously, Walmoor House, on the Queens Park estate, was designed and built by Douglas for his own use around 1896 and two years later he was commissioned to design and build No 7 Grosvenor Street as a home and training centre for city midwives which was commissioned by the 1st Duke of Westminster and in the same year he was also said to have designed St Oswald's Chamber in St Werburgh's Street.

Douglas' most celebrated and photographed creation in the city is the Chester Eastgate Clock, which he designed to celebrate the Diamond Jubilee of Queen Victoria in 1897, but which was only completely erected and working by 1899. That same year, he was thought to have begun the reconstruction of Shoemaker's Row in Northgate Street, which is said to have been designed by a number of Chester's noted architects, often in a fairly piecemeal fashion, between 1899 and 1904.

Back within the area of "Douglasville", the architect was reported to have designed and built the Chester Public Baths complex sometime around 1901 and at the northern end of the same Bath Street, the Prudential Assurance Building, was said to have been completed by Douglas in 1903. To the east of these buildings and once again in the Boughton suburb of the city, Douglas was reported to have undertaken design work on St Paul's Church, Boughton, sometime around 1906.

Shotwick Park was a commission for a House and Stables ordered by Thornycroft Vernon, which were rebuilt after a fire in 1907 and today serves as an Old People's Home. The site was connected with the ancient Shotwick Castle, first built by Earl Hugh Lupus in the 12th century. Douglas was reported to have designed the buildings there, between 1872/1875.

When he died on 23rd May 1911 at his Walmoor Hill home, Douglas was reported to have left a personal estate of some £32,000, as well as title to numerous properties in and around the city. His architectural practice was later absorbed by the less notable Minshall and Muspratt, becoming Douglas, Minshall and Muspratt. The remains of the architect were later interred in the family's tomb at Chester's Overleigh Cemetery where they can often overlooked by visitors. Happily though, many of his works continue to grace the precincts of the historic city, allowing resident and visitor alike to admire skills of the man that Pevsner once described as the "very best Cheshire architect".

Thomas Meakin Lockwood (1830 – 1900)

Much of Lockwood's career and his associated buildings were conducted in the city and along with John Douglas and TM Penson he has been credited with creating the Chester "look", the black and white, half-timbered style which has become synonymous with the city. He was extensively employed by the 1st Duke of Westminster in Chester and he is remembered with a memorial window in the north aisle of St John the Baptist church in Chester. His most famous and photographed commissions in Chester, are the buildings which form the junction between Bridge Street and Eastgate Street at Chester's High Cross which was completed around 1888. On the opposite side of Bridge Street, marking its junction with Watergate Street, the buildings and elevated rows are also Lockwood's work, being completed sometime around 1892.

Despite his obvious talents and his generally sympathetic approach to Chester's historic buildings, even a man of Lockwood's stature occasionally got it wrong and his rebuilding of the section of Bridge Street, including the notable St Michael's Row, was said to be so "foreign" to Chester's look that there was a public outcry, which forced the offending work to be torn down and rebuilt in a more traditional and acceptable fashion, reportedly by the architect's son.

One of Lockwood's earliest commissions was Chester's Northgate Church, built in 1874 and located at the northern end of Upper Northgate Street and today sited close to the much more modern Fountain's Roundabout, which is a by product of Chester's 1960's inner ring road system. The church today is largely associated with the student body of the city's University College in nearby Parkgate Road, as well as the neighbouring communities in Lorne Street, etc.

In 1877 Lockwood undertook the design and construction of the Grosvenor Rowing Club Boathouse which sits alongside the bank of the River Dee. Close by and some 4 years later the architect was commissioned to design the Hall for the church of St John The Baptist which continues to stand in this part of the city, a building he would revisit in 1895, when he designed the Organ Case for the same religious house.

On the western side of Chester in 1885, Lockwood has been credited with the rebuilding and extending of White Friars Lodge, a historic building in the city which owed its title to the former presence of the Carmelite Order which was known to have inhabited this particular area of the city.

Prior to the construction of Lockwood's Grosvenor Museum building in 1885, Chester's Archaeological Society, along with many of their historic finds were thought to have been housed at the Albion Hotel which was located in the Lower Bridge Street area of the city. The new museum building, constructed by the architect was commissioned by the 1st Duke of Westminster and just as this commission was coming to an end Lockwood was reported to be designing the property at No. 3 Upper Northgate Street, which was thought to have been built as a town house for one of Chester's wealthier residents.

Two years later, the architect received one of his most important commissions in the city from the Duke of Westminster, when he was asked to rebuild the adjoining buildings at No: 2 Eastgate Street and No: 1 Bridge Street, properties which formed the south east junction of Chester historic High Cross area. Facing the southern wall of St Peter's ancient church, these buildings which form the convergence of two of the city's most historic streets, along with Douglas's Eastgate Clock, are possibly one of the most photographed city landmarks and is even featured in one of the regions television news broadcasts.

Away from the main shopping thoroughfares, evidence of Lockwood's work continues to exist in some of the city's less obvious but still equally important streets, most notably at 24 to 26 Common Hall Street and numbers 2 to 5 Old Hall Place. All of these properties were reported to have been built as staff cottages for Browns of Chester employees and presumably commissioned by a member of that merchant family in around 1889.

Following his successful work at the south east junction of the High Cross, in 1892, the Duke of Westminster then commissioned Lockwood to redesign the opposite junction of the street, including numbers 2 to 4 Bridge Street, which the architect did, but in a wholly different style.

Further south of these buildings and on the eastern side of the street, today's St Michael's Row and the associated stone stairway and St Michael's Arcade are all attributed to Lockwood, although some sources suggest that the half timbered street frontages are the work of his son, rather than the architect himself. According to contemporary reports, the whole of this area was originally designed and constructed sometime around 1900, in the same tiles and brickwork style as is evident in St Michael's Arcade today. These designs were said to have caused such a furore amongst the local population that the Duke of Westminster, who had originally commissioned the scheme, later ordered the street facades taken down and replaced with the traditional and much more acceptable half timbered look that exists today.

One of Lockwood's most pleasing designs that continue to stand alongside the city's Eastgate is the Old Bank Buildings at numbers 2 to 6 Foregate Street, which is reported to date from 1895 and at one time was said to have been considered for demolition, although clearly commonsense finally intervened to retain such a landmark building. More of his work can still also be seen at numbers 10 to 18 Foregate Street, although only the western section of this property is thought to be Lockwood and dates from 1896.

The Blossoms Hotel, which now occupies a site in St John Street, formerly stood in the city's Foregate Street, at the junction with St John's Street, the site later being occupied by the National Westminster Bank and today, by the "Lush" retail outlet. The later frontage dated 1911 was thought to have been designed by Lockwood himself, but raised by one of the architects sons, sometime after his death in 1900.

Although Lockwood does not appear to have been particularly favoured by the local council for some reason, in 1897 he was the architect that the corporation turned to following a fire in the new Town Hall's Council Chamber which had been seriously damaged by fire. Two years later Bishop Lloyd's House in Watergate Street was restored by the architect and in the final year of his life, 1900, Lockwood was reported to have started his final two projects in the city. Numbers 4 to 10 in the City Road area of Chester was a commission for a new property, which continues to stand today and possibly first served as a bank building for the city's emerging middle classes. His second project of that final year was said to be at numbers 9 to 13 Eastgate Street, on the northern flank of the thoroughfare and including the site of today's famous Boot Inn. Reportedly a renovation rather than a complete rebuild, a number of these historic buildings are thought to date from the 16th and 17th centuries, although their ancient timber frames are now hidden by Lockwood's later work.

E A Ould (1852 – 1909)

The young Edward Augustus Ould was known to have studied in York during the 1870's before becoming a pupil of the noted Chester architect John Douglas. Obviously influenced by his mentor, Ould was known to be an advocate and practitioner of the revivalist style of architecture, which employed the "Black & White" half timbered look, commonly found both in the city and in the surrounding countryside.

He was reported to have established his own architectural practice in 1882 and in 1886 went into partnership with George Grayson, with both men regularly employed designing houses, villas and rectories, in and around the northwest area. They were also known to have undertaken a number of building commissions at the Port Sunlight village established by William Lever, many of which were undertaken between 1888 and 1909. Their works on the new estate were thought to have included, the Auditorium, the Bridge Inn, Church Drive School and the Cottage Hospital.

For his own part, Ould was thought to be a highly skilled and technical architect, who was more interested in the form and function of his designs, rather than just simply how they looked and was said to have received regular commissions from the Grosvenor family.

The Chester Queens School which was completed around 1878 and originally known as the Chester School For Girls, stands on the site of the former County Gaol, which itself had only been newly built around 1807, to replace the infamous Northgate gaol which had been demolished and replaced about the same time. The land for the new school was thought to have been donated by the Duke of Westminster, who along with a number of the city's wealthiest inhabitants was reported to have helped finance the new institution.

In 1882, Queen Victoria herself, was reported to have decreed that the new school should forthwith be called the Queen's School, a title which it continues to retain today. The school building itself is said to be in the Tudor-Gothic style of architecture.

Ould has also been credited with designing Uffington House in the Dee Hills Park area of the city. This particular 4 storey house was thought to have been built for Judge Thomas Hughes, the author of the famous novel "Tom Brown's Schooldays", sometime around 1885 and was named in memory of the family's hometown in Berkshire.

Although not a prolific architect in the historic city of Chester, Ould was known to have been largely employed by a small number of wealthy individual's throughout his career, including the likes of the Grosvenor's and Lord Lever. One of his most important and longest lasting working relationships though, was said to have been with the Samuel Theodore Mander, a member of the family who made their fortune from the manufacture of paints and varnishes. Edward was thought to have been engaged on the redesign and rebuilding of Mander's country estate at Wightwick Manor over a period of several years.

Other Noted Architects

Sir Robert Taylor (1714 – 1788)

Taylor was born at Woodford, Essex in 1714 and having left school, initially followed his father into the family business as a stonemason and sculptor. However, he enjoyed little success in the business and instead turned his talents to architecture, which eventually proved to be a more profitable and successful career.

Fortunately for Taylor, his clients tended to be some of the most important and influential people in society, which inevitably resulted in him being awarded some of the most sought after architectural commissions of the time. Additionally, these contacts also led to him being appointed to at least two important public offices, architect to the Bank of England and architect of the King's Works. Some of his most notable pupils included John Nash, George Byfield and William Pilkington.

Taylor has been credited by some with designing "Forest House" in Chester's Foregate Street which was reported to have been built for the Barnston family of Crewe around 1759. However, a number of other architectural sources have dismissed the idea of the property being the architect's work, most notably because of its age and design. Elsewhere in the city though, Taylor is thought to be responsible for the design of the former Bishop's Palace that once occupied the site, which is now inhabited by Sir Arthur Blomfield's King School buildings that now houses a branch of Barclay's Bank.

William Cole Junior (1800 – 1892)

Reportedly born in Chester, William Cole Junior was thought to be the son of another William Cole who was also an architect in the city. However, William Junior was said to be a pupil of Thomas Harrison and the man credited by some with completing his former masters Grosvenor Bridge, although the names of both James Trubshaw and Jesse Hartley have been attributed to the completed single span river crossing. At the time of its completion, this second Dee bridge was reported to be the widest stone arch in the world and was officially opened by the then Princess Victoria in 1831.

Possibly one of his earliest commissions in the city was the enlargement and restoration of St Oswald's Chapel, in Chester's great former Norman Abbey, which he undertook during 1826. Records tend to suggest that many of William's commissions were in fact funded by either local councils or the church authorities, although he was occasionally employed by individual landowners, such as the Egerton family at Tatton Park.

William is also credited with designing the core buildings of the then newly constructed Chester Lunatic Asylum in 1829 and is noted as being the "County Architect" of the time. Built on ten acres of land purchased from the Reverend Sir Philip Egerton, a Baronet, the plans were drawn up by Cole, who had been selected by the County Magistrates to design the new building, but much of the day-to-day construction work was reportedly undertaken by a Mr W Quay of Neston.

As has been previously mentioned, the now extinct St Bridget's Church, which formerly occupied a site close to Thomas Harrison's modern castle complex, has often been credited to the same master architect, but was probably designed by Cole around 1826. The foundation stone for this popular, but now extinct parish church was reportedly laid on the 27th October 1827, but within 70 years the church was thought to have become unfashionable and was taken down for the second and final time in 1892, the same year that its architect departed this world.

William H Lynn (1829 – 1915)

Although William Henry Lynn is only credited with designing and constructing one single structure in the city, Chester's Town Hall which was generally completed by 1869, is such a notable site that its architect should indeed be mentioned.

William Henry Lynn was born in Belfast and as a 17-year-old was apprenticed to the noted Irish architect Sir Charles Lanyon who was so impressed by the young William that in 1854 he made Lynn a partner in his practice.

In 1872 however, Lynn was reported to have established his own practice in Belfast and set about designing buildings in his favoured modern Gothic and Italianate styles. Much favoured by a number of bank and civic committees, Lynn quickly established a reputation with the commercial, religious and community leaders of the city and was commissioned to design a number of the city's landmark buildings.

Although primarily based within his home city, such was his success and confidence that he was also prepared to compete against his architectural contemporaries across the Irish Sea in the north of England. In 1862, Chester's historic Exchange Building which served as the city's Town Hall was destroyed by fire and the designs for its replacement was put out for competition. Lynn's design which was reported to have been influenced by the medieval Cloth Hall at Ypres proved to be the winner of the contest and although delayed by a series of disputes with the men who were actually building it, the Town Hall was generally completed by 1869. Perhaps as a result of this commission and his ongoing work in Belfast Lynn was thought to have gained further work in mainland Britain, most notably in North Lancashire and Scotland.

Sir Arthur Blomfield (1829 - 1899)

The former Kings School Building (now Barclay's Bank) in Northgate Street was thought to have been converted on the orders of the Dean of Chester's Cathedral around 1875, which resulted in the junction of Northgate Street and St Werburgh Street being widened to its present extent.

The noted architect Sir Arthur William Blomfield was commissioned to undertake the work, no doubt aided by the fact that he was a highly experienced church architect and that his father, who had previously been the Bishop of Chester, later became the Bishop of London. Some five years after completing this particular project, the architect was reported to have returned to Chester Cathedral once again, this time to oversee restoration work within the Abbey, a commission that was thought to have lasted from 1882 through to 1887.

Arthur Blomfield had been born on 6th March 1829 at Fulham Palace in London, the fourth son of Charles James Blomfield, the Bishop of London and who was later educated at Rugby School and at Trinity College, Cambridge, where he received a BA in 1851 and an MA in 1854. By 1861 the architect was reported to have been elected as the President of the Architects Association and in 1883 became the architect to the Bank of England. He received his knighthood from the monarch in 1889 and finally passed away at the age of 70, on the 30th October 1899.

In 1852 he was reported to have been articled to Philip Charles Hardwick and travelled throughout Europe in order to broaden both his horizons and his education. By 1856, the 27-year-old Arthur was thought to have established his own independent practice and no doubt helped by his family connections, within a relatively short time had gained himself a reputation as a leading architect, notably in the design and renovation of church buildings.

The King School for boys which had originally been founded by the Tudor monarch, Henry VIII, sometime after 1540 had previously occupied various locations within the cathedral buildings, including the former refectory of the earlier Norman Abbey. The King's School building, designed in 1875 was thought to have fulfilled this particular role right through to the 1960's, when the school was relocated to a new site on the Wrexham Road on the outskirts of the city.

Harry Beswick

Harry Beswick was reported to have been born in the city of Chester and began his architectural career with the noted local architect Thomas Meakin Lockwood. Beswick was said to have been heavily influenced by the style of his employer and those of his architectural contemporary John Douglas. The young architect was said to have adopted their styles in his early building commissions and between 1891 and 1897 was reported to have trained the nationally renowned architect Ormrod Maxwell Ayrton, who later designed the iconic Wembley Stadium with its famous twin towers. Beswick was appointed County Architect for Cheshire in 1895 and was reported to have been involved with the designs of a number of utilitarian buildings throughout the region, particularly schools and public buildings

Sir George Gilbert Scott (1811 - 1878)

Born at Cawcott in Buckinghamshire to a local builder, George Gilbert Scott was articled to architect James Edmeston from 1827 through to 1831 and later formed a partnership with W B Moffat, a joint architectural practice that would last for some 11 years.

From 1845 onwards however, Scott was reported to have established his own independent practice, assisted by his two sons, George and John. His building designs were thought to be almost entirely in the Gothic style, characterised by its pointed arches, turrets, spires and buttresses, with many of his commissions involving the restoration of early Abbey's, Cathedral's, Churches, etc. Typically, many of his new building designs were generally commissioned by those that admired this particular style of architecture and who wanted their own projects to reflect the grandeur and ornamentation of the Gothic style, as was the case with his two most notable works, the Albert Memorial and St Pancras Station and its Hotel. Despite these successes though, within architectural circles, Scott's designs were not always welcomed and in some cases were known to have caused a great deal of controversy, notably amongst the supporters of the Classical and Renaissance styles of architecture, who more than once accused Scott of ruining the historic fabric he had worked on.

Between 1868 and 1876 Scott undertook a series of restoration projects at Chester's historic Cathedral, which many experts agree was the most dramatic alteration of the building since its foundation in the 11th century. He was reported to have largely rebuilt the Lady Chapel and added the turrets, pinnacles and flying buttresses that adorn the Cathedral's exterior, as well as re-facing much of its crumbling façade with sandstone blocks that were quarried at Runcorn. His most controversial restoration however, was thought to be the reconstruction of the east end of the Cathedral's south choir aisle.

While working at Chester Scott was also credited with designing St Thomas of Canterbury Church which is located on Parkgate Road in Chester and constructed between 1869 and 1872.

Giles Gilbert Scott (1880 - 1960)

The grandson of Sir George Gilbert Scott, Giles Gilbert Scott was born in London on the 9th November 1880, the third son of George Gilbert Scott Junior, who like his more famous father was also an architect. Unhappily for the family, George Junior was thought to have suffered severe mental health problems through the latter part of his life, which ultimately culminated in him committing suicide, reportedly at his own father's St Pancras Station.

For the young Giles however, the illness and later loss of his father does not appear to have hindered his progress towards achieving the aim of following both his father and grandfather into the family business. Educated at Beaumont College, he was then articled to the architect Temple Lushington Moore in 1899, as was his brother Adrian.

Whilst living in Battersea in 1902, Giles entered a competition to design a new church in the city of Liverpool, although with little prospect of actually winning it, which much to his own surprise he did in the following year. Despite the success of his entry, as a relatively untested architect, the authorities in Liverpool were thought to have insisted that Scott work alongside a more established church designer, George Bodley. The two men did not get along, but Bodley's unexpected death in 1907 left Scott alone to design the city's new Anglican Cathedral, which was only finally consecrated in 1924 and not fully completed until 1978, some 18 years after Scott's own death.

In the intervening years, he achieved even greater national distinction with two further landmark projects, Battersea Power Station and Britain's iconic red telephone kiosk. In 1930, proposal's to build a new power generating station at Battersea were tempered with a need to build a plant that was both efficient and generally acceptable to the people and the skyline of the capital city. Because of his architectural style which was thought to have mixed traditional Gothic with both modernism and utilitarianism, Scott was asked to help design an industrial building that was sympathetic to its background, but at the same time, be suitable for its original purpose.

Six years earlier, in 1924, the authorities were reported to have sought a new design for the capital's phone booths, an earlier design having been rejected by them. Whether or not Scott could have ever expected that his highly functional telephone kiosk would eventually become an iconic symbol for everything English is unclear. Nonetheless, the bright red booths designed by the architect have remained a traditional feature of British life for the past 70-odd years and it is only with the advent of mobile communications that their future is now being reconsidered.

In around 1913, Giles was reported to have undertaken a restoration project at Chester Cathedral, parts of which included the design of the "Rood" (Choir Screen), as well as the design of two of the "Reredos" (Altar Screen) which are part of two of the chapels located in the Cathedral's south transept. As part of this same work, he has also been credited with designing the east window of the Cathedral's refectory.

Richard Charles Hussey (1806 - 1887)

Born in 1806, the son of a Rector at Sandhurst in Kent, Richard Charles Hussey entered into a partnership with the noted designer Thomas Rickman in 1835 and continued the practice on his own, following Rickman's retirement due to ill-health in 1838. A gifted artist as well as an architect, Hussey was said to have undertaken restoration work at Chester Cathedral between 1843 and 1844, reportedly in and around the Lady Chapel, during which, previously hidden Norman features was rediscovered and some decayed stonework was also removed. Later in his career, the same architect was thought to have undertaken more restorative work at the equally ancient St John's Church in the city.

James Strong

Reported to have been both a pupil and protégé of Chester's John Douglas, Strong was said to have participated in the rebuilding of Shoemaker's Row in Northgate Street, Chester, most notably at numbers 15 to 17 which were said to have replaced the much older "Cross Key's" inn which had formerly occupied the site. His new building was said to have included a semi-circular window feature that the architect would later employ in his much more renowned, but long since demolished Chester Fire Station.

Strong's picturesque Fire Station which occupied a site at the upper end of modern day Northgate Street and built around 1911, stood on the same spot as had the city's earlier Potato Market. In later years Strong's architectural designs were thought to have been used in the initial phases of the Lache housing estate in 1919, which centred around the present day Cliveden Road, Sunbury Crescent and Abingdon Crescent.

Walter Tapper (1861 - 1935)

Sir Walter Tapper was born at Bovey Tracey in Devon on the 20th April 1861 and later became the chief assistant in the architectural firm of Bodley and Garner around 1882. In 1893 Tapper was thought to have entered into a partnership with J L Davenport and it was only in 1920 that he began to work with his son Michael, who would later complete many of Walter's unfinished designs, including Chester's Newgate. The architect was thought to favour the Gothic Revival style of architecture and he was said to have been extensively employed in the design and restoration of a number of churches and associated religious buildings.

His replica medieval gateway at Chester which was reported to have taken less than two years to complete is constructed of reinforced concrete and faced with sandstone that was quarried at Runcorn. The "New Gate" was reported to have been officially opened on 3rd October 1938, almost three years after its creator had died, on the 21st September 1935.

Ormrod Maxwell Ayrton

Born in 1874 Ayrton is famed for his British Empire Exhibition Wembley Stadium of 1924 and his connection with the city of Chester is said to be very strong, having trained with local architect Harry Beswick between 1890 and 1897, before joining W A Pite in London around the same time and Edward Lutyens from 1897 to 1900. In 1905 Maxwell was recorded to have gone into partnership with Scottish born architect, John William Simpson and Ayrton was generally thought to have been responsible for the partnerships design work. In Chester his legacy remains in the form of St Werburgh's Row, which sits facing the city's historic Cathedral.

CHAPTER FOUR

THE HIGH CROSS

Formed by the conjunction of the Roman's three great internal thoroughfares within the military fortress, Chester's **High Cross**, in common with the rest of the city's historic fabric has been subject to considerable change during its 2000 years of history. Originally, little more than a natural convergence of the Roman's Via Praetoria, Via Principalis and Via Decumana the site of the later High Cross stood in front of what was once the entrance to the legionary's Principia or headquarters building, the remains of which now lie largely beneath St Peter's Church and the generally modern buildings that lie immediately north and west of it.

The actual High Cross at Chester, the stone monument that stands on the site today, is simply thought to be the latest in a long line of such structures that have occupied this particular spot, although its purpose has undoubtedly changed from purely religious to entirely civic over several hundreds of years. The first "Cross" may well have its early origins in the construction of the nearby St Peter's church which was thought to have been re-founded by the Anglo Saxon leader Aethelflaeda around the end of the 9th or beginning of the 10th centuries. This cross was not thought to be in anyway unusual and over the succeeding hundreds of years, numerous such monuments were reported to have been erected both inside and outside of the city, including those dedicated to St Anne, St Stephen, etc. Most of these would subsequently disappear however, notably during the 16th century, when the whole country was wracked by the religious purges and excesses of successive monarch's including Henry VIII, Queen Mary and Elizabeth I.

In 1584 the Cross at the centre of Chester was reported to have fallen down, though whether or not this was due to a deliberate act of religious vandalism or intolerance is unclear. In 1644 a similar event occurred, although most commentators at the time suggested that it was more likely that poor workmanship or general neglect had caused the collapse rather than anything malicious or untoward. However, given the events of the time, the English Civil War and the ensuing siege of Chester, it was perhaps little wonder that when the forces of Parliament did finally conquer the Royalist city that the relatively insecure High Cross was an easy target for Roundhead frustrations who were said to have pulled it down purely as an act of retribution in 1646.

Described as having a seven sided capital sitting atop a 3 metre shaft, the Chester Cross was reported to have been smashed into several pieces by the Parliamentary vandals, who then simply discarded the remnants around the adjoining city streets. The head of this original Cross was said to have been inscribed with ornate tabernacle work, along with images of various saints and been topped with a slightly smaller capital designed in a similar manner. Following its demolition, the broken pieces of the monument were thought to have been buried below the walls of the nearby St Peter's church and seem to have remained largely forgotten for an extended period of time, until they were rediscovered when the stairway to the church was rebuilt in 1804. The recovered fragments were then removed to the care of St Peter's, until finally in 1815 they were handed over to Sir John Cotgreave who relocated the remnants to his new home at "Netherleigh" in the suburb of Handbridge.

According to legend Sir John intended to use the shaft of the cross as the base for a sundial that was being installed within the grounds of his new home, but after being constructed it almost immediately fell down. Re-erected once again, the feature once again fell over and perhaps through disgust and frustration the stonework was simply allowed to remain in the ditch into which it fell. Fortunately however, the pieces were subsequently recovered from the grounds at a later date and returned to the city, although the head of the medieval cross was reported to have been donated to the Grosvenor Museum.

As the central meeting point for Chester's early streets, it seems likely that the High Cross would have been first and foremost, a rallying point for the citizens and defenders of the city. However, as time passed and the city's commerce developed, the area of the Cross would have become much busier as citizens, visitors and traders moved back and forth between the different parts of the city. Consequently, its position became far more central to the city's everyday life and the High Cross was reportedly used to house Chester's Pillory, its Whipping Post and its Stocks, as well as being the place where public announcements were made and decrees issued. A far narrower, dirtier and cramped location than today's representation, due in part to the presence of the previously mentioned instruments of punishment, the city's High Cross was also known to be the site of fairly unpleasant bull-baiting contests, where the unfortunate beast would be tormented and set upon by the dogs owned by Chester's resident Butchers and Bakers. The final bull-bait was said to have taken place in the city in 1803, although such practices were thought to have continued elsewhere in the outlying suburbs for many years after.

Thought to have been located at what would now be the junction of Bridge Street and Watergate Street, Chester's stocks, whipping post and pillory were reported to have been sited on an elevated platform, sufficiently high enough to allow a small shop to be located beneath it. Although the names and purpose of the first two devices are plain enough, the Pillory appears to have been a variation of the stocks, but one where the miscreant was required to stand with their hands and head restrained by the device, often for hours at a time. A second occasional punishment associated with the Pillory was commonly inflicted on slanderers or seditious libeller's who were found guilty of such offences by the city courts. Their ears might be nailed to the retaining board of the device and then simply removed with the use of a razor or sharp knife, as happened to a small number of men whose opinions were deemed to be slanderous, libellous or treasonous.

Although some historic sources suggest that the Pillory had existed in Chester since Tudor times, both the Anglo Saxon and later Norman societies were thought to have employed similar devices for punishing wrongdoers. However, it doesn't appear to have been a regular form of punishment in the city and by 1789, it was reported that no person had been "pilloried" in Chester for some 20 years and during the previous 90 years only 4 people had actually been sentenced to this particular penalty.

As Chester's main streets gradually became populated with stone built cellars, grand halls and their early elevated arcades in the late 13th and early 14th centuries, then maybe this period also saw the construction of the first **Pentice** building, the forerunner of today's Town Hall. Known to have existed by the beginning of the 15th century, this timber and stone construction was reported to have essentially "wrapped around" the southern and eastern walls of St Peter's Church and was little more than a highly impressive two storey "lean to", within which a series of civic and commercial chambers were arranged.

Incorporating a number of civic offices, including the city's Treasury Chamber and the Pentice Court, an earlier building was reported to have been largely rebuilt in 1497. This early administrative centre was the base for the city's Mayor, his Sheriff's and the Clerk of the Pentice, who nowadays would probably be known as the Town Clerk. Within this building, local trading or business disputes would be settled, apprenticeships registered and local taxes paid. In fact, apart from Crown or national matters which were dealt with at the Castle, most of the city's day-to-day commercial activities were brought before the Mayor and his Corporation who were housed within the Pentice.

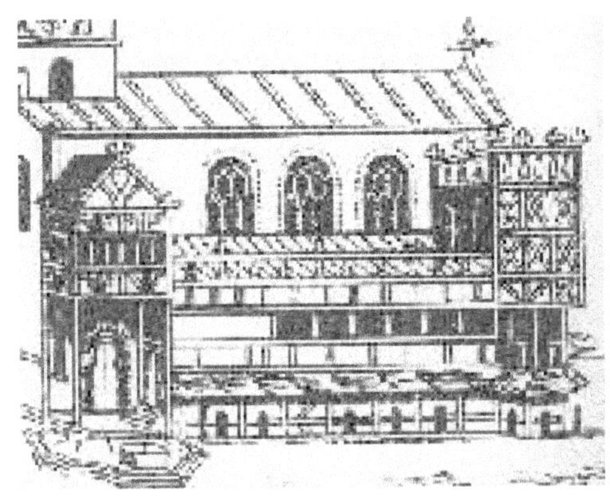

In addition to being the commercial and administrative centre of Chester, the city's Pentice was also the civic heart of the community, the place where nobles and local dignitaries would be entertained by the Mayor and his Council. When King Charles I visited Chester in 1642 prior to the outbreak of the English Civil War, he was heartily entertained by the Corporation and a number of Chester's leading citizens at the Pentice. It was also on this building that Chester's historic Wooden Glove would be hung to announce the start of the city's annual fairs, a tradition that was said to have begun in the 13th century, but was done away with in 1836 by a particularly miserly Mayor, who refused to pay the cost of having the emblem hung out. Unfortunately, the Pentice building failed to survive that late, reportedly being demolished in March 1806, many years after the Mayor and Corporation had finally removed themselves, first to St Nicholas' Chapel and then later to the new Exchange Building on the Market Square which was raised in 1698.

Associated with the Pentice building, was the **Mayor's Balcony**, an elevated platform from which the Mayor and his corporation could deliver local ordinances, election results, civic speeches, as well as watching events unfold at the High Cross which lay beneath their vantage point. Later reports suggest that this mayoral balcony lay slightly to the west of St Peter's church doorway, the site now incorporated into the elevated row which fronts the modern day Deva Hotel.

The modern day **St Peter's Church** lies above the remains of the Roman headquarters building of the former military fortress, the Principia. Although the church was reportedly founded by the Anglo Saxon leader, Aethelflaeda around the end of the 9th, or beginning of the 10th century, it known to have been substantially rebuilt in the middle of the 14th century, with much of the church's current architecture reported to date from between 1350 and 1550. The medieval builders responsible for the construction were thought to have rebuilt the church's north aisle above an existing undercroft, which explains the church' elevated floor, rather than it being set at street level. It is also worth noting, that this later church is thought to have a substantially larger footprint than its Anglo Saxon predecessor, reflecting its increasing importance and status within the city.

The modern day church looks very different from that which existed in earlier years, when St Peter's was known to have been partially obscured by the city's Pentice and its outside stairwell was on an entirely different alignment. Additionally, from around the middle of the 16th century a "Rectory" was reported to have existed above the southern porch of the church. Reported to have been constructed of timber and plaster, this structure was said to have formed two separate chambers and in 1699 a petition was made to erect a stairwell from the south doorway directly to this "Rector's House", a plea which was subsequently granted. Church records are said to recall the individual holders of the post of Rector at St Peter's all the way back to 1195.

The church's looming spire was reported to have been taken down in 1780 having been struck by lightning and the south wall was said to have been damaged by Thomas Harrison during work he undertook in the area in around 1804, possibly with work involved with the then still standing Pentice building. These defects were thought to have been subsequently repaired by the architect John Douglas when he undertook work on the church in 1886.

The first clock to be installed at St Peter's was reported to have been provided by a city clockmaker called William Sampson in 1585 and in return for his gift was thought to have been made a Freeman of Chester sometime later. The clock which currently adorns the south face of St Peter's tower was said to have first been installed in 1813, as part of the re-casing work undertaken on the church by Thomas Harrison in that year. In 1825, the clock face was said to have been adapted so that it could be illuminated by gas light.

On the northern side of St Peter's, the church's ancient burial grounds are generally hidden from view by later developments and are simply marked by a paved courtyard surrounded by a number of city inns and Harrison's two classic commercial buildings. Although part of the church's early graveyard is thought to lie below the extended medieval precincts of St Peter's itself, many other early internments have undoubtedly been disturbed and possibly removed due to the location of the church itself and the subsequent need for building land in the area. During the 17th century, the graveyard was reportedly being used as a regular shortcut by the customers of the three city taverns which stood in the area and records suggest that the churchwardens of St Peter's were being instructed to find a solution to this particular problem. One method of controlling these unauthorised incursions was said to have involved nailing shut the rear doors of the offending taverns, so that customers were forced to use an alternative route, but within a short time these doors were thought to have been forced open again and the problem returned. It was possibly as a result of these issues, that finally the church and city authorities ordered the area to be paved, thereby preventing further damage to the final resting places of these early parishioners.

The other major structure that inhabited the south east flank of the city's High Cross was the main water **Conduit** that served a number of the principal buildings in this part of the city. Some sources suggest that this particular storage tank had existed as early as the 1580's when such water services were becoming popular throughout England, but formal records from Chester indicate that construction of the conduit at the High Cross was in fact commenced around 1622. This reservoir was said to have been constructed by John Tyrer, the same man who was responsible for the Water Tower at the Bridgegate and a second conduit in the suburb of Boughton, on the site of fresh water springs. As the Roman's had done some 1500 years earlier, Tyrer was reported to have transported this fresh water supply through the city streets by way of lead piping and delivered it directly to the conduit. A later reporter described the water house as being built of stone and sitting on four great arches and decorated with the emblems of some of Chester's most notable families, including the Stanley's who were associated with the Earl's of Derby. When the conduit was finally being demolished in 1805, it was reported that a large vat of wine was emptied into the water tank, allowing the liquor to flow freely to the waiting citizens of Chester. The site of the early reservoir is now thought to be marked by the buildings at No 2 Eastgate Street and 1 Bridge Street which were both designed and constructed by the local architect TM Lockwood in 1888 for the Duke of Westminster.

CHAPTER FIVE

NORTHGATE STREET

Running from the city's High Cross northward to the rear gateway of the early Roman fortress, today's **Northgate Street** marks the route of the legionary's Via Decumana which led out of the northern gateway of the camp and onto to both the Wirral peninsula and north east Cheshire. It has also been suggested that in its earliest form, the southern limits of this military roadway, immediately adjoining the modern day St Peter's church and Shoemaker's Row, was thought to have lain slightly east of its present position, simply to accommodate the vast Principia building which was known to have existed at that time.

Representing the main military, administrative and judicial centre of the northwest region of Britain, Chester's **Roman Principia** building was thought to be an extremely important and highly impressive structure, which was designed to reflect the wealth, style and more importantly, the military might of the empire. Comprising a large open courtyard that fronted the main building, the Principia at Chester was also reported to have included a Judgement Hall, suites of administrator's offices, shrine's to the various Roman deities and a strong-room, where the legionary pay chests and valuable equipment could be stored. Known as the Sacellum, this vault was typically flanked on one side by the office of the legionary Signifier, the officer who paid the troops and looked after the legions treasury and its valuables. Often the Sacellum would have been located immediately below the main legionary shrine in the Principia and accessed via a trapdoor or by a dedicated flight of stairs leading to the strong-room. This vault was said to have been guarded day and night and for the men chosen to watch over the treasury, was considered to be a great honour to be chosen for the task.

Today, this 2000 year old former stone cut vault, or Sacellum, can be viewed through a large window located on the southern flank of the 1960's "Forum" shopping centre, which now largely occupies the site of the Roman's Praetorium, the military Legate's or Praetor's accommodations. According to local archaeologists that have studied the now hidden remains of the Principia at Chester, in its final form, the building was thought to have been some 300 feet long and an equally impressive 230 feet wide. Lying on a north-south alignment, its great mass was thought to have been supported by a series of massive stone columns, evidence of which still exist below today's St Peter's church and Shoemaker's Row and its south facing entrance was said to have been deliberately built up with terraces, to further enhance its already imposing façade.

As with many of the great Roman structures that were all but abandoned by their legionary builders in the late 4th or early 5th centuries, Chester early Principia building failed to survive above ground and only relatively small amounts lie below today's street level. It seems likely that as elsewhere, the stonework of this imposing structure was eventually robbed out by the later British and Anglo Saxon inhabitants of the now defunct Roman fortress, to be used on other building projects, including the new Christian churches that were beginning to emerge. With much of the site cleared, the little that did remain was thought to have then been covered over by the body of the newly founded church of St Peter, which is thought to have been established by the Anglo Saxon leader Aethelflaeda in the late 9th century.

Immediately north of St Peter's and separated by the narrow St Peter's Churchyard passage, the **Commercial Newsroom**, which has also been known as the City Club and the Commercial Coffee House was designed by Thomas Harrison in 1808 in his favoured Greek revival style and is highly reminiscent of his castle buildings that stand to the south of the city, overlooking the River Dee. In its original form the street level shop fronts first designed by Harrison met the public footpath directly, but during the 1960's they were deliberately moved back to create an extension to Douglas' arcaded Shoemaker's Row.

Records relating to the post Roman history of this particular site are said to be fairly extensive, with a deed of 1345 noting that the land and the properties associated with it were granted to William of Doncaster and his wife around that same year. By the 15th century however, the property was reported to have been owned by a member of the Bellot family who seem to have had a connection with the area of Great Moreton on the Wirral and a hundred years after that, the land was thought to have been in the possession of the Leech or Leich family.

Prior to the construction of the Newsrooms, parts of this same general area had previously been occupied by a succession of city taverns, the first dating from around 1272 and said to be in the ownership of one Hugh Selimon or Salmon. Five hundred years later, the final two hostelries to occupy the same site were thought to be the "Three Crowns", which was subsequently relocated to Pepper Street in the city around 1782 and later replaced by the modern day "Bridgewater Arms". The "Legs of Man" was said to be the final city tavern to occupy the Commercial Newsroom site, which it did from 1782 through to around 1807 when the whole area was razed to make way for Harrison's two new buildings. It has been suggested that the sign, the "Legs of Man" had some sort of connection with the Stanley family, who were known to be associated with the Isle of Man, from where the sign was thought to have derived its origins.

The Commercial Newsrooms was primarily constructed as a private members club, where Chester's well-to-do, idle rich or the city's wealthy visitors, who had little to occupy their time, could entertain themselves with reading from the club's extensive library, amuse themselves by playing cards or billiards, or perhaps simply by drinking from the club's well stocked cellars. However, in December 1808 just after the new building had been erected, the ground floor of the property was reported to have been occupied by the "Chester Bank", which seems to have been a relatively unsuccessful venture that closed some 19 months later, in July of 1810. The business was then thought to have been taken over by a Mister Roscoe from Liverpool who was subsequently succeeded by the partnership of Dixon and Chilton who seemed to have moved the bank to new premises, next to the White Lion Hotel on the Market Square.

Outside and on either side of the Newsroom building, narrow passageway's led to the northern side of St Peter's Church and to Harrison's own Commercial Hotel, which even today remains hidden away from view by the mass of the Commercial Newsroom building.

The main passageway which leads to the club's entrance and the generally unseen hotel, the Commercial Passage, was reported in the middle of the 19th century to have become a dumping ground for some citizens of Chester and the matter was thought to be so serious that the city authorities were forced to intervene to help remedy the situation.

The site of Harrison's **Commercial Hotel** is thought to have a fairly extensive history as well, with early records suggesting that an inn called the "Rising Sun" had occupied parts of the same site since 1630 and perhaps even earlier than that. This historic tavern was thought to have been so well regarded by a number of Chester's gentleman, who were so horrified at its possible loss, that the inn was completely rebuilt in around 1809, but subsequently operated under the sign of the Commercial Tavern.

Despite the look of the modern day **Shoemaker's Row** at the southern end of Northgate Street, the arcaded parade of shops which exists today bears little resemblance to the original elevated row which occupied the site prior to 1899. As elsewhere in Chester, the original Shoemaker's Row, which was alternatively known as Corvisor's or Cordwainer's Row, consisted of two separate tiers of shop's and private accommodations, at both street and first floor levels with an elevated walkway running along its full length. A painting of the row, undertaken by the renowned artist Louise Raynor during the second half of the 19th century, shows this long extinct row prior to its destruction some 20 years later.

Its modern replacement, which remains with us today, was thought to have been designed and constructed in a fairly piecemeal fashion, preventing its main contributor John Douglas from having any sort of overall control of the project. Douglas himself was said to have designed No's 5 to 13, No 19 and No's 27 to 31 of the modern terrace. Number 9 of the old Shoemakers Row was reported to have housed the "Sun Tavern" in 1675, the hostelry finally being closed in 1900, as the whole row was being redeveloped by the architects.

James Strong, a pupil of Douglas was reported to have designed No's 15 to 17, which replaced the old Cross Keys Inn that contained a semi-circular window feature that he repeated in his 1911 Fire Station building further along Northgate Street. No 25 of the former Row was reported to house the "Woolpack Inn" which was only partially rebuilt by Douglas in 1903, but was later refaced by Strong around 1914. In modern times, the site of this particular hostelry was said to have been occupied by Sidoli's Restaurant and now by Weinholt's the Bakers. Cheshire County architect Harry Beswick, a pupil of T M Lockwood has been credited with designing No 3 and No's 21 to 23 in the modern parade.

Somewhere within the earlier Shoemaker's Row, a tavern called the "Eagle and Child" was reported to have existed from 1540, but after 1721 had been closed down and relocated to Foregate Street in the city. This particular hostelry was thought to have hosted meetings of the city's Minstrel's Guilds. The emblem, depicting an eagle and child is thought to be associated with the related Latham and Stanley families, the latter one having close ties to the city of Chester, most notably as the Earl's of Derby. After 1721, the site of the Eagle and Child in Northgate Street was reported to have been subsequently occupied by another tavern called the "Legs of Man" until 1782, when it too was removed to the site of the later Commercial Newsrooms. As for the Eagle and Child tavern itself, following its move to new premises in Foregate Street it was known to have continued in existence until at least 1758, when the land adjoining the hostelry was sold and the tavern itself was thought to have been demolished to make way for Thomas Lunt's Union Hall building which was constructed in 1809.

On the east side of lower Northgate Street a short elevated row exists above the site of what was once Chester's renowned **Quaintway's** store, which in later years has been occupied by various retail outlets, including in recent times a branch of the "Superdrug" chain. The first floor row is now part of the modern "Rosie's" nightclub complex, but formerly hosted the "Ship and Turtle" inn which was once reported to have been the location for a tavern known as the "Muggeries" and may in fact have once temporarily hosted yet another hostelry called the "Bulls Head".

During the Victorian period, this same extensive Quaintway's property was known to have been the home of one of Chester's most noted wine merchants, Walker and Knight's, who were reported to have utilised the 15th century vaulted cellars which lie below street level and today form part of modern retail premises. It has also been suggested that a notable tavern called "The Cross Key's" had also stood on the site of the later Quaintway's store, before being relocated to Clayton Lane (modern day Duke Street) in the city. However, other reports indicate that the Cross Keys tavern had in fact occupied a site further up the street, closer to the modern day walkway known as Music Hall Passage.

Immediately north of the former Quaintway's building which now houses the Rosie's nightclub complex, there is a narrow alleyway known as **Smith's Passage**, which may or may not owe its name to the city's Ironmonger's who once occupied this section of the city. Seemingly an unremarkable walkway, little used by most pedestrians, a chance discovery in 1892 gave local historians an insight into the past use and former architecture of this particular area of the city. As part of the rebuilding of Walker and Knights property, local workmen were reported to have discovered remnants of previously unrecorded Roman architecture, including the floors and pilae (supports) of a an early legionary hypocaust that had lain relatively undisturbed for hundreds of years. Parts of this same heating system were said to have extended underneath Smith's Passage at a distance of some 30 yards from the main street, but circumstances prevented any further investigation of the walkway. However, at the rear of the wine merchant's property that was being rebuilt, evidence of later, but equally important architecture was discovered, including parts of a 15th century medieval hall and a 16th century Tudor ceiling. Although some of these early architectural treasures were viewed and recorded in part by local antiquarians, perhaps rather typically for Chester, they were later reported to have been simply demolished and disposed of by the contractors employed to rebuild the property.

In between the south east junction of Northgate Street, the more northerly Music Hall Passage and directly opposite to Shoemaker's Row stood the arcade which was commonly known as "**Broken Shin Row**". Reportedly given this name because of the uneven ground and the number of obstacles which daily hindered the pedestrians path, this local name is perhaps more likely to have connections with the city's Ironmongers who were thought to have occupied much of this area. Earlier still, many of these same properties were said to have formed part of Chester's "Cooks Row" which was thought to have been linked to "Pepper Alley" at the northwest junction of Eastgate Street and which itself had one time been called "Country Bakers Row"

The covered alleyway on the eastern flank of Northgate Street and today known as the **Music Hall Passage**, owes its title to the adjoining former chapel of St Nicholas which is discussed below. Around the beginning of the 17th century, circa 1610, this alleyway was thought to have been enclosed within the walls of the city's Cathedral precincts, which were thought to have extended from the site of the Bishop's Palace (now Barclays Bank) to a point just south of the passageway itself. The churchyard walls then ran in a generally eastern direction towards the south transept of the Cathedral, its route possibly marked by part of the modern St Werburgh Street. At around the same time that the passage was reported to be lying within the precincts of the Cathedral, it was also recorded that the alleyway was being paved by the authorities, suggesting that the walkway was in fact one of the main entrances into the churchyard.

At some point in its history, the building which forms part of the south side of the modern alleyway was thought to have been occupied by a building called Mc Hattie's Warehouse, although a chamber within this same property was reportedly called "the Chapel" suggesting that it had once served a less secular purpose. Some historians have proposed that either this building or perhaps an even earlier one had actually been the location for St Oswald's Vicarage, which was known to have existed in this general area and that this might explain the religious title sometimes attached to the site. Others though are far less certain about this idea and believe that the Vicarage in question was in fact located slightly east of the passageway, on the site of St Werburgh's Mount which faces the Cathedral's southern entrance.

St Nicholas' Chapel which lies between both Northgate Street and St Werbugh's Street is thought to have been founded in the 14th century and was said to have first been recorded in 1389, although it has also been suggested that the building may in fact date from around 1280, a full hundred years earlier. Its construction is generally attributed to Abbot Simon of Whitchurch who held that particular office from 1265 through to 1291, so the earlier date is possibly more accurate. The Chapel was specifically built for the parishioners of St Oswald's church, which was then housed in the south transept of the Abbey, but they were said to be so unhappy about their removal from the main Abbey precincts that they refused to worship in the new Chapel.

As a result the building was eventually given over to the city authorities in the 15th century for more secular activities and having been adapted and enlarged became the city's Common Hall for nearly 250 years, between 1545 and 1698. During this period and in common with the earlier Moot Hall which had been located in Commonhall Street, the former Chapel was used as an assembly point for the city's medieval "watches" or guards that were placed in charge of the city's medieval gateways. Made up of chosen individuals, this troop of men would march to each of Chester's gates and leave them in the charge of a group of citizens who would prevent access to any and all unauthorised visitors. These watchmen were also expected to protect the city and its historic fabric from the danger of fire, a well as alerting the authorities to any criminal acts that might occur during their period of duty.

With the construction of the new Exchange building in 1698, the former Chapel of St Nicholas was then said to have been used as a **Wool Hall** for nearly three decades, as well as housing one of the city's Flesh shambles on its ground floor. In 1636 the building was reported to have been used as a meeting place for the city's Smith's, Cutlers and Plumbers Company who purchased the property in 1700, before it was eventually adapted into a playhouse in 1727. Although the building was known to have been used as a place of entertainment from 1600 onwards, it was only formally recognised and licensed for that purpose in 1773 when it officially became the Theatre Royal. Two noted entertainers who performed at the theatre were Joseph Grimaldi, the celebrated "clown" who appeared in a performance of "Mother Goose" and David Garrick, the theatre actor and manager of the famous Drury Lane Theatre in London. However, despite the occasional visits of such luminaries and the obvious popularity of the old theatre, by 1854, its ancient fabric was beginning to show its age and was reported to have been in a fairly dilapidated condition.

Between 1854 and 1855, the noted Chester architect James Harrison undertook restoration work on the chapel building, adapting it for use as a **Music Hall** and including the Gothic Façade which fronts onto St Werburgh Street. It was following these works, that the ground floor of the building was reported to have been used as a warehouse by a firm of carriers called Robins, Mills and Company who operated in the city, whilst the upper floor remained employed as a place of entertainment. A notable visitor for the Music Hall in 1869 was the writer Charles Dickens, who was recorded to have performed readings of two works, "Marigold" and "Trial" in January of that year, but who appears to have been less than impressed both by the snowy weather and the coolness of the Music Hall itself.

In the 20th century the building was adapted once again, this time as a cinema, with the job of converting this ancient building into a modern picture palace reportedly beginning in 1921. The building work was reported to have been undertaken by J E Mayers and during this work a number of skeletons were discovered, relating to its original purpose as a place of religion and interment. Much archaeological evidence of its medieval construction was uncovered and recorded, but by November of 1921 the Conversion of the Chapel had been completed and the new Picture House was officially opened on the 28th of that month. The architects for the new picture house were thought to be Minshull and Muspratt, the partnership who had also designed the "Glynn" cinema in Foregate Street and who had previously been associated with Chester's noted building designer John Douglas. In later years however, the picture house was unable to survive the pressure of competition from the new cinema chains and the rise of television as a form of mass media entertainment and was eventually closed down. During the late 1960's a branch of the supermarket chain Lipton's was reported to have occupied the premises and it has served a succession of high street names in that role right through to the present day.

On the western side of the street, the modern day **Dublin Packet** building was undoubtedly reconstructed at the same time that the adjoining Shoemakers Row was built, with the most northerly point of the arcade indicating a date of 1904. However the hostelry itself is reported to date from at least 1809 when it was recorded to have operated as one of the city's polling stations, although it was then known as the Dublin Packet Vaults. The Tavern was commonly known as "Dixie Dean's", it having being run by a footballer of that name during the 20th century.

During the Roman occupation of the Chester fortress, the area generally marked by the modern day Forum and Victorian Town Hall was the location for the Roman Legate's or Praetor's residence, which was more commonly known as the **Praetorium**. As the man who was ultimately responsible for implementing Roman planning, both civil and military, he was the most important person within the fortress and his accommodation were said to have reflected that elevated status. Reportedly measuring some 200 feet from east to west and an equally long distance from north to south, the Praetorium was thought to have been yet another imposing building within the early Roman camp.

In most permanent legionary camps or fortress' the Praetor's accommodations were known to have been fairly commodious and built to the high standards which befitted his exalted rank and status, not only within the camp itself, but also throughout the wider region. It has been suggested that in some cases, the Praetorium often accounted for up to 10% of the total space within a legionary base, indicating the importance of this particular Roman office holder. However, when bearing in mind that such individuals would almost certainly have had their own household with them, including family members, personal and military advisers, as well as their own doctor and a number of slaves, then the reason for large-scale accommodations becomes clear. It is also worth noting of course, that the Praetorium building itself would have needed to include private accommodations for all of these individuals, along with the necessary kitchens, bathing facilities, latrines, temples, offices and entertaining rooms that were required for its many and varied inhabitants. Located around a large central courtyard, these rooms and spaces would have been added to by the almost obligatory stables and slave quarters that would have housed the animals and servants who were constantly at the beck and call of the Praetor and his guests.

Large scale excavations of the site during the 1960's, in preparation for the construction of the modern day Forum shopping complex, revealed that the Praetorium had initially been constructed of stone, but subjected to several phases of redevelopment throughout its lifetime, with internal walls and doorways being added and removed at various times. At least two Roman altars, which have been recovered from the same general area, were known to have been attributed to two legionary doctors, Hermogenes and Antiochus, suggesting to some historians that the building might in fact have been a legionary hospital, a Valetudinarium rather than the Praetorium. However, the fact that the footprint of the excavated building failed to adhere to the accepted hospital layout and the likelihood that legionary doctors would have lived within the Legate's private residence, all suggested that the Roman building which formerly existed on the site of today's Forum shopping centre was indeed the Praetorium and that the hospital lay elsewhere within the fortress.

As with the neighbouring Principia, the Praetorium would undoubtedly have survived well beyond the final evacuation of the fortress by its Roman builders, being slowly eroded by the British climate and with its stonework being regularly robbed out by the local people for use on other projects. Finally, what little remained of the ancient fabric would have been swept away by local builders, in order to erect the medieval properties that would eventually develop into the likes of the later White Lion, Golden Hart, Saracen's Head, etc. which were themselves sacrificed during the 19th century for the construction of Chester's long lost Market Hall building and the still standing Town Hall.

Further west and immediately behind the Praetorium, stood the remains of an elliptical structure which even today continues to defy clear identification, but which is speculated to have been either a Roman Shrine or perhaps a theatre of some sort. Either way though, following the large scale archaeological investigations of the site in the 1960's all of this whole area was subject to machine-based scouring, creating the car parks and delivery bays that service the Forum shopping centre which now occupies much of the site. In fact what little remains of the highly impressive Praetorium building, assuming of course that it wasn't destroyed during earlier city developments, is probably now hidden below the mass of William Lynn's Town Hall, as well as the city's bustling market square which fronts that particular building.

In 1815 and prior to the construction of Chester's Public Market Hall, the likes of the "Golden Hart" Inn was reported to be standing on the former site of the Praetorium. However, in that same year the inn was said to have been renamed as the "Lord Hill", a title it was known to have held for some forty-odd years before having its name changed once again to the "Great Britain" in 1858. Around 1860, when the idea of a new Public Market was being considered by the city authorities, this whole section of the Market Square, from the end of the original Shoemaker's Row, north to Princess Street, and including the whole of the former Praetorium site was known to have been fully occupied by a number of Chester's most historic buildings. The "Boot Inn", the "White Lion Hotel", the "Market Tavern", the "Prince of Wales Inn", "The Fleece" and the "Eastham Packet" were all reported to have inhabited the area of land which would later play host to the impressive Victorian Public Market and its later Town Hall.

Of the many buildings which were sacrificed for Chester's 19th century Town Hall and Public Market the most significant was the **White Lion Hotel** which was reported to have stood on the Market Square for a fairly extensive period of time and to have comprised at least half of the area of the new Public Market. Throughout its life, this hostelry was thought to have been one of the principal coaching inns within the city and played host to many of the celebrities and high profile individuals who passed through or visited Chester. The entertainer Joseph Grimaldi, the celebrated clown was said to have stayed at the White Lion during his week long visit to the city, when he performed at the nearby Music Hall Theatre. His co-star and close friend Bologna was also a guest at the hostelry and the famed actor and theatre manager David Garrick, part owner of the Drury Lane Theatre was also thought to have enjoyed its fine accommodations.

In 1708, a major conflagration was reported to have occurred in the barn and stables of the White Lion which threatened to spread to a number of other important buildings that stood nearby. Thankfully, the efforts of the city's authorities and citizens prevented the blaze from spreading and the damage was kept to a minimum. The barns, stables and coach houses of the White Lion were thought to have been fairly extensive, notably at the beginning of the 19th century when the nearby Coach and Horses Inn was reported to have transferred all of its coaching services to the neighbouring hostelry. A noted feature of the Hotel was said to have been a mile-stone, which displayed the distances of the major mail coach routes which serviced the city and that was known to have stood outside of the Hotel during its lifetime. With the loss of the White Lion however, in around 1861, this unique mile-post was said to have mysteriously disappeared and has never been seen again.

Sometime later in the hotel's long history the Dixon's and Wardell's Bank was said to have stood next door to the White Lion, but this business later removed itself to new premises just outside the city's Eastgate, in the property now known as the Old Bank Building. Standing to the other side of the White Lion, the Boot Inn was reported to have been located on the Market Square up until 1784 when that particular building was demolished, the tavern itself being relocated to its current home on the north side of Eastgate Street.

Along with the previously mentioned White Lion Inn, another of the city's most notable coaching inns which was ultimately demolished to make way for the new Town Hall and Public Market buildings was the **Saracen's Head**, which may have been established there sometime after the English Civil War siege of the city. This same sign had previously existed in Foregate Street prior to the Siege of Chester, but that building was thought to have been so badly damaged during the conflict that it was subsequently demolished and later rebuilt as the Wettenhall mansion, a private family residence in the city.

In modern day Chester, the general footprint of the old 19th century Market Hall is marked by the utilitarian mass of the Forum Shopping Centre, which itself is soon to vanish, less than half a century after it was first constructed. The Chester **Market Hall building** which was constructed during the late 1860's was reported to have been designed by Mr James Hay, an architect from Liverpool who has also been credited with designing the church at Bidston near Chester. The Public Market having stood for just over a hundred years, from 1862 to 1967, became a centrepiece of the historic city, but was eventually demolished to make way for the modern day Forum shopping centre which stands today and its associated underground car park and delivery bays.

This old Market Hall was officially opened by the Prince of Wales (later King Edward VII) on 10th March 1863 and when completed comprised nine front bays divided by columns. Although most sources accept that Mr Hay was the architect, others suggest that the building was in fact designed by a Mr Roberts of Chester, although this is largely based on his name being attached to a floor plan of the building, which might simply suggest that he was the building contractor, rather than the designer.

Designed principally to house the numerous "markets" and "shambles", many of which had existed in the city since medieval times, the site on Chester's Market Square was originally only one of many that were suggested, others included the city's former Linen Halls in St Werburgh Street and the one located in Lower Watergate Street, but none of these other locations were deemed to be suitable and so finally the present one was chosen. With the building finally erected in 1863, the various city markets were brought indoors, including those traders who had previously sold their fish, vegetables, butter, poultry, etc in clearly defined areas of the city's streets. Up until 1900, potato merchants were reported to have had their own separate market, at the site of the later Fire Station, further along Northgate Street, but in that year they too were selling their goods in the new Public Market building.

The only traders who were not initially housed in the new market building were the city butchers or "flesh-mongers" who were known to have had their own "shambles" on Chester's Market Square. Facing the site of the modern day Library building, their business premises were reported to have been the former Shire Hall, which during the 16th century had stood outside the walls of Chester's then still standing medieval castle. An acute lack of space within the new public building may also have contributed to the delay in adding the butchers markets to the rest of the traders, but a later expansion of the market hall at its northern end finally allowed this to take place sometime after 1864.

Chester's Victorian Gothic **Town Hall** was designed by the Belfast architect W H Lynn in around 1864 and was his entry for a competition run by Chester Corporation to find a replacement building for the city's 1698 Exchange Building which was destroyed by fire in 1862. Thought to have been inspired by the medieval Cloth Hall at Ypres, initially the cost of the new civic structure was reported to have been set at £16, 000, but this was easily surpassed and was undoubtedly added to by a strike amongst the masons who fell into a dispute with the city's Clerk of Works, resulting in the building taking four years to build rather than the planned two. Officially opened by the Prince of Wales, later King Edward VII, on the 15th October 1896, in the following year a fire in the Council Chamber resulted in that particular room being seriously damaged, an event that was later remedied by the local architect T M Lockwood in 1898.

The previously mentioned **Exchange Building** was the predecessor to Chester's Victorian Town hall and was reported to have stood on the south side of Princess Street, somewhere between its later successor and today's Barclay's Bank Building which adjoins the body of Chester's magnificent Cathedral. Constructed in 1698 to replace the much earlier Pentice and Common Halls in the city, the Exchange building existed until 1862 when it was severely damaged by fire and had to be demolished.

Reported to have cost around £1000 to build, construction on the new Exchange Building was thought to have started in 1695 and been finished in 1698. Adorned with a statue of Queen Anne dressed in her coronation robes, this figure was said to have been sculpted by local mason John Tilston, the man responsible for the rebuilding of the tower called Pemberton's Parlour along the city walls, who was said to have died in September 1723 and later been interred at St John's Church in the city. Following the devastating fire of 30th December 1862, which largely destroyed the Exchange building the statue was removed for renovation and later placed on a plinth on the city's Water Tower, from where it mysteriously disappeared sometime later.

Described as a large square brick building with stone facings, the Exchange was thought to have stood on a series of stone pillars, one of which continues to stand in the centre of Abbey Green today. With a central thoroughfare running from north to south, the building also included an eastern entrance and in 1756 four extra rows of stone pillars were added to further strengthen the edifice. Around the same time, additional features were added to the ground floor, including a row of shops on the western side of the central thoroughfare, a shop at the south east corner and an enclosed room at the north east angle of the building. One of the new business premises on the ground floor was thought to have later become a popular city centre coffee house.

The upper floors of the Exchange contained the city's Banqueting or Assembly Hall and the suite of civic offices which housed the many administrators and elected officials who ran Chester on a day to day basis. Including the Council Chamber, the Common or Moot Hall, the Magistrates and Pentice Courts, at the south end of the Common Hall the Mayors Portmote Court was reported to have been located and at its northern end the Sheriffs Court. In later years, the ground floor shops and spaces were thought to have been altered, becoming instead Police Offices, a local Bridewell and the office of Chester's Town Clerk. Much of this later work, possibly undertaken around 1852 was thought to have been supervised by the city surveyor and architect Benjamin Baylis, who was also responsible for overseeing the laying down of the city's drains in Watergate Street in the same period. The reported building contractor for the work supervised by Baylis was thought to be an Aldford man, Thomas Hughes, who undoubtedly undertook similar building projects in the city during that same period.

Around and about the new Exchange Building, much of the area continued to play host to the various open markets that were a common feature of Chester's market square and had been for hundreds of years. Immediately to the south of the new Exchange lay the city's Fish market that was said to have occupied the site close to the present day Forum shopping centre. To its west lay the various taverns, inns and businesses that have already been noted, including the Golden Hart, Saracen's Head, White Lion, etc.

To the east of the new Exchange, Chester's Corn Market was reported to have stood, but in 1707 it was removed to new premises in Eastgate Street, opposite the then still existing Fleshmongers Row. Beyond that again was the **Bishop's Palace**, which had at one time occupied the site of the later Kings School and now houses the modern Barclays Bank premises. The Palace was reported to have been built on the instruction of Edmund Keene, the Bishop of Chester from 1752 until 1771, who was thought to have requested the noted architect Sir Robert Taylor to design his new ecclesiastical property in the city, with the Bishop rather unusually meeting the cost of construction out of his own pockets.

Reports suggest that this early Palace was far less extensive than its later replacement, the Kings School building designed by Sir Arthur Blomfield in 1873, although it was said to have been surrounded by both gardens and graveyards associated with the church of St Oswald's which lay within the Cathedral precincts. The western flank of the modern day Barclays Bank is generally employed as a seating area, where citizens and visitor alike might sit and watch the world go by. During the late 18th century however, when Taylor first raised his new Bishop's Palace, this particular area was said to have been separated from the city and its people by a barrier of iron railings, which only helped to make the crowded street outside even more congested.

At the southern end of the new Palace, the city's fire engine was reported to have stood, being built by the Duke of Ormond in around 1680 and subsequently placed under the control of the Corporation and local Police authority. Its location ultimately proved to be fortuitous for the owners of the White Lion Hotel in 1708 when a major blaze in the taverns barns and stables threatened to engulf not only their own business, but many of those that stood close by. The fact that the city's fire engine stood within yards of the inferno no doubt helped to ensure that a minimum amount of damage was done to Chester's historic fabric.

Founded by King Henry VIII on 16th July 1541, the **Kings School** was initially located within the Refectory of the newly founded Cathedral of Christ and the Blessed Virgin until around 1578 when the old Abbey building became so ruinous that the pupil's safety was at risk. The school had originally been established to educate 24 nominated boys who were a minimum of 9 years of age and who would subsequently spend the next 4 or 5 years receiving a decent level of education at Kings, before going on to further study. Although the Kings School is considered to be the first regular place of education in Chester, it has been suggested that an earlier chorister's school had existed in the city prior to the official founding of Kings, but was abolished when the Abbey of St Werbugh's was dissolved in 1540.

After the move away from the refectory in 1578 the School was reported to have been moved to new premises on the west side of the Cathedrals precincts, today marked by the Georgian houses in Abbey Square and the similarly dated shops which occupy the eastern side of Northgate Street. During the late 16th and early 17th centuries this whole western flank of modern day Abbey Green (Square) was said to have been occupied by a kiln, a drying room and a brew house and it was thought to be in one of these premises that the King School pupil's continued their education.

However, these industrial buildings proved to be little better than the ancient refectory which had been their first home, but because of the dangers and shortages wrought by the English Civil War and the associated siege of the city, it was only at the end of the 17th century that the school and its pupils were finally able to return to the by then restored former monks dining hall.

The later Kings School building which now houses Barclays Bank was reported to have been designed by the architect Sir Arthur Blomfield in 1873, although it is thought to occupy a much greater area than its religious predecessor. At the time of its completion, the roadway which fronted the new buildings south facing entrance, now St Werburgh's Street, was thought to have been adorned with numerous gravestones, marking the final resting places of the dead from St Oswald's Parish.

At the rear of the modern day Barclays Bank, which can be seen from Abbey Green, the sunken area now commonly used as a car park by the bank's staff, was formerly the school playground for the pupils of the kings School. In its earlier role however, as the

Bishop's Palace, this same area was reported to have been occupied by well kept gardens overlying the Palace's cellars, which were generally hidden from view. When Blomfield designed the new school building in the 1870's provision was made to remove the vast amounts of earth from this area and bring the lower floors of his building into plain view, much as they are seen today.

The final noteworthy structure in this southern half of the Market Square is the main **Abbey Gateway**, which in its present form is thought to largely date from the 14th century, although the upper floor, sitting atop the stone vaulted gateway, is reported to have only been completed in May 1590. A local legend suggests that the religious martyr George Marsh was held in a room above the Abbey gateway during his inquisition of 1554 and prior to his execution on the stake at Spital Boughton in the same year, which clearly cannot be the case, if the upper rooms did not yet exist at that time.

Prior to 1820, this first floor area was thought to have been accessed by a spiral staircase which formerly stood on the spot as the modern day flight of steps that serve the same purpose. These upper rooms were known to have housed the Bishop's Registry for a considerable period of time, although it is likely that they will have performed a number of functions during their extensive history. On the southern side of the old gateway, evidence of a blocked up doorway exists indicating the entrance to the Porter's Lodge, which was associated with the 17th century Bishop's Palace that formerly stood on this western flank of the Abbey precincts.

As far back as 1200, Chester's medieval fairs were reported to have been held just outside of the Abbey's main entrance, with traders using wooden stalls constructed by the monks and having to pay a levy to the church on everything that they sold. The Mystery Plays, for which the city is famed, were also performed before the Abbey's gateway and numerous civic festivities and processions involved the great and the good of the city paying their respects to the venerable church at its great entranceway. Just outside the historic gate, the property now occupied by a walk-in cash point was thought to have been the former home of a noted city tavern, the "Bull's Head" which was subsequently demolished to make way for the retail units that exist today.

Princess Street in Chester was formerly known as Parson's Lane during the Middle Ages, no doubt because of its association with the city's clergy, with early records listing the thoroughfare from around 1237, although it had undoubtedly existed well before then and possibly from the foundation of the Abbey in 1093. Around 1295, a Vicar or Parson was thought to have constructed a house in the street in order to serve the St Oswald's Parish, although other records suggest that this house was in fact located close to St Werburgh's Mount, on a site adjoining Leen Lane. It is interesting to speculate, whether or not the title of the street was changed around 1860 to celebrate the official opening of Chester's new public market building in 1863 or the opening of the city's new Town Hall in 1869, both events reportedly undertaken by the Prince of Wales, later King Edward VII, who would have been accompanied by his consort, the Princess of Wales.

At its eastern end and close to the medieval Abbey gateway, the city's Flesh Shambles building was thought to have been situated on what is now the northern side of the street, close to the modern day Coach House. During the late 16th, early 17th century the former

Shire Hall from Chester's medieval castle was purchased from Queen Elizabeth's Counsellor Lord Burghley for the purpose of hosting the city's new Flesh Shambles and was supposedly purchased for the unusual sum of "six Cheshire cheeses". By the time that the new Exchange Building was raised in 1698, the city's Flesh Shambles were said to have been in a "generally filthy condition" with row upon row of covered wooden stalls facing the grand houses which once stood on the site of today's Public Library.

At the western end of this historic thoroughfare and towards the city walls, Parsons Lane was recorded to have been known as "Little" Parsons Lane, the junction of the two lanes marked by a cross of St Stephen in 1509. It has been suggested that the more westerly section of this lane, adjoined the long since extinct St Chad's Lane, which today is marked by Bedward Row and was linked to the church of St Chad which once stood in this area of the city.

During the medieval period the northwest area of the city, from Princess Street to Chester's northern defensive wall was reported to have been used almost exclusively as gardens, with only Barn Lane (later King Street) dissecting the extensive agricultural fields. Earlier still and during the Roman occupation of Chester, much of this same area would have been the location for legionary barrack blocks, workshops and storerooms which due to their generally light construction were easily and quickly swept away by the later inhabitants of the fortress.

It may also be the case that today's Princess Street was formed along the line of the Roman's Via Quintana, an internal military roadway that was thought to have been located immediately north of the legionary's Praetorium. This particular roadway was said to have marked the southernmost limits of the Retentura, the rear third of the fortress where the reserve cohorts of the legion were stationed. According to most records, this military road would have dissected the rear third of the fort, from west to east and in many cases would have led to a minor gateway within the defensive walls, which were known as Porta Quintana Sinistra (West) and the Porta Quintana Dextra (East). Interestingly, in modern day Chester, if you follow a line from the present Princess Street eastward, the monastic gateway known as the Kale Yard gate exists on this general line, although this is reported to be of a much later date.

Back in the main Northgate Street thoroughfare, the property now called **"The Coach House"**, but more fondly remembered as the "Coach and Horses" was reported to have been renovated by the architects Kelly and Edwards, the former pupils of the noted 19th century Chester architect, James Harrison, who took over their teachers practice following his untimely death in 1866. This re-fronting of the property by the architects in 1872 can often hide the fact that the building itself is thought to originate from the early part of the 17th century, although it is first formally recorded in 1690, when a secretary to the king, William III, was reported to have eaten there and found the food not to his liking. The inn was thought to have gained a reputation during the 17th and 18th centuries as one of Chester's most prestigious coaching inns, but by the early years of the 19th century, around 1810, was said to have abandoned this particular service, possibly in view of the competition from the nearby White Lion Hotel.

Adjoining the Coach & Horses Inn, but now replaced by the precincts of the Chester Public Library building, an establishment called the **Elephant and Castle** once stood in this area of the city's Market Square. Prior to its role as a hostelry, this long since disappeared tenement had been home to one Richard Sneyde, a former Recorder of Chester who was reported to have died in 1537. By 1723 the property was said to have been in the possession of one William Willoughby, a city brewer, who undoubtedly began the buildings history as a tavern, but no records exist to confirm this. The Elephant and Castle was still recorded as being in Northgate Street in 1789, but from 1782 onwards was more commonly known as "The Chequers". Following the withdrawal of the taverns licence in around 1920, the building was later employed as the Northgate Café, before finally being absorbed into the site now occupied by the public library. The sign of the Elephant and Castle was known to have stood in Foregate Street prior to 1792 when its former home was demolished to make for Williams' bank building. The sign of "The Chequers" was also later removed to yet another property around the corner in Princess Street, possibly later becoming the "Crown and Anchor" which was recorded there in 1809.

An interesting legend has attached itself to one of the landlord's of the Elephant and Castle, whose 4-year-old daughter was reported to have died at that tragically young age. The child's mother was so distraught at her daughter's loss that she was said to have taken a lock of the young girl's red hair as a memento and placed it into a glass phial. Twelve months later, the parents came across the almost forgotten keepsake and were shocked to discover that the lock of hair had increased in length by six inches and continued to grow over subsequent years.

The original façade of Chester's **Public Library** continues to advertise the Westminster Coach and Motor Works which once occupied the building that stood on the site and is dated to 1914, but could possibly be older than that. The façade is attributed to architect Philip H Lockwood from 1913-14, although the site itself was reported to have been previously occupied by Hewitt and Lawson's Coach & Carriage Builders whose premises had been badly damaged by fire on 1st July 1910. Old photographs of this building show a similar, but much higher frontage, suggesting that the façade was largely rebuilt rather than entirely replaced. Up until the early 1970's the building was used as a car showroom, then occupied by the Chester Arts and Recreation Trust, before being demolished and rebuilt as Chester's main library, replacing the Free Library which had occupied the former Mechanics Institute building in St John Street. In new plans for the renovation and rebuilding of Chester's Town Hall and Market Square area of the city, planned for 2010-12, the Library site is destined to house Chester's new Market Hall.

This particular site is known to have a fairly extensive history, in common with the rest of the buildings that stand on the block bordered by modern day Princess Street and Hunter Street. The plot now occupied by the library was reported to have been inherited by one William Massie during the 18th century and he was thought to have demolished the earlier buildings which stood there, one of which had been a kiln owned by the city's Cathedral authorities. During the English Civil War siege of the city, in the 1640's, the Cholmondley family were said to have occupied a large city mansion that was standing in this area of Chester and which was thought to have been one of the properties later demolished.

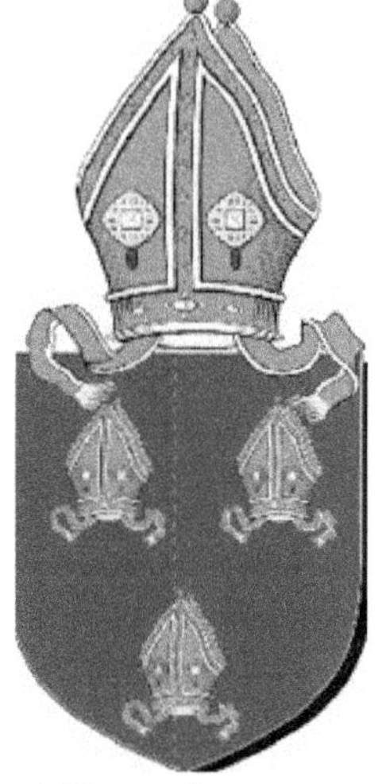

Massie then erected two brand new properties on the site around 1723, one of which was said to have included extensive gardens, a brew house, granary, two stables, outbuildings and a croft totalling three quarters of an acre. The second property, which adjoined the modern day Shropshire Arms, was recorded to have comprised extensive gardens, a brew house, two coach houses and two stables. This second property was subsequently bought and occupied by Robert Davies of Llanerch, with the other house being lived in by Massie and his family.

With both Massie and Davies having died or moved by around 1730, the two individual houses were thought to have been combined into one large family home, although according to a map of 1745 the building was still being referred to as Mr Massie's house. In 1754 the then Bishop of Chester, Edmund Keene, was reported to have been occupying this large townhouse, whilst the Bishop's Palace (site of Barclay's Bank) in the Cathedral grounds was being rebuilt reportedly at Keene's own expense. For the next hundred years or more little is known about this fine building and it was only in 1874 that the site was said to have been purchased by William Hewitt as the location for his new Coach building factory, the fascia of which continues to stand today.

Standing next door to the Public Library, the site of the **Shropshire Arms** has had an equally extensive history, existing in one form or another for around 300 years and having had a number of different names. By 1723 the land was being inhabited by a kiln owned by the Dean and Chapter of the Cathedral and between 1741 and 1758, the first tavern on the site was reported to have been called "The Crown", before being renamed the "Crown and Mitre", a title it held until 1798. From that date until 1820, the house was known as the "Mitre Tavern" and was then changed again to the "Liverpool and Shropshire House", a title it held until 1850, before finally being changed to its modern day title of the "Shropshire Arms". The building that stands on the site today is thought to date from around 1880, when virtually all of this area was rebuilt, possibly as part of the wider development of the previously noted Coach Works of William Hewitt.

The most northern property adjoining Hunter Street and including the retail unit known as **Aldersey Hall** is another relatively new building, which is sometimes known as Hunter's House and was thought to have been constructed at the same time as the Shropshire Arms, in around 1880. This building, which runs westward along the southern flank of modern day Hunter Street was said to have replaced an early narrow passageway called Hunter's Walk, which was last recorded in 1817.

Rather confusingly perhaps, modern day **Hunter Street** now occupies the site of yet another historic building that was sacrificed for the modernisation of the city, when this thoroughfare was first laid down in 1890. It was thought to be in this now extinct property that James Hunter lived and worked as an engraver. Few descriptions of this lost house exist, other than the reports that the southern gable of the property was adorned with a figure of Britannia and along its eastern side, there was a façade decorated with leaded windows and a shop front. It was also in this earlier house that the artist A R Burt was reported to have lived around 1812, giving rise to the confusion over James Hunter being an artist rather than an engraver.

On the eastern side of Chester's Market Square and in between the former Abbey's two medieval gateways, the area now occupied by a terrace of 18th century buildings, a tavern bearing the sign of the "Crown and Mitre" was reported to have been situated sometime around 1744, possibly prior to the name being transferred to the modern day Shropshire Arms. This inn was later known as the "White Hart Inn" between 1751 and 1758, but by 1873 was known to have been renamed as the "**Stag Inn**". In the same general area, a second tavern was reported to have stood on the eastern flank of the Market Square. Called the "Bulls Head", this hostelry was said to have existed between 1741 and 1758 and been located just outside of the main Abbey Gateway, the site now occupied by a modern retail unit.

Chester's now empty Art Deco **Odeon Cinema** was designed by the company's own noted architect Harry Weedon and completed around 1935-6. The building occupies the same site which for well over 1900 years has played host to a number of notable buildings, from the Roman period right through to the early 20th century. The "Hope and Anchor" Inn was reported to be located here in around 1648, being the 4th house south of King Street, but by 1737 the property had become known as the "Golden Talbot", before finally being converted for use as the Judges Lodgings in around 1751. Later reports of this building describe it as one of the most striking in the whole street and give the impression that it probably occupied the whole of the south east corner of the block. The business premises of the solicitors Potts, Potts and Gardner was also said to have occupied the site of the later Odeon cinema and was described as a fairly substantial brick built property which was otherwise known as the Judges Lodgings, possibly indicating that the earlier tavern had indeed been taken over or adapted for other uses.

Prior to the large scale demolition of the site during the 1930's in preparation for the new cinema complex and its associated retail units, No 53 Northgate Street which faced east towards the Little Abbey Gateway was reported to have been a mid 18th century townhouse, built over three storeys and with four windows on its second floor. At the ground floor, this long gone property might possibly have included a covered walkway that formed part of a much more extensive "Lorimer's Row" which today only exists at its northern end, from the Pied Bull to the Blue Bell Inn.

It is also worth noting that at one time, a number of Roman artefacts discovered during the construction of the Odeon and its associated building's, were displayed in the main foyer of the cinema, for the interest of its patrons. Interestingly, archaeological records report that evidence of a Roman hypocaust were discovered in the same general area, lying between modern day King and Hunter Streets, which might indicate the presence of a large legionary building, which has thus far escaped formal and positive identification. As elsewhere in the city, large-scale investigations of the wider area are prevented by the presence of much later buildings, including those that currently occupy the southern flank of King Street and the northern side of Hunter Street. However, hopefully this situation will be resolved as a result of the planned redevelopment of the Hunter Street and Princess Street area of the city in around 2012, which should allow the city's archaeologists to fully explore much of this part of Chester.

During the archaeological investigations undertaken at the old Market Hall site, which also involved the demolition and excavation of the nearby Hunter Street School, the most notable building identified by local archaeologists, aside from the previously mentioned Praetorium and Elliptical building, was a Roman Horrea or granary. This was thought to have been located towards the southern end of Hunter Street, but because of the still standing Victorian and early 20th century buildings, including the now demolished Princess Street chapel, much of the area immediately surrounding this granary site has not been fully investigated up until this point in time.

The **Little Abbey Gateway** which today bridges a narrow walkway on the eastern flank of Northgate Street, adjacent to Chester's Jobcentre is reported to date from around the 13th or 14th century and would originally have served as a secondary access point to the city's Norman Abbey precincts, possibly via an early medieval courtyard. It has been suggested that this narrow gateway also provided access to the Abbey's Tithe Barn and Croft's which lay at the western end of Barn Lane (now modern day King Street).

Today, this ancient gateway leads pedestrians along a narrow walkway, south to the inner precincts of the Cathedral at Abbey Green and around the back of the modern buildings that occupy this eastern section of Northgate Street. This particular passageway however, is thought to date from the late 18th century and to have first been laid down by the builder Thomas Boswell who was responsible for building many of the elegant properties that continue to stand on the north side of Abbey Green. The walkway also represents only a small part of the original, which was designed to help people travel from the city's northern wall through to their new homes in Abbey Green.

Folliot House which sits adjacent to both the Odeon cinema and Pied Bull Inn was designed and constructed by Thomas Harrison in 1778 as his personal residence in the city. Since its construction however the property has been substantially reduced in width throughout its length and today houses offices, principally the Citizens Advice Bureau. In its original form the house was reported as being a three storey property with three windows on each floor facing eastward.

A painting of around 1860 produced by the renowned artist Louise Raynor shows this building extending fully towards the main thoroughfare, level with the covered arcade of the Pied Bull which still exists today. Viewing the east facing façade of Folliot House, as it stands in modern day Northgate Street, it is hard to reconcile the difference or to imagine that the house ever included a covered arcade, so must conclude that this feature was purely artistic licence on the part of the noted 19th century artist.

The name Folliot House is thought to originate from a family of that name who were known to be merchants in the city during the mid to late 18th century. One James Folliot was reported as a merchant living in Northgate Street in 1776, but as that was two years before Harrison constructed the house for his own use, then it was probably his successors who finally acquired the property and gave it its name. Another noted member of the same family was thought to be William Harwood Folliot who lived in Chester during the late 18th and early 19th century who earned a widespread reputation for his quick witted ad-libbing.

The **Pied Bull** pre-dates the year 1660 when it was largely rebuilt, with its current brickwork facade thought to originate from the mid 18th century, although it is known to be a timber-framed building underneath, possibly dating from the 1500's. Features within the hotel itself are thought to date from 1600, but much more of the interior is said to date from around the middle of the 17th century. The noted traveller George Borrow stayed here as part of his "Wild Wales" itinerary and commented about the chambermaid, the local ale and his distaste of the city's famous Cheshire cheese.

In medieval times the site was reported to have been owned by the nuns of St Mary's and a building known as the Bull Tenement was thought to have stood close to the same spot. Following the dissolution of the monasteries in the 16th century however, the land and property was thought to have passed into private hands and new buildings were erected, including lodgings for the Recorder of Chester who presided over the local Assizes during the early 17th century. Following this, the building was renamed as the "Bull Inn" reflecting its association with the nearby Beasts Markets beyond the Northgate, before finally becoming the "Pied Bull", one of Chester's most notable coaching establishments.

King Street, which was formerly known as Barn Lane, was once a simple medieval track which linked the Abbey of St Werburgh with a large tithe Barn which was reported to have stood on crofts that used to occupy the site of today's inner ring road and former infirmary buildings. The terrace of formidable looking Georgian properties which mark the modern streets junction with the ring road at its western end are called King's Buildings and are thought to date from around 1775-6. Undoubtedly fine townhouses of their age, in later years they suffered from general neglect and from the effects of subsidence in the area, which resulted in heavy wooden struts having to be employed to prevent their almost certain collapse into the street, but happily they have been restored in recent years to something like their former glory. Most of the other properties in this narrow thoroughfare date from the same 18th century period, although one or two are thought to pre-date this, but have been restored or refaced in a later style. Again at its western end, this street was also reported to have been the location for one of Chester's many former breweries, the site now lying close to the sandstone archway which was cut through the modern north wall in 1831 and was designed to be used by canal workers. Initially owned by Snape and Bagnall, the brewery was said to have later been owned by an individual called Huxley. The brewery site which lay close to the original north western corner of the former Roman fortress is now covered by modern housing, making it difficult to imagine its former use and layout.

Back in the main Northgate Street thoroughfare, the covered ground floor walkway now known as **Lorimer's Row** was thought to have first been reported in 1155 in connection with the Bull Tenement, nowadays the Pied Bull, which was owned at the time by the Benedictine nuns of St Mary's. At the time Lorimer's Row was thought to have run in front of the earlier Pied Bull site and extended southward to the limits of where the Odeon cinema stands today. Much of this area was heavily redeveloped during the construction of the cinema and its attendant buildings, including the reduction in width of Thomas

Harrison's Folliot House. The skilled tradesmen known as Lorimer's were responsible for manufacturing bits, spurs and the various iron articles generally associated with horse tack and saddles.

The sign of the **Red Lion** Public House in Northgate Street has had an extensive history in Chester, with an early tavern of that name being recorded in Foregate Street in 1738, the property having previously been owned by Charles Walley a former Mayor of the city during the English Civil War siege of Chester in the 1640's. In 1782, the Red Lion was reported to been relocated to Bridge Street in Chester, before the sign was finally relocated to Northgate Street around 1795, where it remains to the present day. However, other sources suggest that an unknown tavern has existed on the present site in Northgate Street since 1600, although its sign, age, etc are currently unknown.

The **Blue Bell Inn** is located in Lorimer's Row, which is a covered arcade, rather than a traditional Row. Although today the two entirely separate houses are regarded as a single property, the southern house is in fact some fifty years older than its northern counterpart, although both are built of sandstone, timber and brick. The outlying booth of the northern property was at one time used as a ticket office for the city's mail coaches and later still as a barbers shop. The Blue Bell Inn was reported to have first been licensed in 1494, although throughout its extensive history has served as many things, including public house, retail shop and today as a restaurant. It is also reported that the city's Spurriers and Girdlers held their guild meetings in this historic property.

The plot of land adjoining Lorimer's Row to the north was formerly the location for Chester's early 20th century **Fire Station**, which was designed by local architect James Strong around 1911. This same architect was reported to have participated in the rebuilding of Shoemaker's Row at the southern end of Northgate Street at the beginning of the same century where Strong, a pupil of John Douglas, was reported to have designed No's 15 to 17, which replaced the Cross Keys Inn. That building contained a semi-circular window feature that he repeated in his 1911 half timbered Fire Station building and a number of his designs were thought to have been used in the initial phases of the Lache estate around 1919, which centred on Cliveden Road, Sunbury Crescent and Abingdon Crescent.

Strong's Fire Station was thought to have replaced Chester's Potato Market, which was said to have included a water reservoir installed by the city's Waterworks Company in around 1828. In much earlier times this land was said to have been owned by the Hospital of St John the Baptists outside the Northgate. However, by 1717 the lands had passed into the ownership of one Samuel Jarvis, a tradesman of little means, who in turn sold the property to a man called Husband, whose wife Dorothy was in possession of the property by 1747 and ten years later she bequeathed the property to one Abigail Allcock. Finally, in 1797 the lands passed into the hands of one Joseph Stones who eventually sold the land to the Waterworks Company.

In 1828 however, the property came into the possession of the city corporation who set about clearing the site to establish a new Engine House and Potato Market there. At the west end of the plot, away from the street, a two storey brick building was said to have been constructed, with the first floor being used to house a water reservoir. Beneath this tank, there were reported to be a number of individual bays which housed the various appliances used to fight outbreaks of fire in the city. These engines were previously thought to have been housed close to the city's new beast market at Gorse Stacks, but being outside of the walls meant that they often took some time to arrive at the scene of a fire and so a new home within the city precincts was thought to be of vital importance.

The remainder of the Northgate Street site, including its street frontage, was reported to have housed Chester's Potato Market, which prior to this date was thought to have been located to the east of the city's Exchange building, close to the Abbey's medieval gateway. Although this new Potato Market was said to have been initially popular with traders, by the middle of the 19th century and following the construction of the new Public Market in 1862, it became less so, as traders inevitably relocated themselves to the new market site. Consequently, by the beginning of the 20th century and with few market traders remaining there, the Potato Market site was reported to have been entirely given over to housing the city's fire fighting services, which led to the construction of Strong's Fire Station building in 1911.

Chester's **Northgate Brewery**, which was reportedly founded around 1856 at the rear of the "Golden Falcon Inn was the last of the city's numerous brewing companies to close, shutting its door for the final time around 1969. The site, rebuilt and renamed Centurion House was later used to house Chester's Magistrates Court, but this too has relocated itself in recent years, with the former brewery site now home to the Chester and District Housing Trust offices. Prior to 1642 a second hostelry, called the "White Bull", was thought to have stood in this area, but sometime around 1711 was absorbed into the later "Golden Falcon".

Archaeological excavations undertaken at the former brewery site prior to the construction of the modern day development, uncovered evidence that the site had once played host to the barrack blocks of the legionary cohorts, who were accommodated in this rear area of the fortress. Separated from the northern defensive wall by the Via Sagularis, the internal roadway which ran along the whole internal perimeter of the fortress, the barrack blocks were further protected from burning missiles that might to thrown over the city walls by the Intervallum, a protective space which also contained the drains and gutters that drained away the rainwater and carried the effluent from the legionary latrines. These barrack blocks were thought to have extended from the later site of the Northgate Brewery southward to the line of today's King Street, giving a far clearer idea of how this area of the fortress was being used some 2000 years ago. This layout was also said to have been repeated on the eastern side of the present day Northgate Street, with more barrack blocks occupying the area of Chester now represented by the Cathedral's Deanery Field.

Early records suggest that the terrace of buildings, which later housed the Golden Talbot, had in fact comprised three separate properties at one point. Robert Skellington, a Slater by trade was thought to have owned the southernmost house, being mentioned in 1660, but reported to have died by 1665. The second and central house was thought to have been owned by one Richard Bavand, who was said to have leased the property to Sir Henry Bunbury sometime around 1598. By 1603 however, the property was thought to have been in the possession of Sir Thomas Gamul who was requested to hand the house over to the city corporation, so that monies raised through rents might be used to benefit the city's poorest inhabitants.

Finally, the third and most northern property was reported to have been the previously mentioned "White Bull" Inn, the foundation date of which is unknown.

During its time as the "**Golden Falcon**" the tavern was run by members of the Kenna family, although the building itself was said to have been owned by a man called Eaton, who was reported to have owned properties in Watergate Street and was somehow associated with the city's Northgate. The building occupied by the "Golden Falcon" had formerly been two separate properties, with the northern half later housing the Northgate Tavern. Between its foundation in either 1704 or 1711 and 1745 the tavern was simply known as "The Falcon" and only became the "Golden Falcon" from 1745 onwards.

The Golden Falcon is reported to be an emblem of the Egerton family, noted landowners and property owners within Cheshire, suggesting perhaps an association between the owners of the hostelry and that particular family. First established in Northgate Street in 1704, although some sources state 1711, under the tenancy of the Kenna family it became one of the most popular and widely used hostelries in the city and was where the composer Handel stayed in 1714. By 1763, ownership of the hostelry was said to have passed to an individual called George Smith who was reported to have substantially rebuilt the property around the same period. Still known as the "Golden Falcon" in 1769, by 1782 the property was thought to have become the home of a local surgeon called Tomlinson. Thirteen years later, in 1795, the house was said to be in the ownership of another member of the Tomlinson family, who was a brewer by occupation and by 1800 the property was commonly described as a brewery, a business which eventually evolved into the Northgate Brewery.

The modern day "**Liverpool Arms**" has formerly been called the "Dog and Partridge", the "Bull and Dog" and in 1789 was reported to have been known as the "Loggerheads Tavern". Although a tavern called the "Bull and Dog" was reported to have existed from 1741 to 1758, its presence on the site of today's Liverpool Arms was thought to have only lasted from 1708 to 1709. For a short period the hostelry was also called "The Wellington" although little is known about this particular period, with some suggestions that this title derives from around 1815 and the city celebrating Wellington's victory at the Battle of Waterloo. As the "Dog and Partridge" the property was thought to have been in the ownership of one Peter Dutton who was recorded to have leased the building to Thomas Clubbe in 1813.

Standing directly opposite to the modern day Liverpool Arms, the site until recently occupied by Sayers the Bakers was between 1840 and 1912 the location for the "Grosvenor Arms" Public House and before that "The Wheatsheaf". As the "**Hen and Chickens**" in the 18th century this tavern was thought to have been a popular venue for the crowds of onlookers who gathered there to watch the execution of prisoners who were hung at the nearby Northgate Gaol which took place up until 1808. Although this particular tavern was thought to date from around 1706, the site's history is thought to be far more extensive, with suggestions that the area had at one time played host to medieval wayfarer's accommodations, a service that was offered by both the early Norman Abbey and its Cathedral successor. It was reported that many of these same buildings were substantially rebuilt in 1782, possibly marking a change in ownership of the properties.

Lying just south of the city's northern wall, today's **Water Tower Street** recalls the time when this particular thoroughfare ran further west to the tower which name it continues to bear, despite the fact that it is now separated from its final destination by the modern ring road system. This modern city street is undoubtedly a successor to the section of the Roman's Via Sagularis, the military roadway which ran behind the fortress' walled defences and that was used by the legionary troops to move around the perimeter of the enclosed camp. At one time during its long history though, the western part of this street was formerly called Ox Lane and was reported to have passed beneath the city's walls before turning north towards Chester's northern gate and then on to the Beast markets that were commonly held in this part of the city. Assuming that this route lay along the line of the much later ravine, created by the construction of the Chester and Nantwich canal which was begun in 1772 then this lane must have become extinct around that time. However, it is worth noting perhaps, that even to this present day there is a strip of land immediately outside and below the city walls, stretching from the Northgate to the more westerly Morgan's Mount, which may in fact be the remnants of this early medieval lane.

CHAPTER SIX

NORTHGATE AND BEYOND

Marking the northernmost point of the early Roman fortress, Chester's present Northgate was designed and built by the renowned architect Thomas Harrison between 1808 and 1810, around the same time that he was overseeing work on a number of his other city projects, including the Commercial Newsrooms at the southern end of Northgate Street.

It has been suggested that the current archway was the architects second design, his first having been rejected by the city corporation and that the pair of stone of staircases, now standing on either side of the bridge, were not part of his original structure, but were added at a later date and as a matter of pure convenience rather than an integral part of the archway's overall design.

Harrison's northern gateway bears little resemblance to the heavily constructed medieval portal which had originally occupied the site and which was thought to have existed in part, from the time of the fortress' original Roman builders. Representing the rear gateway of the former military compound, this entranceway was nonetheless an important route in and out of the base, marking the starting point for Roman troops that were regularly being despatched to their auxiliary forts and ports in both Cheshire and on the Wirral peninsula.

In its earliest form the gateway would probably have consisted of huge wooden gates flanked on either side by imposing stone built flanking towers that formed part of the defensive circuit which protected their base. Undoubtedly altered and improved over time, it seems likely that much of this early gateway would have remained intact, despite the abandonment of the fortress by the Roman legions in the late 4th or early 5th centuries and would have been the foundation for its later reincarnation as a highly fortified medieval gateway.

As seems to be the case elsewhere in Chester and most notably at the city's East Gate, the later inhabitants of the fortress are thought to have largely build around the early Roman structure and taken full advantage of the solidity that these underlying structures provided. Although there is no definitive evidence to support a conclusion either way, it also seems likely that it was only during the later Norman occupation of the city in the 11th and 12th centuries that the gateway finally began to evolve into the heavily protected gateway and city prison that it would ultimately become. Unlike the other three remaining city gates, the northern entranceway was unusual in that it was administered and maintained by the citizens of Chester, rather than having the "serjeancy" held by an often absent nobleman who had been granted the rights by one or other English monarch. A grant of 1360 finally passed the sergeancy of the gate to the citizens, who controlled it in the person of the Mayor and his Corporation and they in turn appointed suitable individuals to undertake the day-to-day running of the gate and prison, including the jailer, the toll collectors, etc.

Eventually the two original Roman flanking towers were thought to have been absorbed into a strengthened, extended, and heightened gateway that was much narrower and longer than its earlier form, with its associated buildings stretching southward and partially incorporating the sites of today's Liverpool Arms and Water Tower Street. Within these grim precincts, city prisoners were often held for extended periods of time and sometimes in the most intolerable circumstances, although in later years those accused of less serious offences such as debt were treated far better than those accused of theft or murder.

The two most notorious cells within the Northgate Gaol were the Dead Man's Room and the Little Ease, both of which were reported to have been rock cut cells some 30 feet below ground level which had to have their air supply delivered through a pipe. As the name implies, the **Dead Man's Room** was used to hold condemned prisoners until such time as they were taken up to ground level to receive their final sacraments and then to the scaffold. Adjoining this, was the **Little Ease**, a tiny cell hewn out of the rock and which barely allowed a prisoner to enter it and often it required the jailer to force prisoners into this tiny space. An added feature of this cell was reported to be the draw-boards which could be fitted into carved slots in the rock and which were sometimes used to further reduce the height of the cell for certain offenders and preventing them from being able to stand up straight.

When the medieval gateway and prison were demolished in 1807/8 to make way for Harrison's new civic archway, elements of the original Roman gateway were discovered by the workmen, but it was only with archaeological investigations undertaken in the 20th century that its exact location was finally established, but further work was prevented by the presence of new buildings that had subsequently been built near the site, most notably the Liverpool Arms Public House. However, the limited evidence available from the dig did indicate that the original Roman gate had in fact occupied a slightly different footprint to its later successor.

Passing under the Northgate arch, on the west side there is a relatively small area of what would have once been the gardens and buildings of the old Northgate gaol premises, that is now occupied by two distinct buildings. The most westerly of the two, furthest away from the modern street, is described as an 18th century two storey brick built property with a slated roof, although its actual construction date and purpose is uncertain. The second property, a single storey building, lying closer to the main thoroughfare and possibly with a similar construction date has been speculated to be a Toll House, but this use has not been confirmed.

On the west side of the street, the little stone bridge spanning the ravine cut by the course of the 18th century canal dates from 1793 and was constructed by local architect Joseph Turner as a means of connecting the medieval Northgate Gaol and the chapel of St John's which stood within the Bluecoat Hospital. Known locally as the "**Bridge of Sigh's**", its name is thought to derive from the misery of the condemned felons who passed over the bridge on their way to receive their final sacraments, before facing the full rigours of the law. It has also been suggested that a number of these ill-fated individuals used the narrow bridge as a place from where they would launch themselves into oblivion, rather than face the hangman's noose and throwing themselves into the canal gorge below.

Originally, the bridge was known to have had iron railings on either side, but these were later removed for use in this country's wartime recycling efforts and they were never replaced. Sadly, in recent years this often overlooked city feature has been allowed to deteriorate to some degree and at the time of writing is overgrown with weeds, allowing the elegant structure to become increasingly obscured.

The modern **Bluecoat School** stands on the site formerly occupied by the 12th century hospital of St John the Baptist, which was established by Earl Ranulph Blundeville sometime between 1188 and 1200, but substantially destroyed during the English Civil War siege of the city in the mid-17th century. There are few records describing the physical precincts of this early religious centre, but it was thought to have included a church, hall and a miscellaneous collection of outbuildings clustered around a central courtyard. Part of the site, which lay immediately adjacent to the modern day Canal Street, was thought to have been used as agricultural land by the hospital to grow their own food or simply leased out to other local farmers.

The central core of the modern day Bluecoat building is thought to date from around 1717 and was established by Dr Nicholas Stratford, the Bishop of Chester, as a charity school for poor boys, under the auspices of the Society for the Promotion of Christian Knowledge, the SPCK, which still operates a bookshop in St Werburgh Street. Although the school buildings date from that particular year, the society itself was reported to have been established by Dr Stratford some 17 years earlier, in 1700, but sadly he never lived to see the first part of the school constructed, as he was recorded to have passed away in 1707.

The original 18th century building was said to have been L-shaped in design, facing both Northgate Street and the city's walls, with the south facing wing housing a chapel and the east facing main building hosting schoolrooms, dormitories and other accommodations. The school's northern wing was reported to have been added in 1733, thereby creating a rear central courtyard and in 1854 the main block of the property was enlarged with a new façade towards Northgate Street. This included the statue of John Coppack, a Bluecoat pupil that continues to stand above the central entrance today and which was said to have been designed by a Mr Richardson from London.

The alms houses which exist at the rear of the school date from around 1850 and were thought to have replaced a number of earlier 18th century properties that had previously occupied the site and served the same charitable purpose.

Today's **Canal Street** was formerly known as Portpool Lane or Way and in its earlier form was reported to have been a much narrower thoroughfare, obstructed in part by a tavern called the "Brown Cow" which used to stand on the site. There is a suggestion that the cellars of this earlier hostelry still lie below this much wider and busier road junction. In its

earlier form, the Portpool Way ran directly from the city's Northgate to the Water Tower and the banks of the River Dee. The name "Port pool" was said to identify the area of the river where ships "laid to" before or after berthing at Chester's busy medieval port. The modern name of Canal Street is associated with the Chester to Nantwich canal which was first begun in May 1772, its route along the northern wall of the fortress following the line of the city's defensive ditch or fosse, which had first been cut by the Roman legionaries some 1700 years earlier. In Elizabethan times, modern day Canal Street was called Narrow Lane, before becoming Dee Lane without the Northgate, then Portpool Lane and finally Canal Street.

Directly opposite to Canal Street and running eastward towards Gorse Stacks is the modern day **George Street**, which as far back as the 13th century was commonly known as Bag Lane or alternatively Sandy Lane. Although the thoroughfare has always been thought to run from the city's Northgate towards Gorse Stacks and on to Flookersbrook, its actual route is thought to have been altered somewhat, not least by the laying down of the new Chester to Nantwich Canal in the late 18th century which pushed the roadway slightly north of its original position. Another casualty of the new waterway was said to be the city's "Pinfold" or animal stockade, which was said to have been located just outside of the Northgate and formed part of Chester's House of Correction that occupied the southern junction of Bag Lane and Northgate Street. During the 13th century reign of Henry III this land was thought to be in the possession of the Hospital of St John the Baptist, which formerly occupied the site of today's Bluecoat Centre and that had been founded by Earl Ranulph Blundeville in the late 12th century.

On the northern side of George Street (Bag Lane), on the site until recently occupied by the city's central Bus Depot, lay a sandstone quarry which was generally associated with Chester's **House of Correction** and the requirement for its inmates to undertake heavy labour. On the opposite side of the road and towards the city walls, stood the House of Correction itself, which was thought to have been rebuilt by the Corporation sometime after 1680, its 16th century predecessor having been deliberately demolished around 1642 as part of the city's defensive strategy during the English Civil War siege of Chester. Up until the construction of the Chester Canal which began in May 1772, the House of Correction was thought to have stood within fairly extensive grounds, but a large swathe of these lands were appropriated by the Canal Company, as part of their excavations for the new inland waterway.

As well as operating as a jail in which to hold and punish offenders, the House of Correction was also used as a place for carrying out public floggings and for holding any loafers or beggars who were arrested for vagrancy on the city streets. Typically such people would be held under lock and key until such time as their place of origin could be determined by the authorities and arrangements made for their return to their hometown, so that they wouldn't continue to be a financial burden to the citizens of Chester.

Additionally, Chester's House of Corrections was also said to have provided a safe haven for the children of city Freemen who had fallen on hard times, although their continuing residency was still based on their willingness to earn their daily bread, by undertaking the arduous work assigned to them. The House of Corrections was thought to have existed on the site through to 1808 when the new County Gaol and House of Correction buildings were constructed in City Walls Road and most of its inmates transferred. Today the site is generally occupied by two 18th century townhouses, one of which was formerly a private school operated by a Mr Wilson and the former premises of the Northgate Bakery which have been broken down into retail units and private offices.

Standing north of these properties and across the other side of George Street, on the site of the former quarry, is the **Bull and Stirrup**, a tavern which obviously derived its name from the beast market's which once occupied this section of the city. Recorded as a Polling Station in both the 1809 and 1810 city elections, this particular hostelry may well have existed from the end of the 18th or beginning of the 19th centuries, but has been much altered and improved over time. In 1809 it was described as a flat whitewashed building with stone steps leading up to its front door, which is completely unlike the property that exists today, suggesting that in the meantime it has been heavily restored, but no information regarding this is available.

Further north, on the eastern side of Northgate Street, modern day **Delamere Street** is thought to have first been reported sometime around 1848 and possibly owes its original creation to the continuing expansion of the city northward and eastward, particularly in the direction of the new suburbs of both Newtown and Liverpool Road. Although it is almost impossible to visualise now, given the redevelopment that has taken place in this particular street over the past 50 years, prior to the 1960's this city thoroughfare looked completely different than it does today. At its most easterly point, the long since disappeared Northgate Railway Station was officially opened in 1875, being operated by the Cheshire Lines Committee, who ran trains to and from the Manchester area. This station was so large, that it formed a connection with the Corporation Bus Depot in Victoria Road, which now lies well beyond the opposite side of the city's inner ring road carriageway. Operating until 1969 when the Northgate Station was finally closed, parts of its former home are now occupied by Chester's Northgate Arena, the civic sports centre constructed during the 1970's.

Elsewhere in Delamere Street, at the beginning of the 20th century much of its southern flank, stretching from Northgate Street to the Northgate Railway Station entrance was lined by a number of generally elegant private houses, some of which were enclosed within secluded walled gardens. By the middle of the 20th century though, virtually all of these houses were gone, only to be replaced by utilitarian office blocks and the functional expanse of the Delamere Bus Station, which has itself recently been demolished to make way for even more modern developments. The opposite northern side of the street has fared little better during the same period; and today it too is currently being subjected to a large scale modernisation project.

Directly opposite the western end of Delamere Street on the west side of Northgate Street stands an 18th century property fronted by a street level arcade. Reported to have been the home of Lady Elizabeth Otway who was associated with the Bluecoat Girls School in the city around 1718, by the mid 1840's the house was thought to have been occupied by the Reverend William Harrison who was the headmaster of a private school which was sited on the other side of Northgate Street, on the spot now adjoining the "Bull and Stirrup" Hotel.

The modern thoroughfare known as **Upper Northgate Street** was at one time called Further Northgate Street and was thought to have ranged from Chester's Portpool Way (modern day Canal Street) to the site of St Thomas' Chapel (now the George and Dragon Public House). During the Middle Ages virtually all of these lands were said to have been used for agricultural purposes, possibly as market gardens, with the exception of the site recently occupied by the Delamere Street Bus Depot and the Bull and Stirrup Hotel, all of which was reported to have been the site of a medieval quarry.

One of the most notable properties which used to stand in Upper Northgate Street was **Egerton House**, built for Sir Philip Egerton and which was formerly sited on the eastern side of the main thoroughfare, before becoming a casualty of Chester's inner ring road system constructed during the 1960's. A 1947 review of the property described it as a large early 18th century property consisting of three storey's, with a carriage entrance on its left-hand side. A second property, owned by the same family and given the same name was reported to have been sited at the eastern end of Foregate Street, near the "Bars" and standing on the eastern side of the northern end of the still existing Dee Lane.

Although nowadays detached from Upper Northgate Street by Chester's inner ring road system, at one time modern day **Victoria Road** was known as Windmill Lane, no doubt because of the mill that once stood within the open fields and gardens which existed in this area of the city. Also known as "Beesome Lane" at sometime in its history, early 18th century records suggest that the Windmill in question stood within several acres of meadow lands and perhaps stood atop a natural incline which was called Windmill Hill. A little to the west of today's Victoria Road stands the elegant **Northgate Church**, which was designed by local architect T M Lockwood and functions as a Congregational Church, primarily used by the students from the nearby Chester University campus.

The most notable building that exists in the area today is the **George & Dragon** Hotel which stands at the junction of Liverpool and Parkgate Roads, the two main northerly routes out of the city. The current building was constructed by the Birkenhead Brewery Company at the beginning of the 20th century, on the site which was formerly occupied by Jolley's Hall, a private residence thought to date from between 1550-1640.

The first property to stand on the site though, was thought to be the Chapel of St Thomas the Martyr (Beckett) which was reported to have existed on the site from the 13th century. Thomas a Beckett was thought to have visited Chester with the monarch Henry II in around 1157 when the English king came to suppress a revolt being led by the Welsh prince Owain ap Gwynnedd. The chapel was thought to have survived through to the middle of the 17th century when it was finally demolished during the Civil War Siege of Chester. Following the end of the conflict the site was used once again for the later **Jolley's Hall** and subsequently became home to John Fletcher. A new chapel, dedicated to the same saint was erected within the Cathedral precincts, but this too was later taken down around 1798, to make way for the Bishop's Palace which continues to stand today.

By 1787 the building was occupied as the "**Recruiting Sergeant**", but was later noted as the "George and Dragon" in an Act of Parliament dating from 1820, which dealt with a road widening scheme. The "Recruiting Sergeant" was thought to have relocated to Cuppin Street prior to 1809, as the sign was mentioned as a polling station in the city in that year.

Just to the north of today's "George and Dragon" the route out of Chester divides into two main roads, Parkgate and Liverpool Road, each indicating their individual destinations. The first, **Parkgate Road** is thought to follow the line of a much earlier Roman road called Blake Street which ran from the fortress at Chester northward to the then thriving coastal site at Meols, which was reported to be one of the most important and extensive settlements of the Roman period and one that remained in existence for hundreds of years.

CHAPTER SEVEN

CHESTER CATHEDRAL & ITS PRECINCTS

Within the grounds of Chester's ancient Cathedral, **Abbey Green** or Square is comprised of two major terraces of mid-18th century houses standing to the west and north of the historic courtyard that once housed the medieval Abbey's bakery, brewery and workshops. Although the current buildings appear to have been built at the same time, this is possibly not the case and as in other places in the city, the houses were probably constructed in phases, possibly over a number of years and by different builders. The northern terrace is known to overlie the remains of early Roman barrack room buildings which date from the 1st century AD and represent one of the first phases of occupation within the military fortress. It was also in this general area that archaeologists first discovered a small number of cremation urns, which were thought to pre-date the foundation of the permanent, much larger military fortress which was begun around 80 AD.

Some 1500 years later, the whole of the area, stretching from the back of these houses to the northern defensive wall was thought to have been site of the Abbot's orchards, a use that was said to have been maintained right through to around 1662. It was in that year that the Dean of the Cathedral granted these lands to a local man called Ralph Bingley for the laying out of a bowling green; such was the fashion and demand for that particular sporting pursuit. As part of his new leisure facility, Bingley was thought to have constructed a large building on the southern part of the site, which between 1770 and 1775 was being used to house the properties which still occupy the site today. A noted 18th century builder, Thomas Boswell, was thought to have constructed a number of houses in this same general area between 1768 and 1775, including those that stand at numbers 1 and 2 Abbey Green. Boswell is also credited with laying down the now partially defunct walkway that leads from Abbey Square through to Northgate Street, via the Little Abbey Gateway. Now obstructed by a modern looking doorway, in its original form this alleyway was said to have ran northward to Chester's defensive wall and was built by Boswell to provide a link for the residents of Abbey Green to the city's northern promenade. Nearby, a number of the buildings that front the eastern side of modern day Northgate Street, including the former home of the Hen and Chickens tavern (until recently Sayer's the Bakers) have also been attributed to Thomas Boswell.

To the northeast of the Abbey Green is the current **Bishop's Palace** which is set apart from the rest of the buildings in the courtyard by a high garden wall and probably dates from the early part of the 19th century. The site on which it stands was formerly the home of a chapel dedicated to St Thomas the Martyr that was said to have existed there until the early 1780's when it was finally taken down. This earlier religious house was then replaced by the Dean's House which by 1787, was thought to have been occupied by an individual called George Cotton, the holder of that ecclesiastical office.

The stone pillar which stands in the centre of the grassed area at **Abbey Square** is reported to be a relic of Chester's historic Exchange building which stood on the Market Square from 1698 until 1862 when it was severely damaged by fire and subsequently demolished, being replaced by the new Town Hall which continues to stand today. This central area of the modern day Abbey Green has itself been put to several uses throughout its long history, including forming part of St Thomas' Court, a separate courtyard and chapel dedicated to the memory of Thomas a' Beckett, which was said to have been relocated to the site of the later Bishop's Palace sometime around 1541. This particular area is also significant for having produced evidence of pre-Roman occupation, specifically prehistoric ploughing, as well as remains of early Roman defensive ramparts which themselves have been linked to the construction of a military stores depot in around 60 AD.

The western flank of Abbey Green which is also occupied by a second terrace of mid to late 18th century houses was formerly the site for a number of privately owned kilns, drying rooms and perhaps worst of all a brew house. Despite having been forbidden by the Bishop of Chester from renting out church property for such purposes, the Dean who was in day to day charge of the Cathedral during the late 16th century did so anyway. However, it seems that at a later date the leases signed by the Dean were cancelled and monies refunded to the tenants, allowing the buildings to be put to other uses, including that of housing pupils from the Cathedral's own King School, who had been forced out of their former home in the Abbey's former refectory, because the building was in such a ruinous condition.

By the middle of the 17th century though and with the Civil War siege in full force, despite their being completely dilapidated and perhaps even dangerous, these industrial buildings no doubt served a purpose by way of storage or as temporary shelters. Once the war had been won by the forces of Parliament however, it was only a relatively short time before rebuilding in the city began again and by the middle of the 18th century this whole section of the historic Abbey precincts was being used to construct the houses that stand today, as well as the adjoining retail units that occupy much of the eastern side of Northgate Street.

Almost directly opposite this elegant terrace of houses, **Abbey Chambers** which stands at the junction of Abbey Green and Abbey Street is a detached 18th century property that sits in front of the next two mentioned cottages. This house itself bears a date of 1754 and may in fact have previously been used to accommodate the various headmasters of the Kings School, which lay just across the Abbey Green.

No's 13 & 14 **Abbey Square** are reported to be a pair of sandstone cottages constructed in 1626 on the orders of Bishop Bridgeman to house lay clerks and "singing men" at the cathedral. The Square was originally the courtyard of the early Benedictine Abbey, which housed the Abbey's bakery and brewery. Initially four such cottages were built on the site of the Abbey's former kitchen, which provided some of the building materials for the new cottages, but only two of the four have survived through to the modern day.

Abbey Street, which links Abbey Green to the ancient Kale Yard Gateway, comprises two separate terraces of houses, the southern flank reportedly being built by a Mr Thomas of King St between 1826-8 and the northern terrace, where most of the properties are 18th

century houses built by individual leaseholders, apart from the one closest to the city walls, which is thought to be a 17th century property, built over an even earlier stone building. Nearby, stands the Kale Yard gateway, an entrance through Chester's medieval defensive walls which is thought to have existed in one form or another since the reign of King Edward I in the late 13th century when the Abbot was given permission to create an access point to the Abbey's vegetable garden's that lay outside of the city's walls.

Despite this Royal assent of 1274 however, the construction and continuing use of the gateway by the inhabitants of the Abbey remained a constant source of dispute and ill-will between the Abbot and the city's corporation. By the 14th century, the matter was once again put before the king, who by this time was Edward of Caernarfon or Edward II, who instructed the Abbot in 1322 to hold the gate in times of peace, but to construct a ditch and drawbridge to protect the entrance, as well as ordering that the gateway should be securely locked each and every night. Around the same time that this external gateway was first constructed about 1274, a second internal portal, from the Abbey's own secluded precincts through to the city walls themselves were built, but this was later sealed up as part of the later agreement made with King Edward II in 1322.

Yet another gateway was thought to have existed close to the still standing Kale Yard gate, being constructed around the same period, but with little evidence of its presence remaining through to modern times. This third portal was reported to have been designed to allow a horse and rider access to Chester's inner precincts and was possibly the root cause of the ongoing antagonism between the Abbot and the corporation who regarded this unauthorised entrance as an obvious risk to the city's security. Regardless of these concerns though, this gateway was thought to have remained in place right up until the start of the 16th century when it was finally removed, although its location is thought to be marked today by the short flight of stairs which lie close to the Kale Yard gateway.

At the time of the gateway's construction, the Abbey's vegetable gardens were thought to have stretched from the city's early medieval east gate right through to the site of today's Phoenix Tower and presumably included the line of the original Roman fosse which had once protected the military fortress. Significantly, in 1264 records suggest that elements of the Abbey's extensive gardens and outbuildings were destroyed by William La Zouche, the agent of the monarch Henry III in order to rebuild Chester's defences, including its town ditches, as part of the king's struggles with the rebellious Barons of England led by the infamous Simon de Montford, a legitimate contender for the English throne.

Everything in this north eastern section of modern Chester centres round the historic **Cathedral of Christ and the Blessed Virgin**, which is the last in a long line of religious centres that are reported to have occupied this particular area of Chester. Although there is little physical evidence to substantiate some of the claims made for the site, it has been suggested that prior to the Roman occupation of Chester, there was a shrine of some sort dedicated to the local native deities. With the arrival of the Legions, this British shrine was then said to have been replaced with a temple dedicated to the Roman god Apollo, which in turn was converted to a Christian place of worship following the conversion of the Emperor Constantine, who decreed that Christianity become the accepted religion of the Western Roman Empire. However, following the evacuation of the British Province by the Roman Legions in the late 4th or early 5th centuries, Christianity was thought to have been largely abandoned by the native Britons in favour of their own local deities and presumably earlier shrines and temples were usurped once again.

The earliest reliable records for the site which later developed into the modern Cathedral appear to date from second half of the 9th century, when a monastery dedicated to St Werburgh, was built on the orders of the Anglo Saxon leader Aethelflaeda in 875 AD. Reportedly replacing an even earlier church, dedicated to St Peter and St Paul, this new monastery was thought to have been founded specifically to house the mortal remains of Werburga, which were put in danger by marauding Vikings. Although little is known about the earlier church dedicated to St Peter and St Paul, the presence in the city of the 7th century St John the Baptist's church might suggest a similar foundation date for this long extinct religious centre. Unfortunately for the new monastery, its life appears to have been as short-lived as that of its predecessor and within 20-odd years of the city being captured by the military forces of William the Conqueror in 1070, the monastery's precincts were being largely re-founded and rebuilt once again, this time as the Norman Abbey Church of St Werbugh's.

Originally granted their charter in 1092 by Earl Hugh D'Avranches, Hugh requested that the Abbey pray for him and his family after their deaths and its foundation was so important to him that he invited Anselm of Bec, who would later become Archbishop of Canterbury, to witness the granting of the charter. From around 1093 to 1116 there was an extensive program of church building and religious dedication throughout much of England, with most church services conducted in either French or Latin.

From the date of its Norman foundation the physical fabric of the church was continually rebuilt and extended around the original Anglo Saxon monastery that it was designed to replace. As each replacement section of the Abbey was built, the corresponding area of the Saxon building was demolished and by around 1211 much of this initial work had been successfully completed. The Lady Chapel was begun in around 1265 and from 1350 onward a new phase of building was undertaken which would last until Tudor times. The cloisters were finally completed at the beginning of the 16th century, barely 10 years before much of the property was seized by the Crown.

Many of the various phases of building work that took place at Chester's great Norman Abbey during the period 1093 to 1540 were personally directed by a succession of Abbots, who oversaw the day-to-day running of this vitally important religious community. Richard of Bec was the first recorded Abbot of Chester's new Norman Abbey and had been appointed by Anselm of Bec, who had been invited to witness the Abbey's foundation charter by Hugh Lupus, the second Norman Earl of Chester. Richard held office between 1093 and 1116 and on his death was interred within the Abbey precincts. It was during Richard's tenure that the construction of the replacement Norman Abbey was begun, enclosing the earlier Anglo Saxon church which was then subsequently demolished piece by piece. The Presbytery, the North and South Transepts of the Abbey, were the first sections to be rebuilt and by the time of Richard's death in 1116, all of these were thought to have been largely completed.

Abbot William was appointed as head of the Abbey in 1121 and on his death in 1140 was buried within its precincts alongside his predecessor, Richard of Bec, the first Abbot. During his tenure as Abbot, the monks living accommodation at the Abbey was constructed and by around 1129 the Chapter House was said to have been completed. The Abbey's Cloisters and Refectory were also thought to have been started during the period, although their construction was undertaken in a series of managed stages. At the time of Abbot William's death, the Abbey's north-west tower was also thought to have been completed.

Abbot Ralph was the Abbot of St Werburgh's Norman Abbey from 1141 to 1151 and was thought to have supervised the construction of the two west towers as well as the Abbey's western façade. He was followed to the office by Robert Fitz Nigel, Abbot from 1157 to 1174, who was thought to have overseen a phase of remedial construction work at the Abbey, which were undertaken to correct earlier mistakes. St Anselm's church, the Abbot's private chapel, was also said to have been built during his tenure.

Abbot Geoffrey was in charge of Chester's Norman Abbey from 1194 through to 1208 and it was during his tenure that the Choir was said to have been started and the Saxon Bell Tower replaced. It was also reported that the earlier Presbytery and Transepts were also replaced and a new entrance to and from the Cloisters was constructed. Lucian was reported to have been a 12th century monk at Chester's Norman Abbey and was thought to have been educated at the nearby collegiate church of St John the Baptist in the city. Much of his work seems to have been undertaken during the tenure of Abbot Geoffrey.

Hugh Grylle was Abbot from 1208 to 1226 and was responsible for the completion of the Abbey's Choir and Bell Tower, both of which projects were started by his predecessor. His next project was the completion of the Nave, which was thought to be incomplete at the time that he took office. He oversaw the demolition of the earlier Saxon Nave and its replacement with a new English style of architecture. Upon his death on 7 May 1226 Abbot Hugh was buried in the Chapter House at the feet of Abbot Geoffrey, his predecessor.

His successor, William Marmion, was Abbot from 1226 to 1228 and it appears that there was a lull in the building activity at the Abbey because his tenure as Abbot was a relatively short one. He in turn was succeeded by Walter de Pinchbeck who held the office from 1228 to 1240 and was thought to have initiated the reconstruction of the Monastery at the Abbey sometime after 1230.

Walter was then succeeded by Roger Frend, who was recorded as holding the office of Abbot from 1240 to 1249 and it was he who was thought to have been responsible for the completion of the Chapter house and the Cloisters. Roger was said to have died on 23 September 1249 and was later interred in the Chapter House of the Abbey.

Frend's successor, Simon de Whitchurch, was Abbot from 1265 to 1291 and was thought to be responsible for the building of St Nicholas's Chapel in around 1280. The entirely separate chapel was initially built to replace the church of St Oswald which was said to have stood on the site of the Abbey's south transept. Unfortunately, this new chapel was not easily accepted by the local parishioners and the building later became a court, then, later still, a theatre which hosted the likes of Charles Dickens when he visited the city. It was also during Abbot Simon's tenure that the construction of the Monastery was finally completed and the next project he initiated was the rebuilding of the Abbey church itself, which included the notable Lady Chapel. Upon his death on 22 February 1291 Abbot Simon was reported to have been buried in the Abbey's Chapter House beneath a marble gravestone.

Thomas de Burchelle was the next Abbot of St Werburgh's Norman Abbey, serving from 1291 to 1323 and was said to have continued the various building projects which had been started by his predecessor, Simon De Whitchurch. Around 1310 Richard 'the Engineer' L'enginour was said to have demolished the Abbey's Presbytery to make way for additional piers within the building. A shrine dedicated to St Werburgh was also built between the High Altar and the Lady Chapel around 1310, but this was later severely damaged during the Reformation initiated by Henry VIII. Abbot Thomas died on 23 December 1323 and was said to have been interred in the main body of the church on the south side of the Choir.

William de Bebington was the next Abbot of St Werburgh's Abbey, holding the office from 1324 to 1349 and thought to have been responsible for the construction of a number of chapels and altars within the Abbey's precincts. In 1349 the Black Death reached Chester and Abbot William was thought to have been one of its more notable victims, succumbing to the disease on 20 September 1349 and later being interred on the south side of the choir.

Bebington's successor, Richard De Seynesbury (Sainsbury), was said to have been the Abbot at Chester between 1349 and 1363 and thought to have overseen the reconstruction of the South Transept of the Abbey. The south bay and southern wall of the western aisle were also reported to have been built during the same period, bringing about the demolition of the south transept. Sainsbury was reported to have been attacked by members of his own community at a time when there was a highly troublesome and violent faction present within the Abbey community and a number of the monks found themselves facing the courts on charges of robbery, arson and assault. So worrying were these troubles, that in 1362 Prince Edward ordered the Abbot of St Alban's to visit Chester and resolve the disciplinary problems that were affecting the Abbey. As a result Sainsbury was forced to resign his post and a number of the more problematic monks were removed to St Alban's to receive corrective training.

Thomas Erdeley, the Abbot of St Werburgh's from 1413 to 1434, had earlier been accused of breaking into Abbot Henry de Sutton's pay chest and stealing 20 marks and three gold rings. He was also thought to have stolen a chest and five marks belonging to Robert de Legh and it was during his tenure that a number of the Abbey's monks were brought before the court for offences ranging from robbery to rape.

John Saughall was the Abbot of St Werburgh's Abbey from 1435 to 1455 and was thought to have derived his name from the outlying area of Chester called Saughall, formerly called Salhare. He was said to have been a clerk at the Chester Abbey, who along with a fellow monk, Thomas Erdeley, displayed a level of violence and dishonesty that might easily have ended their religious careers, yet both men somehow went on to achieve the highest possible office within their community, that of Abbot.

Not surprisingly given its great age, the ancient fabric of Chester's great Norman Abbey has suffered regular bouts of deterioration and deliberate damage throughout its lifetime, not least because of the prevailing British climate and the generally soft sandstone that makes up much of its mass. Consequently, in later centuries it has been subject to a number of major renovation and restoration programs, most notably during the late 19th and early 20th centuries when some of England's most prominent church architects were employed to rescue parts of the aging structure. Between 1843 and 1844 Richard Charles Hussey was reported to have undertaken a relatively small number of restoration projects in the Cathedral, largely centred round the historic Lady Chapel.

Beginning in 1868, Sir George Gilbert Scott was said to have undertaken one of the most extensive renovation projects, which involved rebuilding large parts of the Lady Chapel and re-facing significant parts of the Cathedral's crumbling exterior façade. It was during this same lengthy project, which lasted through to 1876 that Scott was reported to have added many of the turrets, pinnacles and flying buttresses, which continue to adorn the building to this present day and have remained a source of controversy between architectural scholars. Some five years after Scott had completed his mammoth works at the church, Sir Arthur Blomfield, the designer of the adjoining King's School building was also thought to be overseeing work in the neighbouring Cathedral, a renovation project that was said to have lasted from 1882 through to 1887. Finally in 1913, the last of the four great national architects to work at Chester Cathedral began his work there. Giles Gilbert Scott, the grandson of Sir George was said to have undertaken a number of renovation projects within the church, including the design of the Rood Screen and that of two Altar Screens which were linked to two of the Cathedral's smaller chapels.

Lying on an east to west alignment, the modern day Cathedral church of Christ and the Blessed Virgin has been constructed over many hundreds of years, with its ancient fabric subject to regular rounds of large scale rebuilding, renovations and repairs. Beginning at the eastern end of the church, which lies closest to the city's eastern defensive wall, the Cathedral comprises the Lady Chapel, the Choir, the Nave and finally the great Western Door, which is flanked on either side by the church's Consistory Court and Baptistery. The church's South Porch, which faces towards the southern end of modern day St Werburgh's Street leads to the South Transept of the church and is flanked to the west by the Cathedral's ornate War Memorial, as well as the South West Porch of the church. On the north side of the great central Nave; and probably best seen from Abbey Square, is the North Transept, Refectory, Bishop's Parlour and the Chapter House all of which are wrapped around the central Cloisters of the former Norman Abbey.

The west side of the Cloisters is reported to include a 12th century Norman under-croft, possibly one of the earliest features of the modern Cathedral building, although the North Transept of the church is said to include a late 11th century archway, which was built some years before that. The Cathedral's Chapter House now hosts part of the church's extensive library and is also said to contain a cabinet or cupboard that is as old as the 13th century building which holds it. The 14th century North Aisle of the Choir contains remnants of the earlier 12th century Abbey Church which preceded it; and the Cathedral's Lady Chapel still contains partial remains of the stone shrine that once held the relics of St Werbugh, which were the subject of pilgrimage and veneration during the middle ages. The Choir contains a number of elaborately carved late 14th century stalls and the

Cathedral's South Transept, once the site for the parish church of St Oswald, contains a number of interesting memorials and insignia's. These include the Battle Ensign of HMS Chester, the ship on which Jack "Boy" Cornwall won the Victoria Cross at the Battle of Jutland; and the Colours of the Cheshire Regiment, who's Regimental Gardens now lie outside of the South Porch.

CHAPTER EIGHT

WATERGATE STREET

Forming the western section of the Roman Via Principalis, or more correctly the Via Principalis Sinistra, this street has always has been one of the most important thoroughfares in the city, simply because of its connection with the city's early maritime history, founded on Chester's long since disappeared international port. In the earlier years of the Roman fortress, much of the northern side of this street was known to have been occupied by the headquarters building, the Principa, Officers quarters, stable blocks and legionary barracks. As noted in the High Cross chapter, the Principia was reported to have stood on the site of the later St Peter's church and occupied the area between Northgate Street, westward to Goss Street and from the High Cross through to Hamilton Place in the north.

From Goss Street westward to Gerard's Lane, Officers quarters were thought to have lined the main thoroughfare and further west the area between Gerard's Lane and the fortresses western gate was the location for the legionary barracks, constructed of wattle and daub and standing on stone sills, which helped to protect these organic building materials from the worst of the cold and damp climate in northwest Britain.

The terrace of buildings on the northern flank of Watergate Street, which stretch westward from St Peter's church to Goss Street currently occupy the same ground that nearly 2000 years ago marked the southern limit of the Roman Principia, the legionaries headquarters building. However, between the end of the Roman occupation in the late 4th century and the arrival of the Norman's at the end of the 11th century little is known about the use or ownership of these individual plots of lands. Records pertaining to them only seem to exist from around the first half of the 14th century when parts of the site were owned by private individuals or by the Norman Abbey of St Werbugh.

The plot of land which now houses the historic **Deva Hotel** is thought to have first been noted in 1312 when it was reported to have been in the possession of Hugh de Brichulle or Brickhill, but was simply described as "land belonging to" which suggests that the site itself was vacant and undeveloped. By 1345 however, the land and the tenement standing on it were recorded to have been owned by Robert of Macclesfield, who had obviously started to make use of the valuable city property. Nearly 200 years later, the site had passed into the hands of an individual called John Bryne who was reported to have been a butcher by trade, which is significant for the fact that the whole of this northern row would later become known as "Fleshener's Row" in later years.

Sometime between 1534 and 1634 part of the tenement which occupied this city site was given over to housing the "Moon Tavern", a Chester inn that would inhabit this part of Chester right through to 1840. In that year, the hostelry was said to have been renamed as the "Albion Tavern" and that remained its title until around 1912 when it finally became "Ye Old Deva Inn", a name that has subsequently been altered to its present form of "The Deva Hotel".

Within the hotel building itself there are a number of features which testify to its great age, including an Elizabethan staircase from the 16th century and a fireplace which is dated 1509, but most likely dates from the reign of James I at the beginning of the 17th century. In 1943 the building immediately to the west of the "Deva" was taken down to ground level, fully exposing the previously hidden west wall of the "Deva Hotel" and allowing historians to view some of the materials used to construct the early hostelry. A decade later, more building work in the adjacent property exposed more evidence of the wattle and daub materials that had been used at the tavern, both inside and outside of the property. Finally, further work undertaken on the tavern's roof in the 20th century uncovered evidence of substantial rebuilding or restoration work in the early 19th century. Workmen who were employed on the buildings roof discovered a major timber carrying the date 1804 which suggested that the whole building had been substantially re-fronted in that year.

The tavern which immediately adjoins the "Deva Hotel" is the "**Victoria Hotel**", which is reportedly part of the same building as is its neighbour and therefore shares its extensive history. However, its early use and occupation has differed somewhat, as prior to 1670 this part of the building was reported to have been owned by William Bulkeley, the Arch Deacon of Dublin and his family. The predecessor of the "Victoria" was said to be the "Fox and Goose" which was reported to have been in existence prior to 1622, as a city butcher called David Hatton was known to have rented the shop immediately below the tavern in that year. In 1670 Bulkeley was thought to have sold the property to one Hugh Roberts who was a Cooper by trade and following his death in 1687, the house passed into the possession of his brother Robert who was a city butcher. On his death in 1689 the property then passed into the hands of his wife and 2 daughters and it was only some 30 years later that the "Fox and Goose" finally became known as the "Victoria", a name it continues to hold today.

The third and final hostelry that occupied part of this medieval "Butchers Row", but failed to survive through to the modern day, was the "Castle and Falcon". Identified as the third property to the east of Goss Street, the building which would later house this particular tavern was first reported in 1533 when it was in the ownership of St Werburgh's Abbey and was being leased by a butcher called Thomas Hale. By 1542 however and following the dissolution of the monasteries by Henry VIII, many of these minor possessions had been passed to the Dean and Chapter of the new city Cathedral. This was said to be the case with the building in Watergate Street and records indicate that in 1542 the house was being leased by an ironmonger called Thomas Griffiths.

Information on the property for the following 200 years is scarce, but it was undoubtedly during this period that the "Castle and Falcon" was first established on the site. First officially recorded in 1729, by 1760 the tavern was said to be in the hands of one Lawrence Smith and by 1785 was being used to host meetings of Chester's Smith's company. Even as late as 1809 the property was still in the ownership of the Cathedral authorities, but was being leased by members of the Bevan family, although whether or not they were involved with the running of the tavern is unclear. Between 1840 and 1846 and for some, as yet, unknown reason the "Castle and Falcon" was thought to have been renamed as the "Bell Tavern", but by 1846 had once again assumed its earlier title.

The end of the "Castle and Falcon" seems to have occurred in 1874, when a Joseph Salmon applied for a licence on the tavern, but had his application refused, possibly because the property was not simply being used as an inn. However, it appears that another member of the same family was already running another liquor establishment in the street immediately below the site of the "Castle and Falcon", so this too might have been a factor in the authority's decision to refuse Joseph his licence. This second "spirit house" was reportedly called the "Salmon Vaults" and was thought to have operated in Watergate Street from the 1870's all the way through to the 1930's, before finally being absorbed into the retail showroom of the later Aston's furniture store.

Despite the wealth of the families who actually owned many of these properties, in later years this whole "Butchers Row" area was reported to have been generally run-down and a place to be avoided by decent people, a reputation that undoubtedly had something to do with the three taverns which operated there. However, despite this poor reputation one of Chester's earliest banks, the Chester Savings Bank was said to have established its offices around the corner in Goss Street in 1846, prior to its later move to brand new premises in Grosvenor Street.

Standing directly opposite this now much modernised "Butchers Row" and lying on the south east flank of Watergate Street are the elevated rows, and street level shops and offices that were created by the architect Thomas M Lockwood in 1892. Constructed as part of the "beautification" of the city's High Cross and the widening of Watergate Street that took place in the latter half of the 19th century, the site of the modern day Adam's Estate Agent's is thought to have an equally extensive history, as does its northern counterpart. Records suggest that in the 12th century this area of the city was owned by one of the two hospital charities that existed in Chester at that time, either St Giles in the suburb of Boughton, or St John's the Baptist's which formally inhabited the site of the modern day Bluecoat School, both of which were first founded by the 7th Earl of Chester, Ranulph Blundeville. This early site was reported to have been occupied by a large stone house or hall, which was evidently underpinned by the handsome undercroft or cellar that continues to form part of the street level shop premises. A record from the early part of the 16th century indicates that this property was later leased to Sir Thomas Smith in 1507 and that the northern part of the property, immediately adjoining Watergate Street, actually intruded further into the thoroughfare than do the modern buildings and making the eastern entranceway of the street much narrower than it is today.

Formerly called Goss Lane, modern day **Goss Street** adjoins Watergate Street from the north and up until 1962 was the location for Chester's Assay Office, where items made from precious metals would be examined, estimated and authenticated. The Lowe family were thought to have had a long association with this particular office which had first been authorised by King James II in 1685. The property itself is thought to date from 1749 and was first used as a private town house, being occupied by a Dr Samuel Nevitt-Bennett between 1812 and 1826. A Saughall landowner, Nevitt-Bennett was thought to have had extensive property holdings in and around Goss Street during the early part of the 19th century, which he either inherited or purchased from the previous owners, members of the Doncaster family. Two other notable individual who lived in Goss Street were a Bailiff called Richard Pritchard who was reported to have lived there around 1780 and a Proctor called Thomas Store who lived in Goss Street around 1782.

Another member of the Bennett family, a Major John Bennet, was reported to have established a wine merchants business in a property abutting the west side of Goss Street, during which an unspecified treasure trove was said to have been discovered. The property which is commonly known as **Hesketh House**, in memory of Henry Hesketh, a prominent wine merchant, was said to have to have been owned by a William Bearsley in 1765 who is described as being from "Oporto in Portugal", although some other reports suggest that the property had originally been built on the orders of one Henry Bennet of Moston.

Either way, the link between the house and Portugal is interesting, in that during work on the property's cellars there is a legend that a hoard of gold coins were discovered by the occupier of the house, which were purportedly Portuguese in origin. The legend goes on to say that the owner of the house, rather than declare his good fortune, kept its discovery a secret from all but his closest friends and used the treasure to invest heavily in property and assets, thereby guaranteeing his future financial security. Whether or not the story is true is purely academic, but it is interesting to note that this particular property is also said to be linked to a gang of "coiners" who operated in the building's cellars, so maybe the two incidents or activities are related to one another?

God's Providence House which is located at 9 Watergate Street, on the south side of the thoroughfare, is almost an entire replacement for an earlier building which dated from 1652 and in common with a number of early city landmark buildings had been allowed to decay in the years leading up to the 19th century. With the permission of the then owner Mr Gregg, Chester's noted architect James Harrison undertook an almost total renovation of the house during the 1860's which led to it being heightened. It has also been suggested that the letters "HR" which are inscribed on the front of the building may in fact be the original house builder's initials, but this has not been definitively proved.

The inscription "God's providence is mine inheritance" is thought to be associated with an individual called Richard Boyle, made the Earl of Cork in 1620, who was reported to have used this or similar inscriptions on a number of his homes. Consequently, it has been suggested that an admirer or former servant of Boyle, who was then settled in Chester, may well have adopted the inscription for his own property. It is curious to note however, that the plague which gave rise to the dedication was reported to have occurred in 1603, some 40-odd years before the house was even built, which suggests an alternative reason for the dedication. Immediately adjoining this historic building, no 11 Watergate Street is described as an early 18th century house that is known to have been heavily renovated during its lifetime. Significantly though, this much more recent building is reported to sit over a late 12th or early 13th century vaulted and pillared cellar, commonly known as the Old Crypt, which is a grade one listed structure.

Booths Mansion, which occupies 28-34 Watergate Street, actually dates from around the end of the 16th or beginning of the 17th centuries, but today has an early 18th century frontage, which was commissioned by its former owner Alderman George Booth around 1700. In its original form, the property was known to have been two entirely separate townhouses, with the more easterly building being owned by Sir John Booth, who was thought to have purchased it sometime around 1659. Although he owned the property, records suggest that Sir John and his family did not immediately occupy their new house, but instead were known to be living at Cholmondley House in Northgate Street, now occupied by the city's main library building. It is generally assumed that during the period 1659 through to 1678 the property in Watergate Street was simply rented out to private tenants, including Henry Harper, the master of St Giles' Leper Hospital in Boughton and later to another individual called Richard Levinge.

It was only in 1678 that the Booth family, in the person of George, Sir John's son, finally took up residence in their property on the north side of Watergate Street and by 1691 was reportedly being used to host lavish dinner parties and large social events. Prior to 1700 and the complete rebuilding of the site, the western half of the property was reportedly owned by a city Alderman called Bolland, who sold his home to the Booth family in that same year.

Both of these much earlier Chester houses were known to have stood on medieval cellars dating from around 1240 and the lower walls immediately above these under-crofts were reported to be up to 3 feet thick, suggesting that a much earlier and much more substantial stone hall or building had once occupied the very same site. Nothing is known about this possibly long extinct hall or indeed the builders of the two city properties that ultimately replaced it. The two properties that were demolished by George Booth in 1700 for his new mansion house were thought to have been included features contemporary with the reign of King James I which suggests that they may well have been constructed during the reign of Elizabeth I or that of her immediate successor.

The impressive mansion house that replaced these earlier buildings was said to have been built from the ground up, but clearly retained the two medieval cellars which had existed since the 13th century, although at the time one of these was reportedly left filled with rubble. The construction of his new home also brought Booth into conflict with the city authorities, as the much enlarged property now stood slightly beyond its earlier street frontage, a situation that would ultimately result in him being fined and charged a yearly rental for the piece of city land he had unlawfully enclosed within his own property line.

Despite the time, trouble and expense that he incurred as a result of building his new city property, records suggest that sometime between its construction date and 1745 this new mansion was regularly being used by Chester's corporation as their official Assembly Rooms, indicating that Booth had actually sold his interest in the building and was living elsewhere with his family. Clearly though, the new Booth's Mansion had its limitations, because within a relatively short time the corporation too had abandoned the building in favour of the much more modern and extensive facilities at the city's new Royal Hotel in Eastgate Street.

Initially sold to a family called Ward, between 1840 and 1846 the house was reported to have been occupied by a city surgeon called Charles Hamilton who was a close relative of the Ward family. Twenty-odd years later, in

1870, the house was in the possession of one Thomas Faulkner who had a solicitor's practice in Chester, but within a few years he too had moved away from Watergate Street and resettled himself in the Hoole suburb of the city. It is worth noting, that both Hamilton and Faulkner are synonymous with the Hoole area of Chester, being the titles of two of its main thoroughfares.

In 1874, part of the former Booth's Mansion was being used to house the Army's Pensions Office and another section was being used to accommodate elements of the local court services. It was only in 1883, that the property was finally put to some overall use, when the city's Liberal Club were reported to have bought the entire house for the princely sum of £2,500. In 1891 the new owners were known to have carried out extensive renovations on the mansion, thanks largely to a generous donation made by Alderman Charles Brown and helping in part to create the building that stands today. Unhappily though, in 1904 the building was once again abandoned by its owners, who relocated their club premises to another site in the city. As a result the house was subsequently given over to hosting a public billiards hall, before being called into service by the Army during the Second World War, when it was used as a NAAFI Club and as a billeting depot for the servicemen that were stationed in Chester at that time.

During the reign of King Edward III and perhaps even earlier than that, a mansion was reported to have stood at the eastern junction of **Crook Street** and Watergate Street, which has been speculated to be the home of the Earl's agent or "sergeant" of the Watergate. Reported to be hosting the "Caernarfon Castle" inn during the 1780's, this building was last recorded in 1891 as Brooke House and associated with the Lee family who lived in this part of the city. During the 1860's, six Alms Houses were thought to have been built along Crook Street ostensibly to house some of Chester's poorest inhabitants, but these were probably demolished during the slum clearances undertaken in the middle of the 20th century. In its original form this ancient thoroughfare was not connected directly with Watergate Street, but joined the now extinct Gerrard's Lane, which at the time ran northward from Watergate Street through to Parson's Lane (Princess Street) but was subsequently lost during the redevelopment of the Market Square in the late 1960's.

Watergate Wine Bar formerly occupied a series of medieval vaulted bays which are reported to be medieval in origin and were at sometime in their history inter-connected with adjoining under-crofts, once again suggesting their connections with the upper halls which have been rebuilt over time and incorporated into the Watergate Street shopping Rows.

Leche House on the south side of Watergate Street sits atop 13th century medieval cellars and is thought to have its own origins in the 14th century, with substantial rebuilding work taking place over a four hundred year period, during which the property was increasingly improved, heightened and extended.

The house is thought to be named in memory of Sir John Leche, the surgeon or "Leech" to the English king Edward III and possibly to his royal successor, the ill-fated Richard II. The Leche family are generally associated with Carden Park in Cheshire and with the village of Mollington which lies just a few miles outside of Chester along the road to Parkgate on the Wirral. As a matter of interest and perhaps to explain any inconsistencies with subsequent generations of this family, it is worth pointing out that there were thought to be at least 14 members of this family with the Christian name John, which tends to inhibit a clearly defined line of succession.

The first John Leche, the surgeon to Edward III who might have also attended Richard II was reported to have received extensive grants from King Richard in the latter half of the 14th century, including an annuity of £10 paid in 1381 from the tolls of the city's then thriving Dee Mills. In 1386, Leche was said to have been granted the manor of Barrow by the king for a period of 20 years and 5 years later was likewise granted the manor of Moston by the same monarch. It is also interesting to note, that in 1384, a John Leche and his brother Richard, along with a number of other men were charged with attacking one John Deek a citizen of Chester, although only John Leche was thought to have been charged with his murder. Obviously found guilty of the crime, Leche was subsequently pardoned for his act, presumably by the monarch Richard II, which supports the view that the John Leche in question had some connection with the crown, possibly as the king's surgeon.

By around 1550, a member of this extensive family was reported to be one George Leche, who was described as both a merchant and a city Alderman. In his will of 1551, it was noted that he left extensive property holdings to his various relatives, including lands in Watergate Street, which were then being leased to a merchant called Richard Gittens, although whether or not this included the modern day Leche House is unknown. However, it should also be noted that George Leche also left a second property in the same city street, this time in the occupation of an individual called Richard Brynes the younger. Just to confuse the matter even more, in 1583 there was thought to have been a legal dispute regarding a third property in Watergate Street that involved a member of the Leche family. A man called Walter Fox was said to have transferred this as yet unidentified house into the possession of one Robert Leche in that year, but the conveyance appears to have been challenged by Fox's relatives, but all to no avail, as the courts were thought to have upheld Leche's entitlement to the property in question.

A few of the many features that are contained within the historic fabric of the house under discussion include a Priest's Hole and an elaborately decorated chimney piece that is said to date from the late 16th or early 17th century. The house also contains a first floor gallery known as the Ladies Bower and plasterwork associated with Catherine of Aragon, one of the six wives of Henry VIII who was reported to have stayed in the property. The former Great Hall of the house is now thought to stand behind the later street frontage and has no doubt been altered over time to suit the buildings various purposes.

Between 1662 and 1665, Leche House was reported to have been occupied by John Wainwright, the Chancellor of Chester Diocese, but he was later said to have moved to Stanley Palace, a little further down the street. Some 60 years later part of the old house was reported to have been occupied by a tavern called the "Hand and Snake" which was recorded there in 1723, having moved from its previous home in Bridge Street where it had operated from since 1697.

Sadly, many of the earlier buildings adjoining Leche House on the west side were demolished during the first half of the 20th century, presumably because their dilapidated condition made them a threat to public safety. Only number 25 escaped this destruction and that was probably because it was a relatively new 19th century building that had already replaced its early successor. Properties lost were reported to have included no's 27 to 33 on the south side of the thoroughfare, but from there on the historic buildings continued as before. Number 35 Watergate Street is described as a 19th century property rebuilt in the city's favoured half timbered fashion and reported to be the site where a Roman column base was discovered during construction work, although little more information about the find is available. The adjoining number 37 is likewise described as a 19th century structure, but the fact that it sits atop an early medieval stone crypt indicates a much earlier history for the site. The third one of these miscellaneous buildings is number 39, which is thought to be 18th century in construction and that is reported to still include contemporary doors at row level.

Bishop Lloyd's Palace at 41 to 43 Watergate Street, Chester is generally associated with George Lloyd, the Bishop of Sodor and Man, later Bishop of Chester who died in 1615, the very same year that the house is commonly reported to have been completed. There is no evidence that either the Bishop or his family ever took up residence in the property, so it can only be supposed that the house, its decorated gable and Latin inscription was only ever intended to be a testimony to the notable cleric, rather than suggesting that the house ever belonged to him.

Originally built as two separate town houses, only the more western of the two properties is more properly associated with the Bishop, but later work by architect TM Lockwood on No: 51 in 1899 has helped to link the two houses together, including the steps to the first floor rows. Within the interior of the building, evidence of 17th century wood panelling and ceilings still exist to this day, making the house one of the finest of its type in the whole of the city.

The front of the building is adorned with a series of eight carved panels which are reported to depict the history of mankind's redemption, from Adam and Eve to Christ's crucifixion on the Cross. The three centre panels are thought to show the arms of King James I, those of George Lloyd and finally a Latin inscription emblazoned with the date 1615. Although an exact translation of the Latin verse is said to have escaped a definitive answer, the most reliable and acceptable translation to date is thought to be "It is the outward look that shows the true essence of within. As it is without, so it is within"

George Lloyd's eldest daughter was reported to have married two men whose names are inextricably linked with the American colonies and their associated Ivy League system. Her first husband was Thomas Yale, the grandfather of the founder of Yale University and her second husband was Theophilus Eaton, the man credited with founding the settlement of New Haven in 1639, later becoming Governor of the province. Some local sources have suggested that it was Lloyd's daughter herself who was responsible for the decoration and inscription, although there is little historical evidence to support this particular theory.

In fact, there seems to be sufficient evidence to suggest that one of the first occupants of the house was the Bowyer family, who were reported to be resident there in 1616, the year following George Lloyd's death and there is little to say that Sir John and Lady Bowyer hadn't occupied the house since it was first constructed. Although little is known about this particular family's history, they were known to have originated from Staffordshire and may have had a so far undiscovered link to the renowned clergyman which caused them to celebrate his distinguished life and career.

It was reported during the late 19th century that efforts were made to have the historic house moved to America, no doubt because of the previously mentioned links to both Yale University and the colony of New Haven. However, thanks largely to the efforts of city Alderman Charles Brown and the generosity of the public, the house was purchased by the corporation and remains as one of Chester's most outstanding architectural assets.

During the 1880's the house was reported to have been used as a hostelry called the "Palice Vaults" although it should perhaps have been more properly called the "Palace Vaults". The later "Yacht Inn" was also thought to have occupied the same premises for a short time, before moving to a new site at the western end of Watergate Street, eventually becoming a victim of Chester's inner ring road system during the 1960's.

St Ursula's Café building which once occupied the medieval crypt at number 45 Watergate Street is undoubtedly linked, if only by name, with the city hospital dedicated to that Saint which used to occupy a site in nearby Commonhall Street. Although the cafeteria has long since ceased to trade, it's name can still be seen carved into the ornate framework of the premises street doorway and the medieval cellar that it once occupied is now a grade one listed building. This whole section of the Watergate Street terrace is now inhabited by a mixture of miscellaneous 17th, 18th and 19th century houses that have replaced the earlier buildings which once occupied this section of Chester. Number 51 is listed as a 17th century property which has been cemented over in later years and hiding its original façade from public view, whilst the adjoining number 53 dates from the 18th century. Numbers 55 and 57 are described as a pair of 17th century houses, which once formed part of an area, called Coleclough Court, but were then later partially demolished for structural reasons.

Finally, number 59 is thought to have once been one single property, but which was subsequently divided into two separate houses. This seems to be confirmed by the fact that there are a number of internal doorways within both buildings that have been bricked up, presumably as part of the separation of the previously large mansion house. Additionally, the whole front of the original house has been re-fronted, possibly during the late 19th or early 20th centuries. According to some reports, this great house was probably occupied by a wealthy city merchant whose private accommodations sat immediately above the subterranean warehouse that held his valuable merchandise. Along with the house itself, this enormous storage area was also been divided in later years and now plays host to two separate modern retail units.

Prior to its later division, this larger property was thought to have been occupied by a family called Morris and was known to have extensive gardens at the rear of the house which stretched southward to Commonhall Street and the former precincts of the White Friars who occupied this section of the city during the middle ages. In later years the land at the rear of the large house was thought to have been the location for a number of small cottages which collectively were known as **Morris' Place**, which may have fallen victim to the slum clearances of the 20th century and today has been replaced by the parking bays and back streets of modern day Chester. Prior to 1755 the original mansion was thought to have been owned by an individual called Edward Morgan, who also owned another large house further east in Watergate Street.

Immediately adjoining Weaver Street, numbers 61 to 63 Watergate Street are thought to be the former city home of Chester's reforming Lord Mayor, **Henry Gee**. Records suggest that Gee did not actually own the house, but simply leased it from a member of the Stanley family who were the Earl's of Derby. Although today, the house is thought to have been encased with relatively modern 18th century building materials, remnants of its much earlier existence are thought to remain within its hidden interior. During the first half of the 18th century a notable citizen called Henry Prescott was reported to be occupying the house and using it as a place to entertain his friends, including Henry Bunbury who lived on the opposite side of the street in the now extinct timber built mansion which was known as Mainwaring House.

Standing directly opposite to the former home of Henry Gee and on the north side of Watergate Street is an elegant Georgian townhouse that adjoins the narrow city lane known as Trinity Street. Currently occupied by showrooms and shops, as well as an Army recruitment centre, this property is thought to have been known as **Mainwaring House** at one time, but is actually thought to have been built by a member of the Bennett family during the first half of the 18th century.

This current house was said to have replaced a much earlier property which was reported to have been constructed by an individual called Roger Barro (Barrow) sometime around 1522, a man of some repute who was known to have been elected as a city Sheriff during the 16th century. His particular property was once described as a "beautiful example of a timber built mansion", but as with many other such buildings failed to survive the demand for modern brick properties which became so fashionable during the late 17th and early 18th centuries. A city alderman called Henry Bennett was reportedly occupying the house in 1673 and it was perhaps this man who actually demolished the old timber mansion and replaced it with the building that stands today. The person from whom the house derives its name was thought to be Thomas Mainwaring, who was recorded to have died in 1724 and who may well have been the person who owned the house after Henry Bennett.

Although the history of this property and its successor is often unclear, in 1715, a Sir Henry Bunbury was known to be occupying all or part of the house standing on the site, although the very same property was said to have been used by Henry Hesketh the younger, a relative of the Bennett family, for his wine merchants business that he was running in Chester during the same period. It has also been suggested that the property was later used to house a Ladies Boarding School during the second half of the 18th century, which was operated by two people called Tench, but this record might actually refer to an entirely different Watergate Street property.

The modern day **Weaver Street** was formerly known as Albany or St Alban's Lane, recalling perhaps a religious connection with the place or saint of that name. However, in its earliest form this city street would have had its origins in the Roman occupation of the fortress, being part of the Via Sagularis, the internal military roadway that sat immediately behind the western defensive wall. Although the title Weaver Street is generally associated with the brewer and inn-keeper Thomas Weaver who occupied the Old Customs House in 1637 and which is listed below, it is just as likely that the name derives from a Dr Weaver, a physician who was known to have lived in the area. On the eastern corner adjoining Watergate and Weaver Streets and forming part of Henry Gee's former home, low sandstone blocks on the site of a former Locksmiths property reflect a possible link to the White Friars monastery which once stood to the south of Watergate Street.

The south facing route of Weaver Street is like many of Chester's historic backstreet's and has been the subject of widespread development and restructuring, most notably over the past 200 years or so. Linking Commonhall Street, White Friars and Cuppin Street many of the older buildings which once occupied both east and west sides of the thoroughfare have since been swept away, leaving only relatively small and generally modern remnants of its extensive history to be seen by the visitor.

At its junction with Commonhall Street, No's 39 and 41 Commonhall Street are simply described as two 18th century properties, each of two storeys. No 14 Weaver Street is yet another property from the same period, but this time over three storeys each with three windows. Finally, at the south end of the street and adjoining the White Friars building, there is reported to be a section of sandstone wall which is thought to be associated with the historic Carmelite or White Friars who once occupied this section of Chester some 500 years earlier.

Back in Watergate Street itself, the **Old Customs House Inn** at No's 69-71 comprises two former houses which were combined to form the Public House, including their under-crofts which are now used as the beer cellars. No 69 dates from 1637 and was thought to have been responsible for the closure of the elevated row which had previously existed in this part of the street, while No 71 is reported to be 18th century in date. Prior to the 17th century rebuilding of the property, it has been suggested that a much earlier house or tavern had previously occupied the very same site, but details of its name and ownership have been lost over time.

The restored gable of the property which faces onto Watergate Street is reported to carry the initials T & A W, which is thought to signify Thomas & Anne Weaver. Originally called the "Star Inn", the tavern was thought to have been renamed in order to reflect the presence of Chester's long redundant Custom House that still stands on the opposite side of the street, beneath and adjoining Holy Trinity church. Between the Customs House and the generally modern Axe Tavern that sits alongside the city's inner ring road, numbers 77 and 79 Watergate Street are reported to be a pair of late 18th century properties which now serve as retail premises and as part of the adjoining public house.

Chester's modern day **Trinity Street** derives its name from the former church which stands immediately west of the narrow thoroughfare and has probably existed in one form or another since Roman times, when it formed part of the Via Sagularis, the internal roadway which ran behind the defensive walls of the fortress. Although generally altered by modern development and encroachment, Trinity Street still maintains its northern junction with Princess Street (formerly Parson's Lane) as it has done for hundreds of years, although its route is now adorned with a mass of unattractive utilitarian car parks, hotels and office buildings.

Beginning in the first half of the 18th century, Trinity Street became synonymous with the city's non-conformist congregations, the most significant of which, was that led by the preacher Matthew Henry, a non-conformist religious leader and preacher in Chester, who was said to have written a book called "Commentary on the Holy Scriptures", a book that he would never finish. Born at Isycoed in Flintshire in 1662, he had initially trained to become a lawyer, but later changed his mind and gave up his studies to become a dissenting minister.

By 1687 he was reported to have been appointed as a Pastor in Chester and in 1700, friends of the preacher built a chapel in Trinity Street, adjoining the modern day Guildhall, where his message could be heard. Henry was thought to have died at Nantwich in

Cheshire but his body was interred at Holy Trinity Church in the city on 22nd June 1714. A hundred years later, in 1804, the Welsh Methodist's under the direction of the Reverend John Parry were said to have erected a new chapel in Trinity Street, although whether this actually replaced the first one or not is unclear.

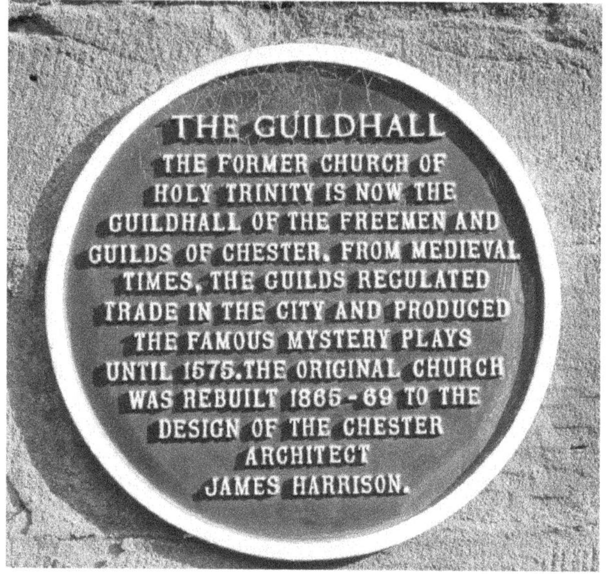

Chester's Guildhall, which was formerly the church of the **Holy and Undivided Trinity** is thought to have its foundations in the 12th century and occupies part of the site of the Roman fortress' west gate, the Porta Principalis Dextra, which once stood in this general area. The church ceased to be used a place of worship in 1961, possibly as a direct result of the city's inner ring road system which was designed to take the increasing road traffic away from the centre of Chester and its numerous historic buildings.

Throughout its life, Holy Trinity was known to be one of the most important parish churches in the city, although the building which stands on the site today was largely rebuilt to the designs of Chester architect James Harrison during the 19th century, but only fully completed sometime after his death in 1866, presumably under the guidance of his two former pupils Kelly and Edwards.

In common with many of Chester's early churches, Holy Trinity was thought to have suffered any number of alterations during its long history, including having its great spire removed in 1811, possibly because of safety concerns for the general public. It was also the site of a tragedy in September 1789, when a local stonemason called Joseph Woodcock was said to have fallen from scaffolding erected at the church and dying at 22-years of age.

The Old Custom House which stands directly below the Guildhall is thought to have been originally constructed around 1633 having been relocated from within the precincts of Chester's medieval castle; and housed the customs officials who were employed to exact the tolls and duties from ships bringing goods into the city from the River and Canal trades. This original building was described as being a brick and stone structure that had several entrances and which had been extensively repaired and altered throughout its lifetime, but by the 1860's was generally said to be unsightly. It was also known to have had a much larger footprint than its modern day counterpart, reportedly extending several feet beyond the present buildings limits and being regarded as an unwarranted obstacle by most pedestrians.

Reportedly rebuilt to the designs of James Harrison, the 2 storey building which stands today was thought to have been completed in 1868, the same year as the adjoining Holy Trinity church. Although large scale maritime trade had disappeared from Chester by the beginning of the 19th century, in 1873 the Custom House in Chester was said to have been staffed by 7 men, including a collector, a chief clerk, an examining officer and 4 outdoor officers.

CHAPTER NINE

LOWER WATERGATE STREET

During the Roman occupation of Chester the current **Lower Watergate Street** would have represented the route between the fortress' western defensive gate and the harbour facilities which at the time lay alongside the River Dee, in the area of today's Watergate arch and Chester Racecourse. Several Roman buildings were known to have stood along the route, including a bath-house, evidence of which was discovered during 18th century construction work on the Georgian properties that still line the northern flank of the main street. Further investigations during the 18th, 19th and 20th centuries have also found further evidence of occupation in this general area, including the identification of stables, animal shelters and terracing features all of which indicated extensive activity in the lands between the fortress and the Roman harbour.

Stanley Palace or Derby House in Lower Watergate Street is thought to date from between 1550-1640, although some sources give a definitive date of 1591 when it was reportedly commissioned by Sir Peter Warburton, city lawyer and MP for Chester, who subsequently endowed the property to his daughter Elizabeth when she married into the Stanley family of Alderley. Elizabeth was reported to have later married again, this time to Sir Richard Grosvenor and when she died in 1628, the property passed into the hands of that particular local family. It has been suggested by some local historians that this great house was built on the former site of the city's medieval Dominican Friary, although in truth it was actually constructed on part of the Black Friars lands that had previously been inhabited by gardens and orchards.

Between 1665 and 1686 the city mansion was said to have been occupied by John Wainwright, the Chancellor of Chester Diocese, following the move from his previous residence, Leche House. However, following Wainwright's death in 1686 the property was reported to have been inhabited by a succession of sundry tenants, some good, some bad, but all of whom were thought to have contributed in part, to a general deterioration in the historic fabric of the building. In fact, by the turn of the 19th century the house was said to be in such a poor condition that at least one local commentator was reported to have referred to it as a slum. This situation was marginally improved in around 1820, when the motley collection of outbuildings that had been allowed to accumulate over the previous decades were finally demolished, creating a similar street frontage to that which exists today. An architectural report dating from around 1856 also noted that within the house itself, a good many of the original fittings and features were still in existence, making the property a true building of note. This is perhaps best illustrated by the fact that ten years later, there was a plan to purchase the house, dismantle it and ship it the United States, where it would then be re-erected. Fortunately for the people of Chester, this plan was prevented by the actions of the city's Archaeological Society, who were reported to have purchased the house from the Grosvenor family, effectively securing its future.

The Palace was thought to have remained in the ownership of the Archaeological Society until 1889 when it was said to have been purchased by the Earl's of Derby, also a branch of the Stanley family, who subsequently leased it to Chester's Corporation in 1931 on a 999 year lease. The building was known to have been substantially restored in 1935, when an extra gable was added and today is reported to be occupied by the English Speaking Union. The house is reported to be underpinned by a series of vaulted cellars, one of which is said to lead to an underground passageway, but no more information regarding the tunnel is available at present.

Standing on the north side of the same street is what little remains of Chester's former Linen Hall which was constructed in 1778 by Chester's cloth merchants and giving the name to modern day **Linenhall Place**. In much earlier times this fairly short thoroughfare was far more extensive, being called "Crofts Lane" and stretching northward as far as today's Bedward Row, which lies opposite to Princess Street and is thought to recall a builder called Charles Bedward who may have first erected properties there.

Up until 1396, Linenhall Place or perhaps more properly called Linenhall Street was said to have been called Berward Street, possibly recalling the route of the Bear Walkers who brought their unfortunate charges into the city, so that they could entertain the local populace around Chester's High Cross. From 1396 until 1480 the thoroughfare was said to have been known as Croft's Lane and then from 1480 until 1665 it gained a new title as Grey Friars Lane, recalling the presence of the city's Franciscan Friars whose religious house was located nearby. Yet another title for this city street was "Monks Lane", once again recalling the association with the monastic house, a local name that was noted in both 1665 and 1691. Finally, the street was also thought to have been known as Lower or Lougher Lane sometime around 1745, before receiving its final and current designation of Linenhall Street or Place in 1778. Sadly, this particular industry, which had once been such an integral part of the city's trading history, diminished over subsequent decades and the great Hall was thought to have been demolished and later replaced by the Racing Stables, which have themselves lately been lost to the city.

At the time of the Roman occupation of Chester, it has been suggested that what later became Linenhall Street (Place) was little more than a external track that lay outside of the imposing defensive walls, possibly linking the western gate of the fortress to the much later "Infirmary Field" where a number of departed legionaries were said to have been interred within a clearly defined Roman cemetery.

Located on the western flank of modern **Nicholas Street**, which is now part of the city's inner ring road system, the terrace of typically elegant Georgian houses, with their deep basements is the longest surviving terrace of such properties remaining in the city today.

The terrace, which has often been known as "Pillbox Terrace", has been credited to the noted local architect Joseph Turner, who also designed Chester's Watergate, Bridgegate and little Bridge of Sighs spanning the northern canal gorge. The name attached itself to the row of properties, because many of its residents were thought to be medical practitioners, the last of which finally moved out in the late 20th century, leaving the properties to be generally occupied by business offices. As with the former Linen Hall site and Stanley Place, the land on which these properties were built was formally in the possession of the city's various religious orders, but which by the late 18th century had come into the possession of a syndicate of linen merchants who were thought to have built the terrace in a fairly piecemeal fashion. In earlier times this street was known as Black Friars Lane, recalling the Dominican order who built their religious house to the west of the thoroughfare, with its more modern designation deriving from the church of St Nicholas, the patron saint of sailors, whose church formerly stood within the Black Friars religious precincts.

Modern day Nicholas Street stretches from Watergate Street in the north to the former site of St Martin's Ash which is now marked by a number of relatively modern buildings and a large traffic roundabout. Two thousand years ago, this same line, along with the more northerly St Martin's Way, was thought to mark the outer limits of the Roman fortress' fosse or defensive ditch which helped to protect its military inhabitants from attack by the native Britons. With the city's abandonment by the legions of Rome and right up until the middle ages this defensive ditch was gradually filled in, but remained as an external route, linking the city's Benedictine Convent, its Castle and the houses of the Dominican and Franciscan Friars with one another, as well as Chester's then still vibrant and bustling early medieval port.

Back in Lower Watergate Street, in 1795 the modern day **Nicholas St Mews** was reported to have been more commonly known as Brooke Street, recalling the name of the Brooke family of Norton Priory who were known to have lived on the site of today's Watergate House. This whole area of Chester is thought to have been constantly employed and built on by successive generations of people who have inhabited the city of Chester, simply because of its position in relation to the city's early port. However, following the construction of "Pillbox Terrace" in Nicholas Street which was started in 1781, rear access to these new properties from their associated stables and coach houses necessitated the laying out of a new byway, which was initially called Brooke Street.

On the south east corner of the mews, adjoining Grey Friars Lane, **Soughton House** is reported to be a late 18th century property, originating from the widespread redevelopment of the area during that same period. At the opposite end of the mews, the site now occupied by Watergate House, was once home to a property called the "Black Hall" which was said to have been owned by a succession of notable and influential families, including the Brookes and the Grosvenor's. The final member of that particular family to own the house was reported to have been a John Grosvenor, who died in 1702 and who was said to have left the house as a legacy for local charities. It is assumed that the "Hall" then came into the possession of the Brookes, before finally being demolished by Thomas Harrison and replaced by the modern day Watergate House. The current name for the thoroughfare, Nicholas Street Mews, is thought to date from around 1800. The property that presently occupies the opposite junction of this narrow thoroughfare, adjoining the western side of the historic Stanley Palace, is simply described as a late 18th century townhouse, which probably dates from the time that much of this whole area was rebuilt.

Watergate House was designed by Thomas Harrison for his friend Henry Potts, the Clerk of the Peace for Cheshire in 1820 and at the time of its completion was thought to have been surrounded by extensive gardens. The house later passed into the hands of the military, being used by Western Command at the beginning of the 20th century, before being used by Cheshire County Council and finally to house business offices. Elements of the property's extensive gardens are now thought to be occupied by the relatively modern Norroy House which itself is reported to stand above remnants of much earlier Roman architecture.

Directly opposite Nicholas Street Mews is modern day Stanley Street marking the eastern limit of the **Watergate Flags**, a terrace of elegant Georgian Houses running westward towards the Watergate Arch. Constructed on the inclined Lower Watergate Street, much of the terrace is known to sit on the site of an early Roman Bathhouse complex, a great deal of which was destroyed during the construction of these same properties around 1779. The house which stands at the western end of the row however, still contains a Roman fuelling arch which is thought to be associated with the complex' hypocaust heating system and is one of the many early treasures of Chester now hidden by later redevelopment.

At the western junction of Lower Watergate Street stands Chester's **Watergate Arch**, which replaced a much earlier medieval gateway that was latterly in the charge of the Stanley family, who were the sergeants of the entrance, but which by 1778 was in a fairly ruinous condition and considered a danger to the public. Purchased by Chester's Corporation in the same year, this old gateway was taken down and replaced by the current archway, which was designed by local architect Joseph Turner in 1788. Its name relates to the historic proximity of the Chester's medieval port on the River Dee and the later 18th century wharves at Crane Bank, both of which delivered goods to the city through this ancient portal.

The **Watergate Inn** which is located just outside of the city's Watergate was formerly called the "Turf Tavern" and in earlier times within the same general area, known then as

Watergate Square, there were reported to have been a number of elegant late 18th century properties, including the impressive three storey Roodee House, all of which have subsequently been demolished to make way for new roadways and car parking facilities. The site of the Watergate Inn was also said to mark the starting point of three of Chester's long gone streets, Paradise Row, Crane Street and New Crane Street all of which have been subsequently demolished or altered beyond all recognition during the 20th century modernisation of Chester. All three of these terraced streets were reported to have been constructed sometime after 1745 and during their lifetimes played host to some of the very wealthiest and very poorest of Chester's inhabitants.

Chester's **Roodee** racecourse is reportedly the oldest horseracing circuit in the country and is also unusual in that its races are run in an anti clockwise direction, as opposed to the usual clockwise. However, the expanse of carefully managed land on which the modern racecourse stands has probably only been in existence since the end of the 16th century when a Thomas Lyniall was granted the lease of the land, in exchange for protecting it from the regular flooding caused by the nearby River Dee.

During the Roman period the area now generally marked by the large central section of the Roodee, as opposed to the surrounding racing track, was said to be little more than a flood meadow that regularly disappeared below the waters of the River Dee at each high tide. Surrounded on all sides by the tidal waters of the river, the area of land that now stands between the home straight of the racecourse and the western wall of the city is thought to mark the line of the deep river channel that served the vast legionary harbour complex, evidence of which still lies immediately below the much later western medieval defensive wall. Rather strangely, during the 19th century a small number of Roman interments were discovered in the area immediately below the walls, on the by then extended Roodee that seemed to indicate that a Roman cemetery had been located there, although quite why remains a mystery. The only identifiable interment was that of a man called Callimorphus and his young son Serapion, which was discovered some 50-odd feet from the brand new Grosvenor Road by workmen digging in the area. The Roman memorial stone that covered the grave confirmed the identification of the two bodies, although little physical evidence of the deceased father and son themselves was thought to have survived over time. Reports from the time suggested that only two artefacts had been found in the grave, a coin from the reign of the Emperor Domitian, which tentatively dated the interment between 81 and 96 AD; and an impressive gold ring that subsequently and rather quickly left Chester along with its finder, never to be heard of again.

Although this particular interment was thought to have lain slightly south of the Roman's main harbour complex, any hopes of discovering more long forgotten burial sites in this area seem slight, given that presence of the generally modern embankments laid down to carry the main Grosvenor Road and the associated Nun's Road thoroughfare, both of which sit many feet above the original Roman ground level. The second interment discovered during the 19th century, in 1881, was found to the north of the first, below the walls and adjacent to the city's Black Friars thoroughfare. Surprisingly perhaps, this would have placed the burial in the midst of the harbour complex itself, but as nothing more than bone fragments were found, its location and identification of the two bodies remains a mystery.

A thousand years after the Roman's had first arrived in Britain and some six hundred years after they had abandoned the province, Chester's Roodee was thought to have remained fundamentally the same, a tidal meadow, surrounded by the waters of the Dee. However, according to a local legend, in 946 AD an event occurred that caused this generally insignificant piece of marshland to gain some notoriety and leading it to be given the name that it still carries to this day.

According to the legend, the wife of the Governor of Hawarden Castle, a Lady Trawst was said to have visited a Christian temple to pray for rain, her prayers being directed at a statue or image of the Virgin Mary, which was commonly referred to as a Rood. Unfortunately for the lady though, the statue was reported to have fallen down and struck her down, killing her instantly. The local villagers were said to be so outraged by the incident that they decided to try the statue for the murder of Lady Trawst, which they ultimately found guilty of the crime. Sentenced to death, the Rood was cast into the River Dee to drown, but eventually found its way to the banks of the flood meadow just outside of Chester, where it was found by the local inhabitants. These Christian citizens then arranged for the image to be properly buried on the flood meadow and marked its grave with a sandstone pedestal and cross, elements of which are said to exist through to the present day.

Although a colourful tale, the likelihood of these events ever having taken place in the first place is slight to say the least. However, it is generally accepted by most historians that the name Roodee actually derives from a combination of the Saxon word "Rood", which means "Cross" and the Norse word "Eye", meaning "Isle" or "Island", giving the name Roodee, a literal meaning of "the island of the cross". The fact that Chester, along with many other towns and cities, regularly placed crosses throughout their precincts, which were variously dedicated to popular saints, might simply suggest that the cross on the tidal meadow was therefore nothing out of the ordinary, just another place to erect a sign of the city's Christian beliefs.

It also seems to be accepted that the height and size of the Roodee was fundamentally altered to something near its present area during the period of 1070 through to 1420, the centuries that were marked by the rule of the Normans and the Plantagenets. Much of this change may be attributed to the harnessing of the River Dee by the Norman Earls of Chester who are reportedly responsible for constructing the weir dam, which helped to drive their corn mills, but which was said to have brought about the almost inevitable decline of the city's thriving river port. By the beginning of the 16th century, most of Chester's trade was being conducted through the smaller ports situation further northward along the banks of the River Dee and the enlarged Roodee itself was thought to have been used for grazing animals or for leisure activities. Indeed, in 1539, the reforming city Mayor Henry Gee was reported to have enforced a local ordinance requiring parents to provide their male children with a bow and arrows during public holidays, so that they could practice their martial skills on the Roodee, for the defence of the city and their country.

Some 50-odd years later, in 1587, Thomas Lyniall was granted a lease on parts of the Roodee, provided that he agreed to erect and maintain a permanent embankment there that would prevent regular flooding of the meadow by the River Dee. This barrier, which is commonly known as "The Kop" and on which the modern area of Crane Bank sits was begun shortly afterwards, but has subsequently been rebuilt and heightened many times since Lyniall and his workers first constructed it. Following its enclosure by the protective embankment however, the site of the Roodee and the adjacent areas of land could be used to house more permanent buildings and it wasn't long before these reclaimed lands were being inhabited by numerous timber and boat building yards, along with the wharves and jetties that served the barges and inland boats which brought goods into the city from the its more northerly harbours.

The area of the Roodee itself appears to have remained relatively undeveloped during the period and was still commonly being used as a site for animal grazing and leisure pursuits. By 1609 though, this open grassland was also occasionally being used for training and exercising horses, which were often owned by the wealthier families of the district; and it was in this particular year that the first horse races were thought to have been organised. Originally competitions between individual owners, where personal wagers were involved, within three years these contests were reported to have evolved into formal race meetings that would mark the history of the Roodee from 1612 right through to the present day. Although there is some dispute as to exactly when the first regulated and articled race was run on the Roodee, with some sources stating 1609 and others 1612, there is no question that the first official horserace was run for a prize of silver bells, donated by a leading Chester citizen, Robert Ambrye, a former Mayor of the city. It is also known that the Chester Races became very well known within a relatively short space of time, so much so that the monarch James I (1603 - 1625) was reported to have attended the event whilst visiting the city and was said to have spent much of his time enjoying the attendant fairs, plays, cock-fights and banquets.

Much of the area now marked by the modern day Roodee, running west to **Crane Bank** and a meeting with the River Dee was generally associated with small scale shipbuilding, both light and heavy manufacturing industries, as well as being the location of the city's **Workhouse** or **House of Industry**. Following the "canalisation" of the River Dee in the mid 18th century and the reclamation of the lands now known as Sealand, for a short time the banks of the River Dee around Crane Street were lined with numerous quays and jetties which allowed merchandise to be landed and brought into the city. Slightly west of the Roodee racecourse and just beyond the railway viaduct which remains today, the site until recently occupied by the city's Gas Works was previously occupied both by a Paper Factory and an Iron Foundry which were thought to have existed between the 1790's and 1840's. Earlier still, the same general area was reported to have been the home of an extensive timber yard and in 1757, the city's Workhouse was established in the same area and would remain there until around 1880 when it was finally relocated to the new Union Workhouse in the suburb of Boughton on the eastern side of Chester.

Although much of the historic fabric in this area of the city has been demolished and swept away in recent years, both for traffic systems and interminable high price housing projects, further along Sealand Road, close to the historic "Cop" river barrier, at least one remnant of Chester's once proud sea trading tradition continues to survive, albeit in a fairly unrecognisable form. The present day "Cop Field House" is thought to have formerly been the home of the clerk who administered the city's vitally important Cheese Warehouses which were once located along this section of the by then "canalised" River Dee. Up until 1875 a series of docks and jetties were thought to have stood along the river bank, being used to load the commercially vital cheeses that were synonymous with the city. Tragically, the site is also thought to mark the site of a young boy's death, the son of a man called Tyler who was reported to have owned the "Sluice House" which was situated further along the river.

CHAPTER TEN

NUNS ROAD AND CASTLE ESPLANADE

Back inside the circuit of defensive walls, today's **Nuns Road** recalls the medieval Benedictine convent of St Mary's which once occupied a site in this part of the city's suburbs, being granted lands in the 12th century by Earl Ranulph Blundeville, but then later dissolved by Henry VIII in the middle of the 16th century. In terms of Chester's extensive history the modern day Nuns Road is a relatively modern thoroughfare, created by the construction of the Grosvenor Bridge and the massive embankments which were built to support the new early 19th century roadway which led in and out of the city. Much of the wider area, including the Castle Esplanade, Thomas Harrison's Chester castle and the same architects St Martins Lodge all date from around the same time and brought about dramatic changes to the historic fabric of the city in this section of Chester.

Although the name **Grey Friars** is thought to have been an earlier title for Chester's previously mentioned Linenhall Place, today it is carried by a lane which links Nuns Road and the more easterly Nicholas Street. It is worth pointing out however, that this designation is confusing, given that the Grey Friars or Franciscans actually occupied the lands north of Watergate Street and so have little connection with this southern area of land. The lane itself has had a number of titles, including Smiths Walk in 1795 and prior to that Black Friars Alley which more properly recalls one of the city's early monastic houses, the Black Friars or Dominicans who occupied this particular section of the city. The later name of Smith is thought to be connected with one Thomas Smith who lived in the city around 1543 and who was reported to have lived in the area of this narrow thoroughfare, presumably after the monastery had been dissolved by Henry VIII.

The modern looking house which occupies the western end of Grey Friars is thought to be largely 18th century in construction, but has been heavily modernised and restored in more recent years. The building itself is said to occupy the site of the medieval Chapel of Saint Nicholas, the patron saint of Sailors which was built by the city's Black Friars and is thought to be the source for the modern day Nicholas Street, which was formerly known as St Nicholas Street, but which has undoubtedly been contracted during its lifetime.

At one time, both ends of the lane were reported to have been graced by stone archways which may well have been gated and helping to isolate the area from the rest of the city. Over time however, these archways have disappeared, with some suggestions that these historic features were later incorporated into the garden walls of the previously mentioned house. It is also reported that these same garden walls contain a boundary marker for the now extinct St Martin's Parish, helping to identify the limits of this former city church. Nearby, the property known as Soughton House, which stands at the junction of Grey Friars and Nicholas Street Mews, is thought to be another 18th century property that sits atop the site of the former Grey Friars precincts, which were finally expunged by the Crown in the 16th century. Directly opposite the eastern terminus of Grey Friars, where it joins Nicholas Street, at the spot now marked by the road entrance to White Friars and Cuppin Street, an elegant townhouse dating from 1844 formerly stood, reportedly housing the **Hastings School** which ultimately fell victim to the modernisation of the area and the ravages of Chester's inner ring road system.

Further south along modern day Nuns Road is the city's **Black Friars**, which correctly recalls the medieval religious house of the Dominican Order which used to occupy this part of Chester's western flank. As with the earlier Grey Friars, this thoroughfare too is thought to have held a number of titles throughout its long history, including Aderne Lane; Hawarden Lane; Walls Lane and Nuns Lane, with its present name being formally and correctly attributed to it in 1858.

The adjoining Nicholas Street has formerly been known as St Nicholas Lane and around 1610 was thought to have been called Black Friars Lane, recalling the Dominicans house in this area of Chester. This early lane was thought to have marked the eastern boundary of their religious precincts, which then ran westward to the walls of the city and the banks of the River Dee. The designation of today's Black Friars Lane as Aderne Lane dates to the reign of King Edward III and is thought to indicate a route or passageway that was associated with the city's medieval quays that were known to have existed in the area; below the line of the city walls. The lane was commonly called "Walls Lane" from 1795 through to 1860, although a large number of locals continued to refer to it as "Nuns Lane", in memory of the medieval Benedictine Convent which once stood within the local area.

Thomas Harrison's **St Martins Lodge**, which presently still stands in the city, although its future fate is uncertain, is thought to mark the site of an earlier building called the "Nuns Hall". This particular building was thought to have been raised by Sir William Brereton, the Parliamentarian commander of Chester during the English Civil War, whose property was badly damaged by those Royalist soldiers stationed in Chester during the military conflict. The Royalist supporter Randle Holme, noted herald and historian in the city, was thought to have occupied the old "Nuns Hall" for a period, possibly during the time that Brereton was absent from Chester because of his political allegiances.

Built around 1829, Harrison's Lodge building later became the **Rectory** for St Bridget's Church which had been relocated from the south end of Bridge Street, where it was said to have stood for well over 800 years in order that Grosvenor Street could be widened. By around 1892 however, the new St Bridget's was once again seen as being unnecessary and was demolished for a second and final time.

Chester's long extinct **Militia Building** formerly occupied the site that sits directly opposite to the main entrance of Thomas Harrison's Castle complex and which until recently was occupied by the unsightly and utilitarian Police Headquarters building, but now replaced by a brand new modern hotel building. Designed by the local architect T M Penson in 1858 the Barracks were constructed to house the soldiers and their families who were garrisoned at the nearby castle and stood on the same ground that some 700 years earlier had been inhabited by the Benedictine Convent of St Mary's. Although the Militia building was thought to be a reproduction of a 13th century style of architecture, it was known to have been altered and improved throughout its lifetime, providing modern comforts for the military families who were stationed within its precincts, but still failed to survive through to the modern day.

Today's **Castle Drive**, which lies below the modern city walls, skirting Chester's largely 18th century castle complex, is a relatively modern invention, built as a direct result of the creation of Thomas Harrison's Grosvenor Bridge and the massive earthen embankments laid down to carry its new associated roadway into the city. Lying close to a much earlier thoroughfare called Skinners Lane, during the medieval period this area of the city was thought to have been occupied by elements of Chester's leather manufacturing industries, including the Skinners Sheds and Tanning Pits which were an integral part of turning animal hides into the boots, gloves and saddles, that were so prized by the citizens of Chester. Along the banks of the nearby river, which provided the necessary water for these commercially vital businesses, lay the numerous jetties and quays which brought the precious skins into the city by boat, many of which were said to have come from Ireland.

With the division of Chester's historic Roodee by the new Grosvenor Bridge embankment, the new Castle Drive was constructed to link the new bridge with its much earlier partner, the still standing Old Dee Bridge. Additionally, this new route also offered the citizen and visitor alike the opportunity to promenade along the banks of the River Dee, as well as viewing the new Castle Gaol designed by Harrison, later the site of today's County Hall and passing the then still standing Dee Mills which lay at the junction of this new roadway and Lower Bridge Street. Today, the smaller section of Chester's ancient racecourse, commonly called the **Little Roodee** which was separated by the laying down of the great earth banks is generally used as municipal car parking and once a year plays host to the visiting Fun Fairs, an annual event that was reported to have first started in 1890.

Back at Chester's Watergate Arch**, City Walls Road** is probably another much more modern thoroughfare which was laid out to access the then relatively new buildings and streets which were built during the late 18th century, including Stanley Place, the Queens School, Royal Infirmary, etc. Prior to the 16th century, this area of Chester housed the enclosed religious community of the Grey Friars and following the dissolution of the monastery by Henry VIII, these lands then fell into the hands of individual families who rented them out for other uses. The later Infirmary site for instance, was said to have been called Lady Barrow's Hey at one time, suggesting an agricultural or arable use, which is supported by the presence of a Grange and Tithe Barn in and around the same area of land.

The elegantly Georgian **Stanley Place** was developed during the late 18th century on land that had previously been in the ownership of Chester's medieval religious houses, including the Franciscan order who were bequeathed lands during the 12th and 13th centuries. Following the dissolution of the Monasteries by Henry VIII in the 16th century much of their former lands and properties were either sold or simply left unattended, which was the likely case for the "Yacht Field" on which the later Stanley Place was built.

Following its construction, Stanley Place along with King Street and Abbey Square was regarded as one of the most fashionable and aristocratic areas of the city, being populated by some of the wealthiest and most influential families in Chester. Close by, the Racing Stables which are associated with the city's Roodee Racecourse were thought to have been rebuilt in the 1920's, during which numerous relics of the long since disappeared medieval Grey Friar's monastery were uncovered. One of the most notable buildings in the area is No. 13, which is otherwise known as the "Sedan House" that is fronted by a porch, under which Sedan chairs would have delivered their passengers directly to their door, the porch ensuring that they were safe from the vagaries of the English weather.

Further north, the present day **Queens School** building dates from around 1870 and was designed by architect E A Ould, a pupil of John Douglas, who was undoubtedly influenced by his former teacher's style. The school was built on the site of the city's former gaol, which had only been built some seventy years earlier, around 1807, but which due to changes in the penal system was thought to have become unnecessary. The land upon which both the former prison and later school stands, prior to 1540 was part of the Grey Friars religious precincts, but following the Dissolution of the Monasteries all such properties were sold off to private interests. Over a thousand years before the Grey Friars even came to Chester, parts of these same lands had been used by early Roman occupiers to bury their fallen comrades in what became a fairly extensive legionary cemetery. Following the expulsion of the Monks and the sale of their lands, this same area of land was thought to have been called Lady Barrow's Hey during the late 16th, early 17th century and was used for grazing or for feed production. By 1860, the general area, including the plot on which the new school was to be founded was commonly called "Gaol Field" in memory of its former murderous past.

The land for the then new **County Gaol** was acquired by Chester Corporation in around 1807 specifically for the purpose of building the new prison. As well as being a gaol, the new building also included a "House of Correction", where incarcerated inmates would be reformed through hard labour and isolation, giving them time to consider their behaviour and their criminal activities, in the hope that such punishments might help the offenders to alter their character and redeem themselves.

The long extinct gaol was described as a brick built building with stone entrances to both the east and west; and at its centre, there was said to be a Chapel which was thought to have catered for the prison's population and more importantly for those inmates that had been condemned to die on the scaffold. As the County town of Cheshire, with the appropriate Courts and Assizes within its limits, Chester was often the final destinations for those that had transgressed against society's laws and were then given its ultimate sentence. It has been suggested that condemned prisoners were hung from a scaffold mounted above the prison's main entrance, with some reporters suggesting this was on the western side of the building, but more likely above the eastern entrance.

A notable local executioner of the 1800's was one Samuel Burrows, who worked within the city as a butcher and as an officially recognised local hangman was regarded as a Deputy Sheriff to the city authorities. Born in Acton near Nantwich, on the 28th June 1772, Samuel was reported to have successively worked as a butcher, surgeons assistant, a member of the naval press gang and finally as a rat-catcher. From around 1800 onwards he held the post of official executioner for a period of some 24 years and during that time was thought to have despatched around 53 people, before his own death on 20th October 1835.

Chester Royal Infirmary which once stood on the eastern flank of this thoroughfare has now largely disappeared, being replaced by modern townhouses and flats and only the façade of the early hospital building has survived the developer's machines. The infirmary was initially founded as a charitable institution following a bequest by Dr William Stratford in 1753 and within 5 years work had begun on the original building which was officially opened in 1761. It was awarded the prefix "Royal" in 1914 following the opening of the Albert Wood wing by the monarch George V in that year. It was reported to be the first hospital in all of England to have separate fever wards, thereby reducing the spread of communicable diseases. Within the same grounds, there once stood the ancient church of St Chad's, formerly one of Chester's many Parish churches, which is now only recalled by a suburban thoroughfare outside of the city. Also within the same general area stood St Werburgh's Grange which was thought to have included a tithe barn, from which the modern day King Street derived its former title of Barn Lane. During the Roman occupation of Chester, this area of the city lay outside of the fortress' defences, but was known to have been used as the main cemetery for those legionaries that sadly ended their lives at the isolated military base.

Bedward Row formerly ran from Crofts Lane, now St Martin's Way westward towards the city walls and at one time was known as Dog Lane. During the medieval period this fairly short thoroughfare was reported to have been connected with St Chad's Lane which was associated with a church of that name that stood in the area. At a point, now marked by the remaining eastern terminus of Bedward Row, which sits on the western side of Chester's inner ring road, the old thoroughfare was reported to have turned south until it merged with Linenhall Place. The line of Bedward Row is also thought to mark the route of a large sewer constructed around 1703 which ran from the city over to and through the city walls, across the Roodee racecourse and terminating along the river bank, close to the still existing Railway viaduct.

CHAPTER ELEVEN

CHESTER CASTLE & COURT BUILDINGS

The Chester Castle complex which stands to the south west of the modern city centre is largely the creation of the renowned local architect Thomas Harrison, with much of its fabric thought to date from between 1788 and 1822. However, there are also a small number of buildings within these relatively modern precincts that can trace their foundations all the way back to the late 12th and early 13th centuries, some few decades after the forces of Duke William had first received the surrender of the Anglo Saxon fortress of Chester.

Although some historians believe that the Anglo Saxon leader Aethelflaeda was responsible for building a "castle" on this site sometime during the late 9th or early 10th century, as part of her recorded refortification of the city, to date little evidence of such a structure has been discovered. The fact that "castles", as we know them, are almost an entirely Norman invention and that Chester was thought to have been fully enclosed with a circuit of protective walls prior to the Norman conquests would both seem to suggest that such a defensive feature never did exist, but is purely the result of misreporting by later writers.

In January 1070, Duke William was reported to have brought a large military contingent across the Pennines to capture the city of Chester and its associated Shire, *"the last remaining part of a free England"*. Some contemporary reports suggest that the city surrendered without a fight, whilst others state that such was the bitterness of the fighting, that William *"wasted"* large parts of the city as an act of retribution against its citizens. It seems highly unlikely however, that had the city's defenders simply thrown down their arms in surrender, then large parts of Chester would have been subsequently destroyed as a punishment, which would suggest that only one of these scenarios can be a true reflection of these long past events.

The first Norman castle which stood at Chester has long since gone, being replaced over time by a succession of Norman Earls and English Kings, until finally much of its historic fabric was finally swept away at the end of the 18th Century by a generation of architects, public figures and private landowners with more than one eye on their own personal legacies and reputations, rather than the preservation of Chester's archaeological past. To emphasize the point, it is perhaps worth remembering that around the same period that a large section of Chester's medieval castle was being razed from the ground; all 4 medieval gates of the city were also being removed and replaced by their modern counterparts. For the great northern architect Thomas Harrison, his impressive Neo Classical - Greek Revivalist castle complex at Chester remains as a highly visible legacy of his life and his imagination, as well as marking a period of closure on Chester's bloody medieval history.

Unlike today, where the city's past tends to be regarded as a vital and equally important facet of Chester's future prosperity, during Harrison's lifetime such considerations were of minor importance to local architects, builders and developers. Consequently, little was done to either record or conserve the numerous historic buildings which were simply "in the way" of the late 18th and early 19th century developments undertaken during the reigns of George, William and Victoria. Instead, the very fabric of Chester's past was very often just "torn out of the ground" and used as foundation materials for their later replacements or transported away to be ignominiously "dumped" in the surrounding countryside. As a result of this large-scale and indiscriminate redevelopment of the castle site, opportunities for modern day archaeologists to fully investigate the area have proved to be extremely limited, hindered as they are by the additional numbers of rudimentary and piecemeal military constructions which have been successively built on the site since 1822.

It has been suggested that Chester's early Norman castle was substantially rebuilt by the 7th Earl of Chester, Ranulph Blundeville, in the late 12th Century. Both the stone built Flag Tower and the first Inner Bailey Gateway, or Agricola's Tower, are thought to date from the period (1190 to 1220) and along with the Inner Ward's outer stone walls might also be credited to Ranulph III. Prior to his death in 1232 and following his return to England from the Crusades in 1220, it seems likely that both Chester and the later Beeston castles may have been substantially remodeled and rebuilt to include features that he had seen on a number of the crusader castles in the Holy Land, which at that time represented the "cutting edge" of early medieval Castle design.

Although not a definitive date by any means, the end of the 14th and beginning of the 15th centuries could be regarded as the period which fundamentally marked the beginning of the end for the medieval castle in Britain. These were the years that saw the arrival and widespread use of gunpowder and its associated weaponry, the new armaments which could easily circumvent or simply destroy the previously impassable curtain walls and their massive flanking towers. It marked the point in time where such static defences were generally accepted to be virtually obsolete, not only because the castle's impressive walls could be bypassed by larger and larger cannonballs, but the sheer explosive power of the gunpowder meant that no length of wall or heavy castle gate could be relied upon to stand against an attacking enemy who happened to have cannons at their disposal. The result of these technological advances meant that few if any new castles were built and those that were already in existence were altered and refortified to take account of this new threat. In many castle's, parts of their battlements or individual flanking towers were altered and adapted to house these new weapons, so offering the castle's resident garrison the opportunity to "fight fire with fire".

As a period of extended peace settled on the country during the late 15th and early 16th centuries, Chester's Castle simply reverted back to its earlier role as an administrative and judicial centre, becoming the site for legal settlements and record keeping. On the 18th July 1494 the monarch Henry VII, along with his mother and his Queen came to visit Chester Castle, but were said to have only stayed a short time and then travelled on to Hawarden, along with a number of Cheshire's leading nobility. With Wales generally peaceful and Chester's historic port fundamentally strangled by widespread silting, the city was beginning to experience the first stages of its almost inevitable slide into national and regional obscurity.

Following the death of the last Tudor monarch, Elizabeth I, the English crown then passed to the Stuart family, beginning with James I of England and VI of Scotland. With Chester castle's basic role having changed from military to primarily civilian over the preceding two centuries one of three military officers visiting the city in 1634, described the castle thus;

"In this city stands a stately and strong, habitable castle wherein the Judges of the Circuit lie. Before you pass over the fair arched into the inner court, on the left hand of the base court stands the great and spacious hall, where they sit on one bench together a whole week. The High Sheriffs place is on one side and the Constable of the Castle on the other.

Adjoining the Great Hall is the Exchequer, where their Court Palatine are kept, wherein sometime sits that old Earl (of Derby), the Chief Chamberlain usually, often too the Vice Chamberlain and constantly and daily the Attorney's, Clerk's, with other Officers as pursuant, Seal Keepers, etc. In this Court are placed the Arms of the 8 Baron's, whereof only one is now extant, the Baron of Kinderton."

Within a few years of this visit, the whole of Chester, along with its medieval castle had been refortified and turned into an armed camp, as the English Civil War erupted between the royalist forces of King Charles I and the opposing army of the English Parliament. The city's ancient Anglo Saxon defences along with the castle's precincts were now equally employed to defend the city and it's much declined historic port from the threat of a puritan army which now dominated much of the surrounding countryside. Throughout much of the hostilities however, the castle simply defended the shipping port which lay on the river below and kept watch on the settlement of Handbridge which stood on the opposite banks of the Dee.

Following the city's surrender to the Parliamentarians in February 1646, Chester's castle was once again pressed back into service, being employed as a prison, court and a tax office. The noted writer and historian Daniel King reported in 1651;

"The castle is a place having privilege of itself and has a Constable. At first coming is the gatehouse, which is a prison for the whole County, having divers' rooms and lodgings. Hard within the gate is a house, which is sometimes the Exchequer, but is now the Customs House. Not far from the Base Court is a deep well and nearby stables, as well as other Houses of Office. On the left-hand side is a Chapel and close by a large and attractive Shire Hall which is newly repaired and where all the matters of Law relating to the County Palatine are heard and judicially settled. At the end of the Shire Hall is the brave new Exchequer building for the said County Palatine and all these are in the Base Court".

"Then there is a drawbridge into the Inner Ward, wherein the divers for the goodly Lodgings for the Justices are when they come to Chester and herein is also where the Constable dwells. The thieves and felons are arraigned in the previously mentioned Shire Hall and having been condemned are delivered by the Constable or his deputy to the Sheriffs of the city, to a certain place outside the castle gate, called the "Glovers Stone", from where the said cities Sheriffs convey them to a place of execution called Boughton".

In the same year that King was describing the precincts and practices of the medieval site, the castle itself was said to be housing two notable Royalist characters from the period. On the 1st Oct 1651, Sir Timothy Featherstonhaugh was reported to have been tried by a Parliamentary military court sitting at Chester Castle, having been charged and later found guilty of "corresponding with Charles Stuart or his party", a crime so seriously regarded that the unfortunate Royalist was subsequently sentenced to death. Three weeks later, on the 22nd Oct 1651 Sir Timothy was reported to have been beheaded outside the cathedrals Abbey Gateway in the marketplace, although it has also been suggested that he was actually shot by a Parliamentary firing squad in the city's marketplace. However, given his noble birth and status, it seems more likely that the ill-fated knight would have met his end at the hand of the state's executioner. Either way, the lethal sentence handed down by the new Parliamentary regime, clearly demonstrated the lengths that the Puritan forces of Cromwell were prepared to go to in order to maintain control and to prove their utter resolve.

A fellow Royalist prisoner with Featherstonhaugh at Chester Castle was Sir James Stanley, the 7th Earl of Derby, who was reported to have raised a military force in the region in support of the king, only to be ambushed and arrested by a troop of Parliamentary cavalry some time later. Held at Chester castle, the Earl was reported to have escaped custody at one point, his supporters in the city having thrown a rope over the castle's defensive wall, but his liberty was said to have been relatively short-lived. Possibly re-arrested a short time later at his family home in the city, he was returned to his confinement at the castle, but only as a temporary measure. Given the potential for future escapes and in order to prevent Stanley becoming a figurehead for the Royalist cause, the Parliamentarian authorities were thought to have rescheduled both the time and place of the Earl's execution.

On the evening of 13th Oct 1651, Stanley and Featherstonhaugh were said to have dined together at Chester Castle for one final time and were thought to have spent the time, perhaps reflecting on their situation, the righteousness of their cause and their impending passage to eternal rest. The next day, the 14th October, the Earl of Derby was reported to have been transported to his home town of Bolton, where he was said to have been beheaded by the royal executioner on the morning of 15th Oct 1651. As with his compatriot Featherstonhaugh, the actual place of Stanley's death is a matter of some dispute, with some sources suggesting that he was actually executed at Wigan, but the Church gate in Bolton remains as the most likely location.

A third, perhaps less eminent royalist figure was tried and sentenced along with the Earl of Derby and Sir Timothy Featherstonhaugh. A Captain or Colonel John Benbow, like his two compatriots was said to be an ardent royalist and to have been charged and found guilty of corresponding with agents of the king and sentenced to die. Because of his lower social rank however, Benbow was reported to have been sentenced to die by firing squad, a sentence which was carried out at Shrewsbury on the 15th October 1651, in the garden below the Castle Mount.

Around the same period, John Shaw who was reported to be a Master Mason in Chester was asked by the Constable of the castle, Thomas Lount, to undertake repairs on parts of the fortress that formerly housed prisoners, specifically the gatehouse of the outer bailey, as well as the Exchequer building. Shaw reported that the castle buildings were in a fairly ruinous condition and that parts of the gatehouse had already fallen down, much to the danger of the soldiers on guard and passers-by. He also reported that the remaining part of the gatehouse, that part still standing, was so seriously decayed that if it was not taken down, then it would surely fall down of its own accord. Within the wider castle complex, the Protonotary's lodgings, the Constables lodgings and the Grand Jury room, the Judges lodging and the ancient Flag Tower were all reported to be in poor condition and all required urgent remedial work which would cost several hundreds of pounds to complete.

In 1681 King James II was reported to have stayed at Chester and taken services at the Chapel of Saint Mary de Castro, suggesting that the Castle was still in relatively good order or had been substantially repaired prior to the King's visit. It has also been suggested that this was the final time that the chapel of St Mary de Castro was employed for religious purposes.

Sometime after this final royal visit, the castle seems to fallen into disfavour once again and from the end of the 17th Century through to the 19th Century it was simply employed as a military station, with its precincts and buildings fundamentally altered for that purpose. The area immediately in front of the ancient Flag Tower was reported to have been used as an armoury and the historic chapel of St Mary de Castro was known to have been used as a gunpowder store or magazine, which might well account in part for its whitewashed walls, as well as the metal lined door, which remain in place today.

In perhaps one of its final phases, before its near total demolition in 1782, the precincts of Chester's historic castle were reported to have been used to hold royal prisoners, who would often be tried and sentenced by the courts that held their assizes at the city's Great Shire Hall. The two Jacobite Rebellions of the period, in 1715 and 1745, both saw high profile prisoners and leaders of the rebellions, held and brought to trial at Chester.

The noted writer Hemingway, in his "History of Chester" recorded for 1715;

"This winter, Lord Charles Murray, with several other gentlemen and a great number of private men, who have all been taken on November 13th in the rebellion at Preston, were brought to Chester castle as prisoners. The winter weather was very severe and the snow lay a yard deep in the roads. Many of the above mentioned prisoners died in the castle due to the severity of the season, with many being carried off by a highly malignant fever; whilst those that did survive were transported to the plantations in America. As the castle was so full of these prisoners, the Lent Assizes were held in Northwich".

A local artist, Moses Griffiths, produced a painting of Chester's medieval castle in 1727 which showed the fortress as still being substantially complete, but events in England continued to remain troubled. For 1745 Hemingway reported;

"Fearing the rebel army from Scotland, Chester and its castle was once again refortified and one veteran regiment and three new ones were raised. However, the rebel forces did not approach the city, but simply passed through a part of the county on their way to Staffordshire. After the surrender of Carlisle however, a number of the rebels were brought to Chester as prisoners in sixteen carts and were held at the castle, which they filled. Once again the Spring Assizes had to be held elsewhere".

Perhaps mindful of such ongoing rebellions, around 1745 the southern curtain wall of the castle's inner bailey was reported to have been either removed or reduced, in order to install a platform for a 4 gun battery which could cover the area across the river near the satellite settlement of Handbridge. At the same time, the castle's Flag Tower, the likely site of the first Norman timber tower and candidate for Earl Ranulph's first Stone Keep, was known to have been reduced in height in order to accommodate a gun platform from which the castle might be defended. Likewise, the castle's Half Moon tower which has been attributed to the monarch Henry III or perhaps to his son and successor Edward I was also reduced in height in order to house a further gun emplacement. Some 40 years later in 1786 the same southern curtain wall was thought to have been refaced, perhaps to rectify some of the damage which had been done during the earlier demolition work.

Around 1780 and just 8 years before much of the castle's ancient fabric was finally torn down to accommodate Harrison's Greek Revival buildings, many of the older buildings still standing in the outer bailey were reported to have been demolished in order to accommodate the soldiers of the Cheshire Regiment who were being garrisoned there.

Finally, in 1785 and because of public criticism over the state of the castle's prison, the decision was made to organise a competition for the design and construction of a new County Gaol within the castle, which was ultimately won by the then relatively unknown northern born architect Thomas Harrison. As it turned out, this first phase of what became the almost wholesale redevelopment of the historic castle begun in 1788 was beset by problems from the outset; and became a highly exhaustive process. Throughout its construction, the prison project was thought to have been the subject of poor workmanship and technique, but given that it was largely built by under-nourished, untrained and badly housed prison labour, then that should have been no surprise. Despite these problems however and after several rebuilds the gaol was finally completed in 1792, with the new prison being exclaimed as one of the finest examples of English penitentiaries in the country.

During the 34 year period, from 1788 through to 1822; and beginning with the notoriously primitive gaol, the medieval precincts of Chester's historic castle were systematically razed from the ground in order to accommodate the elegantly modern complex constructed by Harrison. What little remains of the medieval fortress' inner ward, the Agricola, Flag and Half Moon Towers seem to have been overshadowed and fundamentally forgotten about, hidden as they are, by the monolithic 18th and 19th century structures that supplanted the earlier buildings of the castle's outer bailey. The former sites of the great Princes Hall of Elizabeth, the New Hall (later the Exchequer Court) ordered by Edward I are both said to lie beneath the relatively modern foundations of the city's Crown Court buildings. The main gateway to the castle's outer ward, with its impressive entrance and drawbridge, flanked on either side by massive drum type towers, is today thought to be marked by an entrance to the law courts car park, the impressive medieval castle defences essentially replaced by a modern traffic barrier. The outer bailey's central well, which often featured in pictures and paintings of the ancient precincts, is now said to lie beneath the many layers of tarmac which forms the modern castle's car park, close by the later statue of Queen Victoria.

Even the few parts of the early castle's fabric that remain standing have been treated very badly, often being added to or obscured by later building works of the various military garrisons who have inhabited the site for the past centuries. The Flag Tower in particular seems to have suffered greatly over the past few hundred years and today resembles a decaying bomb shelter, a relic of World War II, which wouldn't look out of place at the bottom of someone's garden.

Aside from Agricola's Tower which still occupies a position on the eastern side of the early Inner Bailey, the most obvious feature in this often overlooked part of Chester's modern castle is the imposing building known as **Napier House**. Credited to a Captain Kitson who was said to have designed and constructed the building in 1832, the eastern side of the property is though to sit on top of the site previously occupied by the various Shire Halls, successively built by Earl Hugh Lupus and his Norman successors. In later years and before the construction of the property which stands today, the site was reported to have been inhabited by the Deputy Governor's House and Officers Quarters which Kitson and his Engineers were responsible for demolishing.

The name "Napier House" is possibly a dedication to General Sir Charles James Napier who was reported to have been stationed at Chester Castle, shortly after the house was first erected. The building itself sits at the rear of the 18th century gun platform which guards the southern flank of the River Dee and is an appropriate position given that the ground floor of Napier House was known to have been used as an arms store, with the upper floors initially being used as additional accommodations for the military garrison, but later given over to office use.

Around the same time that the Flag Tower or castle's Keep was first being constructed, the inner ward's main gateway, the **Agricola Tower**, was also thought to have been built on the site and of the same soft red sandstone which was thought to have been quarried locally, possibly from just outside of the city's North Gate. Standing some 52 feet in height, the tower is comprised of three separate floors, starting with the crypt on the ground floor; the Chapel of St Mary de Castro on the first floor; and finally to an open room on the second floor. Access to both upper floors and to the roof space itself is by way of a single stone cut circular stairwell which is located in a corner of the tower and which has become so worn over time that individual steps have had to be stabilized with wooden slats made of oak. The ground floor crypt of Agricola's Tower is reported to measure some 21' x 16' internally and has an impressively elevated stone vaulted ceiling supported by chamfered ribs, plinths and wall pillars.

Within the ancient Tower and sometime shortly after its initial construction in stone, a small private chapel was installed on the first floor of the tower and dedicated to Saint Mary de Castro, or Saint Mary of the Castle. Occasionally known as the "Great Chapel" this church was thought to have been built for the exclusive use of the Earl and his visitors and was said to have been decorated with frescoes, dating from around 1220 and depicting biblical events and characters. Unhappily, sometime in the towers later history, these paintings were whitewashed over; possibly as a result of the chapel being used as a powder magazine by the resident garrison's and it was only in more recent years that they were once again temporarily discovered. The vaulted crypt which lies beneath and that underpins Agricola's Tower is generally Norman in origin, although sections were thought to have been rebuilt, following a serious fire in 1302. The chapel itself is thought to have had a close association with the Benedictine convent of St Mary, which had been founded in Chester by Earl Ranulph in the 12th Century, before being finally suppressed in the 16th century on the orders of Henry VIII.

The rediscovered frescoes were said to have included; the Visitation to and the miracles of the Virgin Mary, including the story of Theophilus, a priest who reportedly sold his soul to the devil, but who later had it retrieved for him by the Blessed Virgin. It has also been suggested that the wall paintings include the heraldic symbols and coats of arms of a number of the Palatinate's leading Officers, as well as individuals who were placed in charge of Chester's historic castle. One of these symbols was said to be that of Roger de Clinton, the Bishop of Coventry, Lichfield and Chester who was reported to have been appointed to the See in 1129. Bearing in mind that the structure of the tower, the architecture of the chapel itself, all seem to indicate an original date of around 1200, then the tower would appear to be entirely the work of Ranulph III. Although the date and origins of these "lost" frescoes have often been attributed to England's Plantagenet Kings, some experts speculate that the paintings were actually completed on the orders of the 7th Earl following his return from crusading in the Holy Lands in 1220.

It has been suggested that the chapel within the rectangular Agricola's tower is perhaps typical of the early Romanesque architecture much favored by the Norman occupiers of the site, but is also of a date that places its first construction right on the "cusp" of the beginning of the Early English style of architecture. Experts point out that certain features within the chapel, including the ribs, bases and capitals are of a type which might indicate a date of between 1190 and 1210, the very period that marked the change between Romanesque and Early English architectural style. Also, the presence of the Chapel within the Agricola Tower has led some historians to suggest that it was this tower, and not the Flag Tower, which was the Keep of Chester's early Norman castle. This hypothesis is largely based on the usual custom of housing the Chapel within the final defensive redoubt, in other words the Keep. However, it would not have been unusual to have located the Castle's Chapel within the main gateway, as this would have essentially forced an enemy to fire upon or directly attack the "House of God", something that most Christian soldiers would have been extremely loathe to do.

Around 1825 and in conjunction with the general redevelopment of the whole castle complex by Thomas Harrison, the ancient Agricola's Tower was reported to have been encased in brickwork by the Board of Ordanance, although the work itself is generally credited to the renowned architect Harrison.

It's likely that the initial timber and earthworks motte and bailey castle which was built at Chester on the express orders of William the Conqueror developed in a fairly piecemeal fashion and over an extended period of time. The wooden keep, which had surmounted the motte or mound in the earliest defensive enclosure, was later rebuilt in locally available red sandstone and is thought to remain in place today as the modern day **Flag Tower**.

The castle's Keep identified the tower which was located in the most heavily defended part of the castle precincts and was regarded as the final defensive position, in the event that all other defences had been overcome by an attacker. Stone buildings were extremely expensive to construct, explaining the widespread use of timber in the first instance, but as the Normans started to gain full control of the country and raise increasing revenues from the native population through taxation, so much more money was spent on erecting these military installations. The Keep, as the most vital building in any such military compound would have been rebuilt in stone first and only once this was completed would the baileys other internal buildings be constructed in a similar fashion.

Stone Keeps were often built on a solid base within the inner bailey, rather than on top of the motte or mound, which were generally unable to support the weight of a much heavier stonework building, which might typically be between 2 and 4 storeys high. Most stone keeps were thought to have contained a water well, a garderobe or privy, a hall, as well as a private chapel. The individual floors were often linked by a spiral stairwell which was located at the corner of the building and on the ground floor were the store-rooms and guard rooms. On the first floor was thought to be the hall along with private apartments and above them the kitchen, where in the event of attack, hot liquids could be prepared and thrown down on the heads of any would-be attackers.

The actual location of the Flag and Agricola Towers, both of which stood within the inner ward of the castle, protected by high curtain walls and the newly constructed outer bailey, would have made it virtually impossible for a potential enemy to attack them, which is perhaps the main reason why they were not rebuilt or replaced by the much more formidable circular tower. It is also worth bearing in mind, that both of these substantial towers would have been in daily use by the garrison, so their potential loss or replacement would not have been straightforward consideration.

However, the Flag Towers later partial demolition in the 18th century to accommodate a gun platform has seriously reduced the importance and imposing nature of this particular tower. Its early construction and importance though, is indicated by its two vaulted cellars which are clearly of Norman Romanesque design. The early and overall dimensions of the tower is now unclear, given that it has been reduced in height, but was known to have been at least 30' square at its base. Although it was known to have had external stairwells which accessed the upper storeys, these were thought to have been introduced later in the towers life and to have replaced an earlier internal staircase, which was likely to have been located in one corner of the tower.

Standing along the western side of what remains of the early Inner Bailey, the Flag Tower today is generally hidden amongst a swathe of building rubble which can be largely attributed to a succession of 18th and 19th century military properties that were erected by the different garrisons to serve as bake-houses, store-rooms and guard houses.

Another much later survivor which continues to stand just north of the Flag Tower is the **Frobisher's House**, which is thought to occupy the same site as an earlier "Armourer's Shop", a vital craftsman within any military fortress. Between 1696 and 1698 this house, along with the now extinct "Old Mint" building which itself was joined to the medieval Half Moon Tower, were all employed in the re-coining of the nations currency, under the watchful eye and control of Edmund Halley, he of comet fame. The mint at Chester was one of a handful located throughout the regions, not because London couldn't cope with the work, but because local people and businessmen were suspicious of "southerners". By establishing regional mints throughout the country and putting them under the control of trusted public figures, the authorities ultimately gained the trust and confidence of the general public and helped the nation's economy to remain stable. During that two-year period Chester's mint was reported to have handled the re-coining of Cheshire, North Wales, Shropshire and much of Lancashire. Following the closure of the mint in 1698, the Old Mint building was thought to have been used as an Orderly Room by the resident garrison of the castle.

In what was formerly the Outer Bailey of the old medieval castle, little remains of the curtain walls, flanking towers and defensive ditch that once protected the Great Shire Hall, stables and buildings of the Plantagenet kings and their successors. The two most dominant features of the new and enlarged lower ward are the massive pillared gateway located on the west side of the parade ground and Harrison's impressive County Hall and Assize Courts with its 12 columned portico.

The main entrance to the new castle complex, commonly referred to as the "**Propylaeum**" or "Pillared Entrance" was thought to have been designed by Harrison around 1808, the same time that he was building the Commercial Newsrooms in the city and has been

compared to the Brandenburg Gate in Berlin which was reported to have been built some 20 years earlier. However, despite this earlier record, the first stone of the massive portal was actually reported to have been laid on the 20th June 1811 by Colonel Trafford of the Congleton Militia and the gateway's final stone was laid on 26th August 1813.

Harrison's **County Hall** and **Assize Courts** which flank the eastern boundary of the castle complex were reportedly built in a classical Grecian style, its west facing portico supported by 12 Doric style columns each measuring 23 ft in height, the first of which was reported to have been laid on the 13th October 1797. Before raising this first pillar onto its plinth, a lead casket containing a white Wedgewood cup and holding a small number of coins was placed into a cavity and then covered by the great column, with the obvious expectation that they would remain undisturbed for perhaps hundreds of years.

A short time later and under a second column, a brass snuff box reportedly belonging to Admiral, the Lord Nelson was interred within a similar plinth cavity, once again with the expectation that it would not see the light of day for a considerable period of time. Sadly, despite Harrison's skills at designing his landmark buildings, clearly his engineering and construction abilities did not reach such great heights. In the 1920's, just some 120-odd years after the impressive façade was first raised, huge cracks began to appear in the outer stonework of the building which were later identified as having been caused by subsidence.

Harrison and his construction team were thought to have erected the 300 ft central section of his new Shire Hall and Assize Courts directly over the ditch of the old medieval castle and failed to ensure that the filling materials within the ditch were sufficiently compacted to withstand the great loads that were being placed upon it. Although much of the footprint area for the new civic buildings had been strengthened with wooden piles driven into the ground, unforeseen water seepage along with an unknown geological fault that created weaknesses in the underlying sandstone bedrock all contrived to make these generally new buildings structurally unsound.

As a result, between 1921 and 1922, a number of the great Doric columns were taken down and extensive remedial work was undertaken to underpin the foundations of the building and to try and solve the water seepage problem that had gone unrecognised for so long. Finally, at the end of the project the columns were reinstated in their original positions and the Wedgewood cup was once again re-interred in its base, although this time with extra coins from the time of the later works. The brass snuff box attributed to Nelson however, was not replaced, but was instead gifted to the Castle's regimental museum, presumably because it was considered too valuable to be left inside the column.

The central block of Harrison's new castle initially housed Chester's new Shire Hall and Courts, including the Grand Jury Room, Prothonotary's Office, Records Office and the many associated law offices, all of which were designed to serve the twice yearly Assizes. The main courtroom itself was described as a *"splendid semi-circular room with coffered ceiling supported by 12 Ionic columns which measured some 80 ft by 50 ft, was 44 ft in height and capable of accommodating around a thousand people"*. Although now largely unknown and sealed away, this new building was said to have included an underground passageway which allowed prisoners to be moved between the courts and Harrison's newly built gaol which formerly lay on the site of today's County Hall.

Although Chester's Crown Court has played host to some renowned cases and defendants, it continues to be strongly associated with the trial of the infamous "Moors Murderer's", Ian Brady and Myra Hindley who were jointly tried for the murders of several young children (John Kilbride, Lesley Ann Downey and Edward Evans) during the mid 1960's. Because of the heinous nature of the crimes, the trial was held at Chester to help ensure the safety of the two defendants and to ensure that there was no incidents of civil disorder. It was reported that Brady and Hindley were held in the cells of Chester Town Hall and then transported to the court building to attend the trial during April and May of 1966. Finally on the 6th May 1966 the jury returned a guilty verdict on both defendants and they were duly sentenced to life sentences, a lucky escape when one considers that capital punishment had only been abolished the previous year. Hindley ultimately spent the remainder of her life in prison, finally succumbing to illness and escaping further punishment by dying in jail, whilst Brady himself continues to serve out his sentence in Broadmoor Hospital.

At each end of the main Shire Hall building, Harrison's designs included separate wings that were intended to house the military offices and installations that were associated with the various resident garrisons based at Chester castle. Initially this included an Armoury, which was reported in 1817 to have housed over 30,000 stands of arms, including rifles, pistols, bayonets and swords, all held in readiness for use by the numerous regiments and militias that existed at the time. As the principal military base in the region, Chester Castle was known to have been the main rallying point for many of these regular and irregular army units and would therefore have been the place where they received their weapons.

From around 1832 however, the Armoury was said to have been removed to the ground floor of the newly built Napier House within the castle's old Inner Bailey and its former home was then altered and given over to much more mundane purposes, such as a clothing store, offices and military quarters. Records as to which of the two wings actually housed the Armoury tend to differ, but on balance the southernmost wing, possibly known as **Colville House** and dating from 1807, is the most likely site of the arms store and later used as Officers Quarters and Judges Lodgings. A noted inclusion at Chester's Armoury was said to have been 2 cannons captured at Sebastopol in 1857, although these were later removed and their current whereabouts is unknown.

Standing in front of the grand façade of Harrison's Chester complex and in the centre of the former military parade ground is a bronze statue of Queen Victoria which dates from 1903. Although it was erected some 2 years after the Queen's death, the statue itself is notable for having been designed by Pomeroy, with the attendant stonework attributed to the noteworthy county architect Harry Beswick. Paid for by public subscription, the official unveiling of the statue was said to have been carried out by Earl Egerton in October 1903, reportedly because a member of the royal family was unavailable for the engagement.

Although the replacement of Chester's medieval castle was reported to have begun around 1788 with the construction of Harrison's Gaol, by 1877 National Government was thought to have taken over responsibility for criminal offenders and many of these early county gaols were ultimately closed. At Chester, the castle's prison was said to have remained in use until 1884 when it was finally closed and its last inmates transferred to HM Prison Knutsford, although it continued to hold military prisoners until some years later.

In 1895 though, Cheshire County Council was reported to have acquired the military prison in order that the city's law courts could be extended and additional council offices built for the burgeoning number of clerks and administrators used to run the authority. The rest of the former Felons Prison, which lay outside the limits of the castle were said to have been employed as a training ground by a local artillery company, with some of the prisoners cells given over to store supplies and being used for office space. Later still, in 1938, much of this same site, along with the historic Skinners Lane, was used to construct the present County Hall building which was said to have taken some 19 years to build (1938 to 1957) owing to it being interrupted by World War II and the financial restrictions that followed that particular conflict. Designed by the County architect E Mainwaring Parkes, the building did not receive a good reception from either conservationists or architectural critics when it was completed, many of whom believed that the office building did little to enhance its riverside location.

It was reported that in 1954 the military finally gave up possession of Chester Castle and subsequently passed the site into the hands of the civil authorities, although the older parts of the base are thought to be in the guardianship of English Heritage. Despite representing some of the most important and ancient parts of Chester's 2000 year history the former inner bailey of the medieval castle complex, containing Agricola's Tower, the Flag Tower and the Half Moon Tower seem to be simply maintained, rather than included, within the historic fabric of the city and that is truly disappointing given the part they have played in Chester's past.

CHAPTER TWELVE

CASTLE LANE & GLOVERSTONE

Nowadays called **Castle Street**, this Chester thoroughfare was formerly part of an area called Gloverstone, a county township which marked the legal boundary between the city authorities and that of the crown and owes it name to a long since disappeared boulder which was said to have been used by the city's leather workers to dry their animal hides. In its original form, the township of "Gloverstone" lay between the main gateway of the Norman Castle and the main trading streets of Chester and was said to have been populated by numbers of disparate tradesmen who made their livings outside of the city limits, often because they were not freemen of Chester and therefore not legally entitled to trade within the walls. However, because "Gloverstone" lay within the county's jurisdiction and was therefore free of many of the city's restrictive practices a large number of itinerant and foreign born traders were forced to settle in this particular area of Chester.

At the "Glovers Stone", an immense ice age boulder that had been deposited in the area many thousands of years before, the city Sheriffs would call on the Constable of the Castle to deliver his prisoners to them for their sentences to be carried out. The condemned felon might then be whipped through the streets of Chester, placed in the stocks or for those sentenced to death, transported on a hurdle or on the back of a cart to the gallows at Boughton Spital or later to the Northgate Gaol. Although more commonly called "Gloverstone", this area of the city was also occasionally referred to as "Castlegate", no doubt because of its close proximity to the medieval castle's main entrance. Following the redevelopment of the castle site in the 1790's however, this historic stone was said to have been simply buried in the castles ditch and then forgotten about. Other sources though, suggest that the boulder was actually removed to an area below the city's 14th century Water Tower, where it later became part of an ornamental garden feature.

Although lying outside of the defensive walls of the Roman fortress, excavations in the 20th century have uncovered evidence of an early Roman building in and around the site of the medieval castle which has generally considered to be the remains of a "Mansio" or Roman guesthouse. Lying on a site, to the south of no's 11 to 15 Castle Street this early building was thought to have existed, in one form or another, for the hundreds of years that the fortress itself existed and was only abandoned in the late 4th century when most of the Roman forces finally withdrew from Britain.

A second series of archaeological digs, examining a site bounded by Castle Street to the south, Bunce Street to the west, Grosvenor Street to the north and Lower Bridge Street to the east uncovered evidence of post Roman Anglo Saxon industrial activity. Undertaken as part of a general redevelopment of the area, these investigations were reported to have discovered the remains of an Anglo Saxon leather manufacturing complex, including its sunken tanning pits and suggested that much of this general area, lying between the fortress' southern wall and the River Dee, was sparsely populated and generally used for early industrial processes, especially those that required easy access to a water supply.

It has also been suggested that much of this same area, along with the newly enclosed lands to the west of the former fortress were given over to commercial agriculture or market gardening and were thought to have been granted to those who volunteered to defend the city from any outside threat. It was only with the arrival of Duke William and his Norman army in 1070 that much of this land was appropriated by the new rulers of Chester, during which many of the earlier Anglo Saxon structures were simply razed from the ground, leaving little evidence of their presence, save for the post holes, pits and evidence of burning that was left behind following their destruction.

Although Castle Street is inextricably linked to the site of Chester's early Norman, medieval and modern day castles, it undoubtedly existed well before a stone was laid by Duke William's engineers in 1070. It seems entirely likely that it actually developed as an early byway, possibly in connection with the previously mentioned Roman "Mansio" and offering a route between that particular building and the first bridge across the River Dee. The ancient church of St Olave's, located directly opposite the eastern junction of Castle Street, is thought to date from the late 8th or early 9th century, suggesting that the route which later became Castle Lane (now Street) would have been in existence by that period.

As elsewhere in Chester, this modern city street would be barely recognisable to its early inhabitants, such has been the level of change and redevelopment over the past few hundred years. Beginning at the western junction of Castle Street, which adjoins the far more modern Grosvenor Street and inner ring road roundabout, the mass of Harrison's Chester Castle continues to dominate much of the southern western flank of the street. Apart from the northern wing of the complex and the remnants of its associated ditch, the most significant feature in this area of Castle Street, surprisingly enough is the entrance to the castle car park which is controlled by an automated barrier. It seems hard to believe, that less than 250 years ago, the **medieval Castle gateway** would have graced this site, rather than the utilitarian and uninspiring portal that exists today.

Marking the entry into the medieval outer bailey, which formerly housed the horses, troops and buildings of England's greatest monarchs the main gatehouse was reported to be a grand entrance, protected by drawbridge, portcullis and ditch, as well as being flanked on either side by impressive drum type guard towers. Thought to have been built around the end of the 13th or beginning of the 14th century for the monarch Edward "Longshanks", this great entrance, along with all of its associated defensive curtain walls, was thought to have stood for around 500 years before being demolished to make way for the buildings which currently inhabit the site.

In between the site of the old castle gateway and the church of St Mary's on the hill, a spot now occupied by a modern day housing mews, populated by relatively modern townhouses a timber mansion, reportedly called the **"Gatehouse"** was thought to have stood, until it was demolished in the 1790's as part of Harrison's castle redevelopment. Little is known about the date or ownership of this obviously early building, save for the fact that it existed and was in this general area. It is also likely that the eastern side of the site, now inhabited by these modern townhouses, had formerly hosted the Foulkes Mansion that later on became the now extinct Royal Standard Hotel and later till may have hosted a city tavern called "The Crow". It is worth noting however, that a later review of Castle Street suggested No 25 in the street had formerly operated as a tavern and might well be the site of the aforementioned hostelry.

It is also interesting to speculate, whether or not this same plot of land had been home to a building called the **"Stone Hall"** which was thought to be in existence at the end of the 12th or beginning of the 13th centuries. Reportedly the home of Earl Ranulph Blundeville's chancellor, known as Peter the Clerk, this administrator was thought to have served the 7th Norman Earl from around 1180 through to 1228. Also called Peter the Chancellor, he was thought to be the founder of the Thornton family in Cheshire and associated with places such as Thornton-le-moors in the county. This hall was still in existence in 1494 when it was said to be in the possession of Sir Peter de Thornton, presumably a distant relative of Peter the Clerk.

St Mary's Church which stands on the south side of the street and at the junction with St Mary's Hill is more commonly known as St Mary's on-the-hill and is thought to originate from around the middle of the 14th century and has a strong connection with Chester's castle's, both medieval and modern. Originally called the church of St Mary de Castro, because of its close proximity to and association with Chester's medieval castle, it should not be confused with the "chapel" of St Mary de Castro that continues to exist within the ancient Agricola's Tower and was thought to have been built entirely for the use of the Earl and his household.

The SE Chapel of St Mary's-on-the-hill, dates from the middle of the 15th century and the oak roof is thought to date from around 1500, with the Nave being supported by a Tudor oak beam taken from the derelict Basingwerk Abbey in Flintshire around 1535. The church contains a number of monuments dedicated to notable characters including Sir Francis Gamul and the various members of the Randle Holmes family, both of which are noted below. The church was heavily restored during the 19th century by the notable architect James Harrison, who was reported to have raised the tower by some 9m during the renovation. A century or so earlier, the soaring spire of St Mary's was said to have been taken down by the military authorities based at Chester's medieval castle because it was high enough to overlook the defensive walls and outer bailey of the castle, providing a vantage point from where enemy snipers might attack members of the garrison.

There was further work on St Mary's carried out by John Pollard Seddon between 1890 and 1892, including the rebuilding of the church's north porch. It lost its status of parish church in 1887, but was reinstated four years later when the historic St Bridget's was demolished for the second and final time. By the mid 1970's the Church was no longer being used for religious services and the city council negotiated to purchase the building from the church authorities with the intention of transforming the property into an Urban Studies Centre. Having finally purchased the former church and following a program of renovation and renewal the new urban centre was finally opened in June 1979.

The **Troutbeck Chapel** in the south aisle of the church is dedicated to a family of that name, who were important figures in Chester during the 15th and 16th centuries and is said to contain fragments of ancient glass in its main window. Records suggest that the cost of building the chapel was funded by one William Troutbeck in 1433, possibly as an extension to the already existing church. The Troutbeck estates were said to have passed into the possession of the Talbot family, the Earls of Shrewsbury, by the middle of the 17th century, ostensibly through marriage and it was during this period, around 1661, that parts of the Troutbeck Chapel were reported to have collapsed, following a fire. This part of St Mary's was said to have remained generally ruined until 1693, because of a continuing dispute between the Earls of Shrewsbury and the parishioners of St Mary's, who only agreed to fund the cost of rebuilding the chapel, provided that ownership was passed to the church itself, which it finally was in 1693.

Associated with the general area, a later generation of the Troutbeck family were reported to have owned a large townhouse or mansion at the bottom of St Mary's Hill that included fairly extensive lands and incorporated the by then relatively defunct Shipgate which by 1534 was said to be obsolete. This area of the city now houses the Bear and Billet which dates from the middle of the 17th century and was formerly the townhouse of the Talbot's, the Earls of Shrewsbury who were the historic "Serjeants" of the Bridgegate.

St Kathryn's Chapel which formerly occupied part of the north aisle of St Mary's commemorates members of the renowned Gamul family, who prior to the English Civil War were major political figures and landowners in the city. The church contains a monument to the family, depicting Thomas Gamul and his wife Alice attended by the kneeling figure of their notable son, Sir Francis, who ultimately brought the family's fortunes to ruin through his support for the fated monarch Charles I. The family were known to have been related through marriage to at least two of Cheshire's leading families, the Grosvenor's and the Cholmondley's and it has been suggested that every member of the Gamul's, up until the middle of the 17th century were interred at St Mary's.

The chapel's dedication to St Kathryn (Katherine or Catherine) may refer to St Kathryn of Alexandria, a Christian maiden who was beheaded on the orders of a pagan Emperor, but whose veins produced milk rather than blood. Legend tells how, after her martyrdom, her body was carried off by angels to Mount Sinai, where a church was founded in her memory.

An early instrument of her torture, in order to force her to recant her beliefs, is thought to remain with us to this day, in the form of the "Catherine Wheel", a popular feature of every Guy Fawkes Night. According to Christian reports, the saint was tied to a spiked wheel, which presumably when it was rotated inflicted pain on her, although the exact methodology is unclear. However, according to the same legends, instead of causing her pain, the wheel was said to have exploded into hundreds of pieces killing many of her accusers who were standing nearby. St Kathryn is reported to be the patron saint of both Preachers and Librarians.

The third noted Chester family who were known to have had a long association with the church of St Mary's were the Randle Holmes, four generations of heralds, painters and antiquaries who were all identically named and pursued the same profession in the city. The third member of the family, commonly known as the "Great Randle" was thought to be the most significant individual to hold the title, being the co-author of an incomplete work, the Academy of Armour which was published in an unfinished form around 1688. A devout supporter of the ill-fated monarch Charles I, he was reported to have written several reports and articles describing the suffering of Chester's inhabitants during the Civil

War siege of the city. He was also said to have been heavily fined by the authorities following the surrender of the city to the Parliamentarians and like his Royalist companion, Sir Francis Gamul, found his estates seriously reduced by the sequestrations and penalties inflicted by the new government.

Neither would his financial status have been improved by the construction of his property known as the Old Lamb's Row, which occupied much of the site lying between the Bridge Street and Lower Bridge Street, today the location of a major traffic junction. Having agreed its construction with local builder William Hughes around 1670, the two men then fell into a dispute over the terms of their agreement, which finally had to be resolved by the courts and undoubtedly cost Holmes even more of his dwindling fortune.

When he died in 1699, Randle Holme III was interred along with his father and grandfather in the family church of St Mary's, although even after his death his estate was still quibbled over by his family and the authorities. It was little wonder then that his son, the last Randle Holme struggled to survive financially and was eventually forced to sell the family's priceless collection of historic manuscripts to Robert Harley, the Earl of Oxford, who ultimately donated his own entire collection to the British Museum. With the thousands of pages of the Holme collection sold and with his heraldry trade failing to provide him with a living, finally in 1711 Randle Holme IV was reported to have sold the family business to a man called Francis Bassano who subsequently made his living in Chester. As for Randle himself, he was recorded to have died some short time later and been interred at St Mary's church along with his father, grandfather and great grandfather.

Lying adjacent to the historic church is the even more ancient thoroughfare from which its name derives, **St Mary's Hill**. Possibly formed by the quarrying activities of the Romans or the later Normans, much of the sandstone bedrock surrounding the castle site is known to have been extensively quarried right up until the 13th or 14th centuries. However, St Mary's Hill's association with the River Dee and its long since redundant Shipgate (which some suggest is a derivation of Sheep Gate) suggest that this former track is indeed an ancient one and possibly pre-dates the 11th century castle site. Modern day archaeological excavations undertaken during the second half of the 20th century have indicated that areas of the wider site, notably those lying alongside the banks of the river, were being used for agricultural purposes during the immediate post-Roman period. It is not inconceivable therefore to believe that this particular byway originates from that time, or indeed before the Romans finally abandoned their fortress at Chester. Bearing in mind that the graveyard of St Mary's and most notably its cemetery walls are thought to sit atop the remains of the previously mentioned Roman "Mansio" building, it seems entirely plausible to suggest, that what is now St Mary's Hill, was at one time some sort of access route to this long since gone property from the river or from the first Roman bridge that crossed the Dee.

Although the thoroughfare is lined today with a number of small cottages, records of earlier occupation are extremely limited and date generally from around the 15th century. In 1468, there were said to 4 properties and their gardens along the route and noted to have passed from the Erney family to the Norris' of Speke, presumably by sale or through marriage. The fact that they were thought to be existing properties in 1468 suggests that they had in fact been constructed well before that date, although no evidence regarding as to exactly when these properties were first built is currently available. The only other details with regard to these same houses comes from 1488, when the properties were sold by the Norris family to an individual called Birkenhead.

The only other building that was noted on St Mary's Hill was the Rectory of St Mary's, which occupied the northernmost point of the thoroughfare, directly opposite to the church and graveyard of St Mary's. Described at the time, as an extensive timber built property, this early house was thought to have become virtually obsolete during the late 19th century when the neighbouring church of St Bridget's was demolished and Thomas Harrison's former home, St Martin's Lodge, became available for use by the clergy of St Mary's.

The **Golden Eagle** Public House was formerly thought to have been known as the "Spread Eagle" during the first half of the 18th century, the same time that the buildings façade was said to have been substantially rebuilt. In 1852 the tavern was thought to be in the possession of a man called Foulkes, whose son William, was recorded as the organist at Chester Cathedral and who was thought to have occupied or built a house that later became known as Foulkes Mansion. Reportedly standing on the south side of Castle Street, this property later housed the Royal Standard Hotel, possibly sometime after 1871 when Foulkes was said to have travelled to America, ostensibly for health reasons.

In earlier times the Golden Eagle site was reported to be the location of the **"Green Hall"** a fairly large timber house which was thought to have its earliest origins in the 15th century when it was owned by one Henry Ball (or Bell) who was noted as a city Sheriff in 1469. The Ball family were said to have owned the mansion until 1593 when the property was sold to a renowned Parliamentarian figure in Chester called Gilbert Gerard. Although most historians agree that Gerard owned and lived in the property around 1660, a city Barrister called Philip Oldfield was known to be resident there up until his death in 1616, suggesting that he may have rented the property from Gerard, or perhaps had bought the house from the Ball family in 1593. Upon his death Oldfield was said to have been buried at St Mary's church, which is thought to still contain the monument dedicated to the renowned lawyer by his family and friends.

Even though the Golden Eagle itself is known to be a truly historic building, Castle Street itself is thought to contain a number of both 17th and 18th century properties; although as elsewhere in the city this thoroughfare has been subjected to extensive redevelopment, most notably in the 20th century. The narrow thoroughfare which lies immediately west of the tavern, Bunce Street, is yet another city road that can probably trace its origins all the way back to the 12th or 13th centuries. Possibly deriving its name from one William Bunce, a city Sheriff who was recorded in 1244, this city notable was thought to have held lands south of Chester and close to the village of Eccleston. In 1270, a Richard Bunce, probably a relative of the aforementioned William, was reported to hold lands close to Chester's medieval Ship-gate and making a local connection with the thoroughfare that still bears this particular family's surname. Mentioned once again in 1328, by the 18th century Bunce Lane (now Street) was simply known to mark the westerly limit of the extensive gardens that formed part of John Williams' Bridge House property, which had been constructed in Chester's Lower Bridge Street area. Prior to 1826 and the laying down of the then new Grosvenor Street, Bunce Street was known to have ran northward to join the equally ancient Cuppin Street, but this connection was severed by the new city thoroughfare, built to link the developing Grosvenor Bridge with Chester's historic centre.

The final two significant houses which exist, at least in part, in Castle Street are Gamul House which is located at the south east junction with Lower Bridge Street and the tavern the "Old Kings Head" which lies at the northeast junction of the same city street. Because both of these properties are generally situated along Lower Bridge Street, then information regarding their individual histories are dealt with there.

However, before closing this historical review of Castle Street it is perhaps worth noting a reference to a property called the Dedwood Mansion, which used to occupy a plot of land along this old thoroughfare. Records suggest that this noted family's timber built mansion was located to the west of the "Old Kings Head", presumably with its stables, gardens, etc running westward and the house itself facing onto Castle Street. The site of this earlier house might now be marked by no's 1 and 3 of that street which are known to be two separate properties that were formerly one building.

The Dedwood family were thought to be able to trace their Chester ancestry all the way back to 1390, when an individual called Roger del Dedwode (Roger of the dead wood) was noted in the city. Less than 20 years later one Richard del Dedwode was recorded as being involved with the control of the forest of Mara, which once formed part of the modern day Delamere Forest and in 1408 a second member of the family, a John del Dedwode, was reported as the Governor of Chester Castle. Given the close proximity of the long extinct hall to the medieval castle, it was probably this member of the Dedwood family who built the mansion which is the subject of this discussion.

A second John del Dedwode was said to have been elected Mayor of Chester on two separate occasions, firstly in 1468 and then again in 1483, perhaps indicating the family's power and influence throughout that particular period. In 1497 another member of the Dedwood's was reported to have been buried at the nearby St Mary's church, suggesting that the family were still resident in that parish, at least up to that date. Little else is known about the family, other than much of their estates were later said to have come into the possession of the Bruen family, presumably through marriage.

By 1590 the Hall was thought to be occupied by a man called Edward Planckney, although he does not appear to have been the owner, but simply a tenant and implying that the property may still have been in the hands of the Bruens or their successors. In 1599, Sir John Egerton was recorded to have sold the mansion and its lands to one William Aldersey with the property being described as lying on the north side of Castle Lane and its gardens located to the west of the house.

CHAPTER THIRTEEN

BRIDGE STREET

In its earliest Roman form, modern day **Bridge Street** was known as the Via Praetoria and marked the southern approach to the Roman Principia, the headquarters building which sat at the centre of the fortress, its front entrance facing down the Via Praetoria, towards the southern gateway, the Porta Praetoria and onto the main Roman highway known as Watling Street. The military buildings that lined the street were reported to have included the Praetentura or Bath House Complex which lay on the eastern side of the thoroughfare and was said to have occupied the space now inhabited by much of the modern Grosvenor Shopping precinct. On the opposite western flank, it has been reported that an Officers Club and Bath House, or Scholae, was located and beyond that, towards the western wall of the fortress were the vitally important Horrea or granaries which held the food stores of the legions. Throughout Chester's long and colourful history, this ancient thoroughfare, along with both Eastgate and Watergate Streets has played a central role in the social and business life of the city, although today's spacious and generally clean Bridge Street would be barely recognisable to Chester's earlier inhabitants.

Reports and records appear to indicate that for many centuries Bridge Street was virtually enclosed at its southern junction by the area known as the "Two Churches" which comprised the modern day Heritage Centre, formerly St Michael's and the long extinct church of St Bridget's that reportedly owed its foundation to King Offa in the 8th century. From that point, northward to the present day High Cross area, both sides of the medieval street were said to have been occupied by the predecessors of the buildings that stand today and were themselves fronted by numerous "seldae" or stalls that were erected by the various merchants who plied their trades in this part of the city.

The northern half of the thoroughfare was thought to have been particularly crowded up to and including the 16th century when it played host to the many and varied markets that were common to the city. It was only with the opening up and development of Chester's Northgate Street, notably after the Dissolution of the Monasteries in the 1540's, that many of these same markets and fairs were moved away from the Bridge Street area, allowing the thoroughfare to become much more open and accessible. It was also during this same period, in 1586, that Bridge Street was reported to have been paved, thereby helping to improve conditions for traders and shoppers alike.

Early leases and grants for many of the buildings and lands in Bridge Street, notably between the late 13th and early 16th centuries seem to indicate that a good proportion of both were in the possession of the city's various religious houses. Lands stretching from modern day White Friars, northward to Commonhall Street and bounded in the east by Weaver Street were said to have been held by the Carmelite Order from the 1290's onwards and only passed into public and private hands following the Dissolution of the Monasteries in the 1540's. A number of the street facing properties in Bridge Street, along with their extensive rear gardens were said to have been in the possession of St Mary's convent, located close to the medieval castle and established in the 12th century by Earl Ranulph Blundeville. These too though were sequestered by King Henry VIII during his religious purges and along with virtually all other church lands in Chester ended up in the possession of a London Salter called John Cocks (Cokks) who was thought to be an agent of the Crown.

It is also apparent from these same early records, that the elevated Rows for which the city of Chester is famed and that continue to exist in Bridge Street and elsewhere were constructed and developed over an extended period of time, rather than emerging as a completed feature. This is witnessed by the fact that individual sites, along both sides of the street, were often described as "void parcels of land" as opposed to identifying distinct or previously existing properties. Two examples of this, are a grant of a "void parcel of land" made to John and Randle Bothe in 1483 and a grant of a "parcel of land" made to Robert Leche, a fishmonger by trade, in 1506.

Members of the Leche family, who are perhaps more commonly associated with Leche House in Watergate Street, were also known to have inherited considerable property interests in Bridge Street as well. Thought to have been related to the Barnston family through marriage, by the first half of the 16th century these relatives were said to have acquired a number of properties on the eastern flank of Bridge Street, including one that adjoined a city tavern called "The Cock" which was located within the main thoroughfare.

As with Chester's Eastgate, Watergate and to a lesser degree Northgate Street, the great age of Bridge Street is testified to by the number of under-crofts or cellars that exist there. Although they have a number of suggested origins, including being designed to circumvent the problem caused by pre-existing Roman structures and rubble, the fact that most of these cellars date from the 13th century is also notable. A major conflagration of 1278 that destroyed many of the city's early timber buildings has been identified as one possible cause for the development of these stone built under-crofts, although this fire is not the only explanation for their construction. It seems just as plausible to suggest, that most cellars date from that time, simply because building technology had developed to that particular degree and where individual property owners could afford to, they chose to mount their timber houses and shops on stone foundations. As a matter of interest and in relation to the subject of the cellars themselves, in 1355 one of these basements was reported to have been called "Helle". Reportedly owned by an individual called William de Shavynton (Shavington) it has been suggested that such names were commonly applied to such cellars, although whether it was for purely religious reasons or not is unclear.

The most northerly point of Bridge Street, on its western side, has previously been noted in discussing both the city's High Cross and Watergate Street areas, being largely redeveloped by T M Lockwood in 1892 as part of the Victorian modernisation of that era. However, his buildings at numbers 2 to 4 Bridge Street, which currently stand at the northwest junction with Watergate Street, still contain the 13th century cellars that testify to the sites great age, a time when a much more ancient stone hall occupied the very same site. In 1507 this first early hall was reported to have been granted or leased to the renowned city Alderman Sir Thomas Smith, a man who was elected Mayor of Chester on eight separate occasions and who was known to have held possession of a number of properties in this part of the city during the 16th century.

On the opposite side of the thoroughfare and marking the northeast junction of Bridge Street is yet another Lockwood building, undertaken around 1888, along with the adjoining properties on the south side of Eastgate Street. Noted just prior to its later rebuilding by the architect, the property at No 1 Bridge Street was reported to have been occupied by a tinsmith's shop, but no further information regarding its earlier history has been found thus far. From this point southward, the next few city buildings are thought to be generally late 18th or early 19th century constructions; although in one or two cases there might well be internal structural features that have managed to survive from earlier times.

The former **Bookland's Crypt** at 12 Bridge Street, Chester incorporates a 13th century under-croft which comprises six vaulted bays, located at the rear of the shop. Above this stone built vault, the timber building which exists from the 17th century was formerly known as Cowper House, the former home of Thomas Cowper, a former Mayor of Chester in 1642, who was a prominent Royalist supporter during the English Civil War siege of the city. There is an inscription "TC 1664" which is thought to indicate the date of repairs carried out after the devastating siege. In its original form, Cowper's House was thought to have been a far more substantial building and included the adjoining No 14 Bridge Street, but was probably divided during the 18th century to suit the prevailing fashions.

The **Dutch Houses**, at No's 22-26 Bridge Street are thought to date from between 1660 and 1670 and sit over under-crofts which were undoubtedly associated with earlier town houses which had become dilapidated and later demolished. By the 1970's, along with a number of other city buildings, the Dutch Houses were said to be in such a perilous condition that they had to be rescued by the city council. However, the subsequent restoration project resulted in the whole façade being deconstructed and the internal timber supports being removed and replaced by steel replacements. The property's title is thought to reflect an architectural style, rather than any sort of direct connection with the Dutch people, although it has been suggested that from 1700 onward Chester did include a relatively small but vibrant Dutch business community. In 1873 the architect Thomas Lockwood was reported to have restored part of this property and in 1947 the building was noted for its then still intact architectural features, but the later 20th century rescue of the site has undoubtedly reduced its historic importance.

Shuttleworth's Crypt, at No 36 Bridge Street, Chester is an early 14th century undercroft or cellar comprising two vaulted arches which are overlaid by early and enormous beams which once supported a grand town house that was reported to have been rebuilt in both the 16th and late 18th centuries. At the first floor Row level there is an example of a studded door which is thought to date from the 16th century.

As a matter of interest, a family called Shuttleworth is thought to have existed in Chester since the 16th century, or perhaps even earlier, with one Sir Richard Shuttleworth being recorded as the Chief Justice of the County in 1593, although whether or not this is the same family is unclear. However, one of the main supporting beams forming the roof of the cellar is reported to carry the date 1593, marking a connection between this family and the building.

Somewhere within this same general area of Bridge Street, during the reign of Henry VIII a particularly unlucky Welshman called Tudor ap Thomas was reported to have owned a mansion in Chester. Unfortunately for him, in 1491, it was reported that his young child was killed when an object fell from St Peter's church and struck them, presumably as they played in the street below. As if that was not unlucky enough, it was also said that the same man then suffered a second tragedy, when his wife fell down the stairs of the house and subsequently died of her injuries. Clearly, the city of Chester was not a happy or indeed fortunate place for this particular family, although whether or not Thomas remained in the city in unknown.

The most northerly side street on the western flank of modern day Bridge Street is **Commonhall Street**, which derives its name from Chester's long since extinct Common or Moot Hall that used to stand in this area of the city. In the 15th century various plots of land, in and around Commonhall Street were reported to be in the hands of a family called Loyaldon, who in 1446 was granted a void plot of land and in 1488 purchased a second site close by. Although it isn't entirely clear who owned the properties prior to these dates, it has been suggested that were probably owned by members of the prominent Norris and Smith families who were thought to have owned substantial assets in the city.

During the Roman period much of this section of the military fortress was reported to have been given over to food storage, most notably the cereal grains which formed a staple part of the legionary's diet, principally in the form of bread. Stored in stone built buildings known as **Horrea's**, a great deal of time and money was spent on constructing these grain stores, because their content was so important to the health, well-being and perhaps more importantly, the loyalty of the Roman troops who occupied the fortress. It was not unheard of for legionary's to mutiny because their grain supply was reduced or spoilt by pests, so it was important that these granaries and their contents were well built and maintained by the fortress' commanders.

Typically, the ground floor of these great storage houses stood aloft from the surrounding land, reducing the likelihood of it being infiltrated by pests, such as rats; and allowing a free flow of cooling air to circulate below the stored grains, thereby reducing the incidence of damp or mould. Within the inner space of the building itself, there were thought to be a large number of individual bays, each of which held large wooden containers to hold the valuable crops, which presumably could be used to hold entirely different types of cereal grain, from corn to barley. It has also been reported that in some instances, parts of these great food stores was also given over to the storage of other legionary foodstuffs, including the various vegetables and fruits eaten by the soldiers, as well as the various meats which formed part of the regular legionary diet. According to archaeological records the Roman Horrea's were located on the northern side of today's Commonhall Street, a site now inhabited by terraced housing, car parking and the offices of the Chester Chronicle.

Chester's **Common Hall of Pleas** or Moot Hall which was recorded as early as 1318 was noted as a Court that dealt with entirely civil matters relating to Corporation business, including property disputes, ownership and local regulations, with cases being heard by the Mayor and a number of the city's Aldermen. The Common Hall was also reported to have held the city's Coroner's Court, where inquests were heard before two local Coroners who would determine an individual's cause of death, their offices having existed at Chester since 1299.

The city's Public Assizes were also said to have been held within the Common Hall, with the visiting judges holding court in both the city itself, for local criminal matters and also at the Castle for those miscreants who were charged with having committed crimes against the Crown. By 1545 however, these courts were reported to have been relocated to the former Chapel of St Nicholas in Northgate Street, leaving the old Common Hall to be used for a variety of other purposes. Following its demise as the city's Moot Hall, the building in Commonhall Street was said to have been used as a secure storage facility, to hold goods brought into the city for sale, but on which taxes or tolls were still outstanding. By 1547 though, the use of the building was reported to have been granted by the city's Mayor and Corporation to one Ralph (Rauff) Goodman.

Later still, this same general area was said to have been partially inhabited by a Shot Tower and Lead Works which was reported to have been owned by a Mr Mellor and was thought to be the predecessor of the much larger and more modern Lead Company that was established in the Boughton suburbs around 1800. According to some local sources, Mr Mellor was more notable for the fact that he was said to be the final person to be buried in the ancient St Bridget's churchyard, which stood at the southern junction of Bridge Street until 1826, when the church was relocated to the Castle Esplanade to make way for the new Grosvenor Street.

Another early property that was known to have stood on the southern side of Commonhall Street was the "Sugar House", which along with many of the other industrial buildings in this area, occupied lands that prior to the 1540's had been in the possession of the city's Carmelite Order or White Friars. According to early records, this Sugar House had been established by a merchant called Anthony Henthorn in 1697, but became far more notable for being the birthplace of the architect, artist and designer Sir John Vanbrugh, whose father lived and worked there.

During an architectural survey conducted around 1947, several notable properties were noted in Commonhall Street, including No's 39 and 41 at the junction with Weaver Street, which were described as adjoining late 18th century houses. Additionally, No's 24 and 26 are reported to have been designed by the architect T M Lockwood in 1889, as staff quarters for the city's Brown's Department Store.

At the south east junction of Commonhall Street and Bridge Street, a city tavern called the "Harp and Crown" was reported in 1707, later still becoming the "Grotto Inn" and in modern times occupied by Liberty's retail clothes outlet. In 1590, this very same site was thought to have been in the possession of one Sir Rouland Pole who was reported to have leased or purchased the property from another city notable, William Aldersey.

The hostelry, the Harp and Crown, is somehow associated with the legendary "Blue Posts Inn" which was thought to have been located on the opposite side of Bridge Street and was famed for its notable landlady Elizabeth Mottershead, who was said to have outwitted the agent of Queen Mary, by substituting the monarch's royal warrant for a deck of playing cards. During the 18th century, the second house north of Pierpoint Lane was reported to have been in the possession of Ellen Fletcher, who was possibly related to the family commonly associated with the local "Observer" newspaper. Another man with the same surname was thought to be one Robert Fletcher, a native of County Cork in Ireland, who made his fortune in the city and was reported to have left his mansion in Chester to help maintain a charity that he had founded there.

Pierpoint Lane which leads from the main Bridge Street thoroughfare through to Commonhall Street is thought to be another fairly ancient byway, which has previously been known as Dirty Lane and Mill Lane during its lifetime. The title "Dirty Lane" possibly describes the look of the early passageway, which at the time was little more than a muddy track that had evolved from an even earlier boundary ditch, which was thought to have marked the limits of each individual building plot. As for its other title of Mill Lane, that appears to be self explanatory, although few records or little evidence of a mill having existed in the area have come to light thus far.

The title "Pierpoint" has a number of possible origins, including being named after a family called Petraponte who were reported to be resident in Chester during the 12th century and may have owned a property within the area. However, during the same period, a man called Richard the Clerk de Perpont was mentioned in the first half of the 12th century and one Alice de Pierpoint was reported to be the prioress of St Mary's convent around 1292, suggesting that any, all or none of these might be the source of the modern street's title.

Between Pierpoint Lane and the more southerly White Friars, during the 14th century a property known as "Godweyt" (Godeswine) Hall was reported to have existed. Although its specific location is generally unknown, this early Hall is thought to have been owned by a family called Godweyt who were residents of the city in the 13th century. Although the property itself was thought to have been noted in 1289, during the reign of Edward I, some sources suggest that the family's connection with the city began as early as 1267, in the reign of Henry III.

In Bridge Street itself, Pierpoint Lane was also thought to have marked the northern point of Chester's **Saddler's Row**, the area of the city where the saddle-makers made their living. Although the title Row assumes a location at first floor level, some historians believe that in common with their contemporary tradesmen, the Lorimer's, who inhabited shops and buildings in Northgate Street, the Saddler's actually occupied a long since disappeared street level Row which ran from Pierpoint Lane southward to modern day White Friars. A reference to this part of Bridge Street in 1342, recorded that a man called John Erney, had granted 2 "messuages" and their shops in Saddler's Row to a relative, suggesting that the Erney family were prominent landowners in this area of Chester. This is generally confirmed by an even earlier recorded grant of lands in the Bridge Street area, when one Richard Erney was reported to have granted a property lying alongside the main thoroughfare and running westward to the Common Hall to a David Shipbrook in 1337.

During the Roman period, much of this area of the legionary fortress was thought to have been occupied by a fairly extensive legionary building, possibly a "Scholae", which was an Officers Club, accommodations and bath houses. Archaeological excavations and civil construction work in and around Pierpoint Lane have confirmed the presence of these very early military buildings, with numerous artefacts, including roof tiles being recovered from the site, many embossed with the motif of the 20th Legion Valeria Victrix.

The most striking feature on the eastern flank of Bridge Street is undoubtedly **St Michael's Row**, with its flight of steps leading to the city's main shopping precinct. St Michael's Row and Arcade were originally built in 1910 by T M Lockwood who designed the frontages, rows and arcade in white and gold tiles which were so out of keeping with the "Chester Look" that there followed a vociferous campaign to have the façade taken down and replaced with the much more traditional and publicly acceptable frontage that stands today. The existing façade was said to have been designed by William Lockwood (Thomas' son) and the building work undertaken by local contractor John Mayer & Co. Prior to the construction of T M Lockwood's initial designs, this section of the eastern flank of Bridge Street was said to have been occupied by four individually historic properties, including the Plume of Feathers coaching inn and London House, both of which were demolished to make way for his new development and are noted more fully below.

The much later route of St Michael's arcade which runs eastward from the centre of Bridge Street may mark the line of a much earlier passageway called the "**Black Dog Entry**" that was reported to have linked Bridge Street Row with the now extinct Fleshmonger's Row in the east of the city. Deriving its name from a tavern called the "Black Dog", this hostelry was later reported as a "Coffee House" in Bridge Street in 1782, before the sign was said to have been transferred to another tavern in the suburbs of Boughton at a later date.

The still existing Feathers Lane in Bridge Street recalls an old Coaching Inn called "The Feathers" or perhaps more fully **"The Plume of Feathers"** which was located on the eastern flank of the street, directly opposite to today's Pierpoint Lane. Finally demolished sometime around 1863 to make way for the St Michael's Row development, "The Feathers" was reported to have existed for well over 300 years, although the earliest record for the hostelry is thought to date from 1652, which actually gives it a lifetime of some 200 years. This inn stood over the western edge of the then largely undiscovered Roman Bathhouse complex, although work in the tavern's lower floors was reported to have unearthed various artefacts indicating that Roman architecture was indeed present on the site.

The associated passageway, **Feathers Lane**, is so named because it marked the entrance to the stables and coach yard of the Feathers Inn which were set back from the main street. This thoroughfare was recorded in 1534, although at that time it was known as "Dublin Lane" suggesting an even earlier association with both travel to and trade with Ireland. The inn later became a central coaching and parcels collection centre within the city, but by 1782 it had diminished in status and was being eclipsed by the likes of the White Talbot and Golden Talbot Inns which had sprung up to serve the highly lucrative coaching routes. As for "Feathers Lane" itself, in its earlier form this narrow byway was said to have linked Bridge Street with the more easterly, but now extinct, Fleshmongers Lane, which now lies below the mass of Chester's main shopping precinct. Prior to Thomas Lockwood's redevelopment of St Michael's Row and Arcade around 1910, the houses that sat on either side of this narrow passage were reportedly owned by members of the Goodman family, who were thought to have been responsible for finally closing off the eastern end of this historic lane with their own formal gardens and effectively severing the link between Bridge Street and Fleshmonger's Lane.

Close by and on the same eastern flank of Bridge Street, the "**London Bridge**" Inn was yet another notable tavern of its age which has long since disappeared into the city's vast and extensive history. Reported to have occupied the site of today's no 57 Bridge Street, the 7th house from St Michael's Church in 1542 was owned by Richard Goodman, a Mayor of the city and was a designated Christmas Watch House, obliging its owner to guard the inner precincts of Chester throughout the festive period. Goodman was reported to have leased the property, or at least part of it, to an individual called Percival who was a card maker. The property's later existence as the "London Bridge", firstly as an Inn, then a Tavern, a Vaults and finally as a Hotel all took place within the space of a hundred years or so and as the hostelry finally closed in around 1901, it seems likely that it was first established in around 1800.

Rather than having any connection with the capital's London Bridge, the inn at Chester was reported to have derived its name from adjoining business premises, which were thought to have been called London House and the footbridge which spanned the nearby Feathers Lane. This wooden bridge was removable, so that hayricks carrying feed and bedding to the horses in the nearby Feathers Hotel stables, behind the main street frontages, could make their way through unhindered. As soon as the wagon had passed the bridge would be moved back into place and rejoining the northern and southern walkways. Following the closure of the "Plume of Feathers" around 1863 however, this bridge was said to have been removed and an uninterrupted walkway constructed, although a permanent solution was only introduced sometime around 1891. When the London Bridge property was largely rebuilt in 1901, it was thought to have been renamed as the "London Bridge Hotel", but failed to survive for any length of time and was reported to have closed a short time later.

Although the previously mentioned Goodman (Godeman) family undoubtedly existed in Chester from earlier times, they were thought to have become fairly prominent members of the city's political and business communities in the late 15th and early 16th centuries. Beginning with Richard Goodman, a merchant in Chester around 1498, a William Goodman was reported to have been elected Mayor of the city in 1550, succeeding Edmund Gee who was said to have died of the plague in that year. Around the same time, a man called Rauff Goodman was reported to have been granted an old house called the "Common Hall" and lands alongside, by Sir Thomas Smith, another major Chester landowner. This same grant was also said to have mentioned the Chapel of St Ursula, as "lying close by the Common Hall", with modern day excavations having identified the site of St Ursula's Hospital as being at the south east junction of Commonhall Street, where it meets the equally ancient Pierpoint Lane.

Although the Common Hall, St Ursula's chapel and hospital have long since disappeared and been replaced by successive generations of increasingly modern buildings, the Hospital and Chapel of St Ursula is worth a special mention nonetheless. The hospital was reported to have been founded by Sir Thomas Smith, an eight times Mayor of Chester, who was said to have bequeathed one of his own properties and a number of smaller Alms houses to the charity in the late 15th century. A later property, known as St Ursula's Café, was thought to have been located in nearby Watergate Street, suggesting that although the hospital and chapel were located on the south side of Commonhall Street, they also held properties on the north side of the street, possibly as far as Watergate Street itself.

Number 43 Bridge Street, on the eastern side of the thoroughfare, was formerly **St Michael's Rectory** building which replaced an earlier undercroft and townhouse in 1659 and is associated with the parish church of St Michael's which lies at the south east junction of Bridge Street, but today serves as the city's Heritage Centre. The old Rectory is described as a mid 17th century property, built of timber and plaster and comprised of 4 storeys. It is said to include a fine 18th century staircase and in later years housed an antiques emporium. On the opposite side of the street, No 40 Bridge Street was reported to have been rebuilt by the local architect James Harrison in 1858, the same year that he rebuilt both numbers 51 and 53 on the east side of the same city street.

The **Three Old Arches** in Bridge Street are reported to be the oldest shop front in England, proclaiming a date of 1274 and making them contemporary with a number of the early crypts and under-crofts that exist within this section of the city. The frontage has however, been refaced sometime during its history and more modern windows, frames and sills introduced. The old medieval stone walled hall retains its original late 13th century under-croft which has been employed as part of the street level shops. In its original form, it has been suggested that this building, or another long extinct one, ran on southward, past White Friars, but was later demolished as part of a redevelopment of the area. In 1697 a man called Francis Skellern was reported to have ordered the construction of a stairwell at the south end of the Saddler's Row and perhaps suggests a date for the disappearance of the building which once sat alongside the south end of the Arches property.

On the eastern side of Bridge Street, directly facing the Old Arches, close to and possibly adjoining St Michael's church, an ancient townhouse called **Fitton's Mansion** was reported to have existed in the first half of the 17th century. Reportedly old by the time Charles Fitton inhabited the house around 1617, he was Mayor of Chester in that year and was said to have lived there, up until his death in 1633. Although there are no reports that the house was seriously damaged during the Civil War siege of the city, by 1658 the property had passed into the hands of a man called William Jones who was said to have demolished the old mansion house and replaced it with a number of separate city properties.

Modern day **White Friars** is yet another city thoroughfare that has a long and colourful history and possibly marks the line of the Roman's Via Sagularis, the military roadway that ran immediately behind the defensive walls of the fortress. As with other Chester streets, lanes and byways, White Friars has been known by many historic names and in the 14th century was said to have been referred to as Fustard's Lane, reportedly deriving from the trade name "Fusterer" or saddle-tree maker and marking its connection with the nearby Saddler's Row in Bridge Street.

Prior to the foundation of the Carmelite Friary in around 1290, this street was thought to have been known as Alexander's ("Alysaundres") Lane and possibly reflected the lands ownership or tenure by one Alexander Hare or Harre, who was reported as being the Clerk of Chester. Even earlier than that, it has been suggested that the ancient byway was known as St Bridget's Lane, reflecting its connection with the now long extinct parish church of that name that was said to have existed since 797 AD having been founded by King Offa.

However, from 1290 through to around 1541 the Carmelites inhabited lands granted to them by a Chester Sheriff called Hugh Payne, which comprised 7 "messuages" and the title of the lane was thought to have changed accordingly. Records seems to indicate that the White Friars were busily rebuilding and redeveloping their new religious precincts well into the 14th and 15th centuries, as well as receiving a number of wealthy endowments with which to fund their ongoing work. Unfortunately for the Friars however, by the middle of the 16th century the monarch Henry VIII began his religious purges that saw many of England's historic religious communities dissolved and their assets seized. By the time of its closure, the White Friars property, although relatively small, was said to have extended from White Friars Lane in the south, to Commonhall Street in the north and been bounded by Weaver Street in the west and to the back gardens of Bridge Street in the east (now generally marked by the line of the relatively modern 19th century Bolland's Court)

A member of this particular family, Arthur Bolland, was reported in 1691 as a brewer, although they seem to have been generally associated with Watergate Street by 1700, when members of the family were said to have owned a property next door to the previously mentioned Booth's Mansion. A Thomas Bolland, another beer brewer was noted as a Sheriff of Chester in 1695 and Mayor of the city in 1725 and was probably the son of Arthur, although this has not been confirmed. In 1755, an Alderman Bolland was thought to have built a new property in Bridge Street and in 1817 a passage called Bolland's Entry was recorded, suggesting that the passageway had been constructed by the family in order to access buildings at rear of their new townhouse, possibly the previously noted Bolland's Court.

On the northern side of modern day White Friar's Street Bolland's Court is now the name given to an entry that directly links White Friar's with the more northerly Pierpoint Lane, primarily through the removal of a city building that once stood on the site of the new passageway. The western junction of this new thoroughfare is inhabited by White Friar's Lodge, which displays a construction date of 1884, although the rear gable of the property has obviously been rebuilt in more recent times. This particular house has been credited to the skills of the renowned 19th century architect T M Lockwood. Embedded into this rear wall is a stone plaque recording that when the house was first constructed a number of Roman artefacts were discovered, including remains of a Roman hypocaust. It is also noted on the stone recording that these items were found some three feet below a tiled the floor, which was thought to have belonged to the Carmelite monastery that later inhabited the site. On the west side of White Friar's Lodge is the property known as White Friar's Cottage, which may in fact be of a much earlier building, but its specific construction date is unclear.

The discovery of Roman remains on the site of today's White Friar's Lodge would not be of any great significance, had it not been for the presence of the remains of a hypocaust, which are generally associated with more important and better quality Roman structures that were often built within a permanent legionary camp. Added to the fact that this unidentified building appears to have lain relatively close to the southern wall of the fortress is also interesting, given that in most cases any important buildings would have been sited close to the centre and not close to the defensive ramparts. However, it has previously been reported that an Officer's Club or Scholae had existed to the west of today's Bridge Street, so the artefacts discovered in White Friar's might well be associated with that particular building and account for the remains of the hypocaust heating system.

Following the Dissolution of the Monasteries by Henry VIII, many, if not all of the seized religious properties in Chester were said to have been held in the possession of one John Cocks and it was only in May 1544 that parts of the former White Friars lands were returned to local ownership when they were granted to one Fulk Dutton and Edmund Gamul in 1583. Although they were reported to have occupied the living quarters of the former Friary for an extended period, eventually the substantial property was thought to have been sold to Thomas Egerton in around 1597, who at the time held the office of Attorney General and later had the whole White Friars property demolished to make way for a brand new city mansion.

Although this new Egerton Mansion was reported to have been one of the finest in the city, it was said to have been little used by the family, although it was known to have remained in their possession right through to the 18th century, before it too suffered a similar fate to its predecessor and was taken down. Its former site is now occupied by a property called "The Friars" or "Friars House" which is described as a detached 18th century house, standing within its own large gardens. According to architectural sources the front of the building is generally late 18th century, whilst the rear is slightly earlier, suggesting that the house has been extensively renovated and enlarged during its lifetime. The western side of the formal gardens is said to include a sandstone wall that marks its boundary with Weaver Street and is thought by some historians to originate from the 13th century and the long disappeared Carmelite Friary.

Throughout the length of modern day White Friars, the street is generally inhabited by a large number of 18th century terraced properties, most notably on the southern flank and many of which have now been transformed into city centre office spaces. The odd exception to this is No 1 White Friars which is reportedly known as and often called the "Old House", referring to its recorded construction date of 1658 and its description as a two-storey timber frame and plaster built property. In 1962 this house was reported to overhang the sidewalk and was said to once been the former home of the renowned dissenting minister, Matthew Henry, who was such a prominent figure in Chester during the 17th century.

However, on the north side of the narrow lane, there are a number of individual properties that can either trace their origins much further back in time, or have a much more interesting history than their more southerly counterparts. This includes the previously mentioned "Friars House" and the property known as "Bank House".

The latter named property is notable for its relatively short-lived history as a Chester bank, which was founded in the second half of the 18th century by two businessmen, called Thomas and Hesketh. The bank itself was unusual in that it issued its customers with bank notes that had a black background and white lettering, which led to the business becoming known as the "Black Bank". Regardless of this particularly unique feature though, the bank was reported to have stopped paying people in 1793 and was subsequently liquidated. In a bitter twist of fate perhaps, the man given the task of liquidating the business, Thomas Williams, went on to found his own highly successful bank in Chester with a Mr Deacons and ultimately established the "Old Bank Building" that remains in Foregate Street today.

In 1750 the "**White Horse Inn**" was recorded to have stood at the junction of White Friars Lane and Bridge Street, presumably close to the now extinct St Bridget's Church. Existing since 1673 this tavern was reported to have been owned by the Heath family, but by 1810 this particular hostelry had been removed to a new location in Eastgate Street where it was recorded as a city polling station in that year. Prior to carrying the sign of the White Horse, the site was said to have been occupied by yet another tavern called the "Horse and Baggs", although little information is known about this much earlier hostelry.

Following the relocation of the White Horse in 1810, its former home in Bridge Street was then occupied by the "King's Head Hotel", a city hostelry that subsequently managed to survive right through to the late 20th century. This hotel was notable for the fact that John McCafferty, the leader of a Fenian gang that planned a raid on the armoury at Chester Castle, was reported to have stayed there as part of his preparation for the armed incursion. Unfortunately for McCafferty and his compatriots, one of their accomplices had forewarned the authorities about the planned assault and troops were rushed to Chester, leading to the planned attack being abandoned by the Irish sympathisers.

Chester's Heritage Centre, formerly **St Michael's Church** is thought to date from the end of the 15th century and was largely rebuilt by architect James Harrison in 1850, but was finally deconsecrated in the early 1970's and re-opened as the city's Heritage Centre in 1975. More information on this building is noted in the chapter dealing with Grosvenor and Pepper Streets.

On the opposite side of Bridge Street, standing slightly south of St Michael's Church and towards Pepper Street, the ancient **St Bridget's Church** was reported to have stood in the city since the reign of King Offa and to have first been raised on the site sometime before

the monarch's death in AD 797. Sitting atop the western side of the former fortress' southern gateway, this church was thought to have been closely associated with the city's resident Welsh congregation, although it was known to have been a popular place of worship for the many citizens who lived within its parish boundaries. This first church was reported to have been taken down during the middle of the 17th century, possibly as a result of damage it suffered during the Parliamentary siege of Chester during the English Civil War, but more likely to improve the fabric of the ancient church, which by then would have existed in Chester for nearly 900 years.

Less than 150 years later however, in 1786, St Bridget's was once again in need of repair and in conjunction with this restoration work, the church's physical footprint was thought to have been altered, to allow greater and wider access to Bridge Street from the south. Some 40 years later though, in 1826, the decision was made to take down St Bridget's church and a number of other historic buildings to make way for the new thoroughfare called Grosvenor Street, which linked the soon to be opened Grosvenor Bridge with the heart of the city, and at the same time deliberately ignored the uniform grid-like layout which had been successfully employed at Chester for the previous 1800 years.

However, the future of St Bridget's in Chester was thought to have been assured, when the decision was made to construct a new church, dedicated to the same saint, at a site close to Thomas Harrison's brand new castle complex. Work began on the new church on October 27th 1827, to the designs of Mr William Cole Junior, a local architect who had formerly been a pupil of Harrison and the man who would ultimately complete the construction of the nearby Grosvenor Bridge. With the new church completed by its builder Mr John Wright, the city's old parish of St Martin's in the Ash was reported to have been amalgamated with the new St Bridget's to serve the community in this particular sector of Chester, despite the presence of the nearby church of St Mary's on the hill which had been serving this part of the city for centuries.

Possibly as a direct result of these earlier, pre-existing parishes, with their already well established congregations, the new church of St Bridget's failed to flourish in its new home and so in 1892 the decision was made to do away with this reportedly unfashionable church for the second and final time, ending over a thousand years of existence in the city. Recalled only by occasional parish marker stones which exist throughout the general area, the most tangible record of this ancient church's existence is the single archway that still stands as a visitor attraction in the city's Grosvenor Park and the large traffic roundabout which stands close to Chester's 18th century castle. When the city's new inner ring road system was laid out during the 1960's a number of those who had previously been interred at the long extinct church of St Bridget's were reported to have been moved to the new cemetery at Blacon, including the remains of perhaps Chester's greatest architect Thomas Harrison.

South of the historic church and lying close to the still standing Falcon Inn, an old building called the "**Old Lamb Row**" was in existence until 1821 when it suddenly and unexpectedly collapsed into the street. Reported to have been owned by a member of the

Randle Holme family, this historic building was said to have included a hostelry called Ye Old Lamb, from where it derived its name. Few local inhabitants were thought to have mourned its loss however, as this ageing property was said to have been little more than an obstruction for many years and its disappearance finally allowed the main thoroughfares to be opened up.

The "Old Lamb Row" was reported to have first been constructed in 1670 on land that was owned by a man called Hunt, but which was leased by members of the Randle Holmes family, who engaged a local builder called William Hughes to build the new property. Beset by legal problems from the outset, the terrace only remained in the possession of the Holmes family until around 1707 when it was sold and was subsequently owned by a succession of private individuals, most of whom allowed its fabric to deteriorate over time.

Comprising the "Old Lamb" hostelry, from where the building gained its name, the remainder of the terrace was said to have been given over to private accommodations which were rented from these private landlords. Finally, by 1821 it was thought to be in such a dilapidated condition that a large section of the property unexpectedly collapsed into the street, mercifully without injuring anyone in the process, but requiring the whole edifice to be demolished for safety's sake. Although the building was not replaced, the name and memory of the "Old Lamb Row" was thought to have been retained in the "Old Lamb Vaults" tavern which was established in the area sometime later.

CHAPTER FOURTEEN

LOWER BRIDGE STREET

The modern day **Lower Bridge Street** continues to mark the route southward out of the city and in Roman times was thought to have led to both the first bridge thrown across the River Dee and to a shallow fording point which was reported to have lain between the site of today's County Hall and Edgar's Field on the southern bank of the river. Apart from a previously discussed Roman "Mansio" building which was thought to have stood close to the site of Chester's later medieval castle, the only other Roman feature of note in this area was reported to be a raised platform of some description which lay in the area of modern day Duke Street and has been speculated to be an embankment associated with their early bridges or possibly an as yet unidentified defensive or settlement feature.

Lying immediately outside of the southern gate of the fortress, the Porta Praetoria, the legionary roadway which later became modern day Lower Bridge Street was thought to have linked this early military base with the Roman's Watling Street, which lay further to the south. It has also been suggested that at its most northern limit, that is to say just outside of the southern gate, this roadway formed a junction with a long disappeared minor road that was reported to have run in a southwest direction towards the site of the later castle, but was possibly directly linked to the Mansio building which was known to have stood in that same general area.

Although during the Roman occupation of Britain, this roadway or street was known to lie outside of the fortress' defences, it was undoubtedly under the legionaries control and was probably inhabited by relatively small numbers of civilians, both Roman and British. Even after the Roman's had largely abandoned the base in the late 4th century, this area still lay outside of the main civilian settlement; and remained so until the late 9th and early 10th centuries when it was finally enclosed by the Anglo Saxon leader, Aethelflaeda. It was King Alfred's daughter, who was reported to have ordered the construction of the first extensive timber and stone palisade that finally incorporated this southern area of the much larger post Roman settlement into the city's historic limits.

Even after its inclusion within Chester's military defences, the area still appears to have been sparsely populated in comparison to the northern half of the city that was formerly occupied by the Roman fortress; and was reportedly inhabited by a relatively small number of people who were employed in the leather manufacturing industries, coin production, as well as seafarers who based themselves on the River Dee and traded goods throughout continental Europe. This was thought to especially true for the small, but vibrant Hiberno Norse community which was thought to have existed in this southern part of the city during the Anglo Saxon period and whose presence is still recalled by ancient St Olave's church and Chester's historic "Wolf Gate", both of which continue to stand in the city today.

By the middle of the 11th century Chester was known to be one of the principal sea ports and trading centres in all of Britain; and was generally celebrated as the premier city of northwest England. It was also noted as the final English city to fall to the armies of the Norman Duke, William the Conqueror, who was reported to have captured Chester in 1070, nearly four years after he had beaten the Anglo Saxon leader Harold at the Battle of Hasting's. Although the city was said to have been "wasted" because of its resistance to his rule, this retribution may in fact have been largely confined to the southern section of the city and was not so much an act of revenge, but a clearance of the area that would later house his castle. It has been suggested that many of the earlier Anglo Saxon properties that stood in the area, which were almost entirely timber built, were destroyed by fire to provide a defensive zone around the new Norman Castle site, which would have housed the then new and undoubtedly nervous foreign garrison.

As elsewhere in the city, it was the during the reign of the Norman Earl's and their cohorts that much of Chester began to be extensively laid out and developed, with single plots and large swathes of land being granted to and purchased by individual noblemen and wealthy merchants, all of whom were well placed to take advantage of this new property bonanza.

By the 17th century this part of the city was reported to have been occupied by a number of fairly luxurious and important private houses, a small number of which continue to stand through to the modern day. At the same time this particular section of the city had the less than desirable distinction of being sited within Chester's "Beast Market" ward, attributed to the presence of the city's livestock markets which were thought to have existed on land bounded by the gardens of Lower Bridge Street and Chester's eastern wall. The northern boundary of these beast markets were said to have been marked by the gardens of Pepper Street and to the south by the ancient St Olave's Lane. The presence of Fleshmonger's Row lying nearby, as well as a number of the city's leather workers operating within the immediate vicinity, would all seem to indicate that this beast market was a well established feature of the city prior to the 17th century and one that was only finally done away with when the Gorse Stacks market was established in the first half of the 19th century.

The **Falcon Inn** site is thought to have been the location for civilian occupation from around the time of the Norman Conquests and possibly even before that. The buildings medieval undercroft or cellar includes a beam which has been dated from the mid 13th century, whilst two others are thought to pre-date this wooden support and may in fact be 12th century. Significant amounts of the lower stonework is also thought to be 13th century, while much of the timber structures above ground level is reported to be 16th and 17th century.

Having ordered the reconstruction of the townhouse in 1626, in 1643 Sir Richard Grosvenor applied to enclose the public walkway (Row) which fronted his property and began a trend which inevitably led to the loss of most of the Rows in this southern part of the city. Grosvenor was a noted Royalist supporter at the time of the English Civil War and had purchased the house to accommodate his family during the conflict.

The Falcon was reported to have first been licensed as an Inn around 1778 and continued in that role until 1878, when it was restored by John Douglas for the Grosvenor family and turned into a Temperance House, which served its clients only non alcoholic beverages. In 1785, the Falcon Tavern was reported as being run by an individual called Richard Lloyd.

By the mid 1970's the building was deserted and in such a dilapidated condition that it was having to be supported by wooden struts on its northern front, to prevent it's almost certain collapse onto the public footpath which fronted it. In 1980 the building was finally transferred to the ownership of the Falcon Trust and money was raised which allowed the property to be restored to its present condition and once again serving as a Public House.

Bridge House which occupies No's 16-22 Lower Bridge Street was built for Lady Mary Calveley around 1676 and was a replacement for her earlier home, which was said to have included a traditional row. The resulting building was reported to be the first correctly proportioned neo-classical structure in Chester and it was only in the 19th century that the ground floor was extended forward to accommodate retail units. During the 1950's, 60's and 70's these ground floor shop units were said to have been occupied by booking offices for the local Crosville Bus Company. In its original form, the front of the house was reported to have been adorned by an elegant dual staircase, via which both resident and visitor would have accessed the building. Around 1811, the property was said to have accommodated the Bridge House School, which was run by a Mrs Keate's and was said to have boasted substantial gardens at the rear of the house.

In more recent years the building has been called the "Oddfellows Hall", having previously housed the Oddfellows Lodge and Club. The property is primarily associated with the Williams family of Bodelwyddan and in particular one John Williams who was the Attorney General for Chester and Flint, and who was said to have owned this particular townhouse.

During the 20th century, much of the western section of Lower Bridge Street, between Bridge House and the Old Kings Head has been subjected to extensive decay, demolition and rebuilding. Within the terrace, No 36 is described as a late 18th century house built over 4 storeys and No's 38-42 is thought to have previously been one single property, later divided into separate houses.

Tudor House, which is located at no's 29-31 on the eastern side of Lower Bridge Street, was built in 1603, despite its sign previously claiming a date of 1503 and was extended to the rear in the 17th century. The building's present façade was rebuilt around 1728 when its second storey walkway was fully enclosed by its owners. This property is said to stand atop a medieval cellar, which may in fact be contemporary with the building itself, although the neighbouring undercroft at No 27 Lower Bridge Street is thought to originate from the 13th century. It may well be the case that both of these cellars were formerly part of a much larger and earlier medieval building that has been lost over time and subsequently replaced by Tudor House and its adjacent properties.

The house was thought to have been originally built for a wealthy Chester merchant but throughout its history has been employed in various roles, including as a bakery and has also served as the "Britannia Inn". The property was generally restored in 1907, but by the 1940's it had been allowed to deteriorate so badly that the whole structure was leaning badly and parts of the building were deemed to be unsafe. It was only in the second half of the century, with work beginning in 1973, that it has been restored once again to its present condition. For most of the 20th century, as it does today, the house is known to have been occupied by a series of antique emporiums and one of its most notable owners or inhabitants was reported to have been Catherall's of Chester. Next to Tudor House, an old passageway called "Hawarden Castle Entry" is thought to recall an earlier tavern called the "Hawarden Castle" which stood close by.

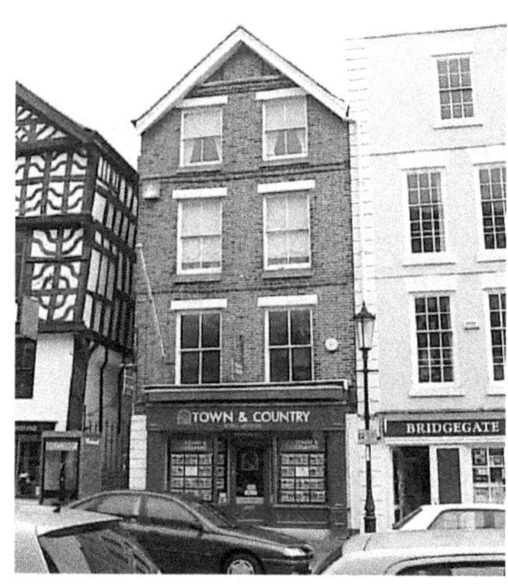

Reported to have been the fifth property down on the east side of Lower Bridge Street, the "Hawarden Castle" was accompanied at one time by another inn called the "Red Lion" which was thought to date from the 17th century and noted as being the third property down from Pepper Street on the east side. In between these two hostelries in 1810 a third tavern, the "**Black Horse**" was reported in that year and was said to have been used as the meeting place for the city's bricklayers company. Although it was said to have been in existence between 1826 and 1827, by 1860 the licence for this particular tavern was said to have lapsed.

Numbers 37 to 41 Lower Bridge Street are commonly known as **Park House**, which was built in 1715 for one Elizabeth Booth who was resident in the city and a niece of George Booth, the Lord Delamere, a notable Royalist figure of the age. The house itself was first noted in Elizabeth's will of February 1732, when she made a charitable bequest of £10 per year to the nearby St Olave's church, which was to be charged against the property. When she died in 1736, Elizabeth was reportedly unmarried and therefore without issue and so her property passed into the hands of her relative Thomas Ravenscroft, while Ms Booth herself was said to have been buried in the nearby village of Hawarden.

By 1769 the Park House property was reported to have passed into the possession of one Bagut Read of Chester and was said to have remained in his family's hands up until 1820. However, by 1809 the property was thought to have been occupied by one Joseph Dale, who lived in the house with his wife until his death in 1814 and who was said to have extensively landscaped the grounds of Park House, creating formal gardens and orchards which were reported to have become known locally as Dale's Park. Following Joseph's death, his widow was said to have remained in the house, until she too passed away in 1818, when the property once again changed ownership.

Having been further extended and improved in the late 18th and early 19th centuries, the house was subsequently purchased by a group of local businessmen who intended to turn the private house into an Inn with a bowling green and billiard room, becoming the **Albion Hotel** in 1818 and later in 1831, the Talbot Hotel. It has also been suggested that No 35 Lower Bridge Street once formed part of this much more extensive hotel complex. At the same time, this same group of investors were reported to have purchased another property, situated directly opposite Park House, which was said to have been occupied by a family called Hunt and that the new owners intended to convert into the Albion Newsroom, which was completed in 1827.

By 1855 the hotel's large central hall was commonly being used as a ballroom and as the largest public rooms in the city it also served as Chester's main Assembly Room and played host to many of the most memorable civic events held in the city. It was also said to be one of the main coaching establishments in Chester, with its extensive stables and coach houses being used to accommodate many of the horses and carriages from other city taverns and hotels. Such was its reputation at the time that it was reported to have no superior in all of Chester and in December 1820 was the site for a civic banquet held in the honour of the Duke of Wellington who was visiting the city.

Between 1849 and 1887 the hotel was reported to have played host to Chester's Archaeological Society, although by 1859 the hotel was reportedly up for sale and by 1873 the licence had ceased to exist. In 1887, the Archaeological Society had relocated to the brand new Grosvenor Museum building and by 1910 Park House was reported to be occupied by the Chester Working Boy's Home, before being inhabited by the Libraries Department of Cheshire County Council.

At No 44, on the west side of Lower Bridge Street, remedial work during the early 1970's found evidence of a much earlier timber framed building, which had been set further back, than its current successor stands. Almost opposite to this house, numbers 45 to 47 on the eastern side of Lower Bridge Street is known as **Liverpool House** and is simply described as an 18th century property which has been extensively refurbished during the 19th and 20th centuries. Interestingly, this name has now been transferred to a generally new building that occupies a site on the eastern side of Lower Bridge Street, but is unconnected with its former namesake.

On the western side again and adjoining Castle Street, the **Old Kings Head Inn**, which is located at 48-50 Lower Bridge Street dates from around 1622 and is generally associated with the Randle Holmes family, heralds and historians in the city. Earlier still, the site was reported to have housed the former home of Richard de Paris, a master mason who undertook work at the nearby medieval castle and whose properties were being sold by his daughter in around 1317. It is perhaps worth noting that this hall was entirely separate from the much more renowned Paris' or Hawarden Hall which stood on the opposite site of the street and was sited next to the ancient church of St Olave's which remains today.

In 1524, the site of the Old King's Head was reported to have been generally uninhabited and was recorded as gardens which were sold or granted to one Randle Brereton, who was then the Vice Chancellor of Chester. Immediately prior to his ownership, these lands were said to have been in the possession of two brothers, Joseph and Thomas Aston, although little more is known about these two individuals. However, it is Brereton who has been largely credited with constructing the first houses on these former gardens, which by the early 17th century was reported to have been inhabited by William Ball, Randle Holme, Thomas Wright and Margaret Hooker.

In 1622 however, Randle Holme was reported to have rebuilt his own property, a fact that is noted above the doorway of the present day building, presumably because Brereton's original houses were either too small or poorly constructed. Having rebuilt their family home though, by 1670 the Holmes' were thought to have relocated to the Old Lamb's Row, which formerly occupied a site at the junction of Bridge Street and Lower Bridge Street; and which resulted in the city Herald being sued in the courts by his builder.

Much of the frontage of the Old Kings Head is 17th century, which has been restored on a number of occasions and the early Public Walkway or Row on the buildings first floor level was thought to have been lost during the 18th century when the trend to enclose these previously public thoroughfares was led by the Grosvenor family who had set the precedent at the nearby Falcon Inn. The Old Kings Head was said to have first been licensed around 1717 and during the 20th century the building has undergone two distinct phases of restoration, in the 1930's and then again in the 1960's.

Although the Old Kings Head remains one of Chester's most historic and popular taverns, only a relatively small part of the building is thought to be used for that particular purpose. Within the remainder of the property and generally unseen by the patrons, the house is thought to include a number of important features which directly relate to its past and to the Holme family's former occupancy. These are said to include, oak panelling, an oak staircase and a fireplace bearing the arms of the Randle Holmes family.

Gamul House, at 52-58 Lower Bridge Street, is thought to have its foundation in the early 1500's, but has since been heavily refurbished in the 17th century, when it was re-faced in brick and had elliptical windows introduced. Thought to contain the remnants of a late Jacobean hall of around 1620, it was later used to house individual shop units and high density living accommodations. By 1760, Gamul House and Cottage was no longer a private family residence, but instead were being used to house a city dancing academy and in 1819 part of the house were being used to host a local Baptist congregation. It was thought to be from this period onwards that much of the buildings historic fabric was allowed to deteriorate and it was only in the late 20th century that affirmative action was taken to rescue it from almost certain collapse.

By 1831, the building had been sub-divided into a number of low quality residences, with other parts being used as an Organ builder's workshop, an antiques showroom and finally an architect's office. In the early 1970's the roof of the main hall was said to have collapsed, forcing its tenants to abandon the building. So concerned were the local authorities, about the condition of the building that in 1973 they purchased the hall and set about rescuing the property.

The early Great Hall, which is said to stand on the left hand side of the extensive building, was generally restored by the local authorities, although they were unable to replace the gallery which had been lost over time. However, they were able to conserve the ornate ceiling, painted panel work, elaborate carvings and perhaps more importantly the Jacobean chimney piece which is a central feature of the Hall. This particular element is thought to include the arms of the Gamul family which was said to have been designed by the equally notable and Royalist Randle Holme, whose family home lay on the opposite side of Castle Street.

The building bears the name of the Gamul family and is perhaps more commonly associated with Sir Francis Gamul, the Mayor of Chester in 1635, who entertained King Charles I at his home during the English Civil War period when the fated monarch visited the generally Royalist city. It was said to be as a direct result of Gamul's Royalist sympathies and active participation against the Parliamentarian forces that much of their fortune and political influence was inevitably lost or sequestered.

On the opposite side of the street to Gamul House, No 53 Lower Bridge Street is a small 17th century timber cottage building which is on the corner of **St Olave's Street**. It is a 3 storey property dating from around 1700 and may have once formed part of the later mentioned Old Coach Row, which used to occupy this section of the main thoroughfare. It has been suggested that this house was constructed by an individual called Mather who lived and worked in the city, although whether or not this was a John Mather, who owned a malt mill in nearby Clayton Lane (Duke Street) during the 18th century, is unclear. The modern day property is said to sit on top of an undated medieval cellar, suggesting that the building which stands today is simply a successor to a much earlier structure.

The ancient sandstone church of **St Olave's**, from which the lane derives its name, is thought to date from the pre-Norman period and is generally associated with the Christian monarch and martyr, Olaf, the Norwegian king who was said to have been killed at the Battle of Sticklestadt in 1030. Reportedly dedicated to the quickly canonized martyr by Chester's local Scandinavian community, just a few years after Olaf's death, some sources have suggested that this church was not recorded in the Domesday record of 1086 and may therefore not have existed prior to that date.

However, the church and its lands were certainly noted during the reign of Earl Richard D'Avranches who held Chester between 1101 and 1120, when a nobleman called Robert Pincerna (the Butler), who held the manor of Poulton, was reported to have granted St Olave's to the newly founded Abbey of St Werburgh's. It seems possible therefore that the church had indeed originated from the pre-Conquest period, but had been dedicated to another, as yet unidentified saint and had only been rededicated to St Olaf sometime after 1030, but before the Norman capture of Chester in 1070.

It is also worth noting, that in 1216 several other parcels of lands in St Olave's Lane were reported to be in the possession of a family called Lippard, which later passed into the hands of Roger the Falconer through his marriage to their daughter Lucy. Later still, these same lands were thought to have passed to members of the prominent Egerton family, sometime during the 14th century. Standing close to this historic church and lying southward on the same sandstone plateau there formerly stood a Great Hall built by the renowned 13th century mason and military engineer, Richard L'enginour. A prominent Chester citizen of the 13th century, the engineer was thought to have been involved with the redevelopment of Chester Castle during the reigns of both Henry III and his successor, the militaristic Edward I. L'enginour was also said to have been involved with the creation of Edward's ring of Welsh castle's and in later years was elected as a

Mayor of Chester. Following his death, the Hall adjoining St Olave's was reported to have passed into the hands of one of his children, Almaric Le Gynour, who subsequently sold the property.

L'enginour's former home was then said to have been purchased by another master mason called Richard de Paris who renamed the property Paris' Hall. He was also thought to have owned another hall on the opposite side of Bridge Street, now occupied by the "Old Kings Head", which was reportedly sold by his daughter sometime at the beginning of the 14th century. Richard's son was thought to have been called Robert and traded in Chester as a Boot-maker and it was his son, also called Robert who was later thought to have become Chamberlain of the city.

Paris' Hall was alternatively known as Pares Hall or Hawarden Hall and in earlier times, it has been suggested that this land had been owned by an individual called "Richard the Skinner", which given the presence of the leather industries in this part of the city, both before and after the Norman conquests might well be true. Its later designation as Hawarden Hall is thought to originate from the name of the "Aderne" family, whose title was occasionally corrupted or altered to Hawarden.

From the time of its original construction by L'enginour, this Hall was known to have been rebuilt and altered by its various owners, including Paris and the later Aderne family. By 1752 therefore, the building was generally described as being Elizabethan in style, a fact that was particularly noted when much of it was destroyed by fire in that year. Despite such calamities however, elements of the early buildings were still in evidence by 1820, when the remaining parts of the Hall were reportedly being used as the site for one of Chester's many 19th century breweries, but this too has long since disappeared. Operating from around 1820 this brewing business was reported to have been owned and run by a partnership of two individuals called Newell and Gamon, one of whom was a city Alderman.

By 1831 though many of these buildings, including the old Hall and the later mentioned Old Coach Row were all swept away in another round of city modernisation, their former home being marked today by the relatively modern mass of the Quick's Car Showroom, which is now occupied by one of Chester's local newspaper businesses.

Prior to 1831, a fairly historic hostelry known as the "Crown and Angel" was reported to have stood in St Olave's Street, possibly when the **Old Coach Row** was still in existence during the first half of the 19th century. This tavern may later have become known as the "Old Coach Inn" which was reported to have been located there between 1809 and 1817. Otherwise known as "Rotten Row" this raised pathway was said to have run southward from the northern flank of St Olave's Lane to Duke Street and included; the Old Coach Inn, a plasterers business and the house of a man called Ankers Smith. As noted earlier though, this whole area now lies buried beneath the mass of the previously mentioned car showroom building, but evidence of its former presence still exist on the south face of the retaining wall to St Olave's main entrance.

Today's **Duke Street** was formerly known as both Claverton Lane and Clayton Lane; and during the 16th century was reported to be occupied by two generally large plots of land that stretched from the eastern side of the main thoroughfare to the eastern wall of the city itself, all of which was said to be in the possession of one Robert Brerewood. Today, Duke Street runs eastward from Lower Bridge Street towards the city's walls, where it adjoins the relatively modern day Park Street. However, up until the late 18th or early 19th century the whole of this thoroughfare, running from Lower Bridge Street to Chester's old "Newgate" (or Wolf Gate) was known as Claverton's or Clayton's Lane and only became Park Street after the gardens of Park House (later the Albion Hotel) were laid out by Mr Dale between 1809 and 1814. The six of nine original Alms Houses which continue to occupy the western flank of modern day Park Street, close to Chester's current "Newgate" arch, were first constructed by Robert Harvey in 1662, when the thoroughfare was still commonly known as Clayton Lane.

This early lane can reportedly trace its origins back to the first years of the Norman occupation of Chester, purportedly being recorded in the Domesday record of 1086. A hundred or more years later, in 1202, it was said to have been recorded again, although some sources have suggested that both of the "Claverton Lane's" in question were in fact outside of the city and associated with the long disappeared village of Claverton, which now lies below the lands of the modern Eaton Estates.

Although there were known to be a limited number of shops, tenements or "messuages" in the area which were generally associated with a long since extinct "Capel" or "Horse" gate that existed in the area, these particular lands seem to have only been developed during the 17th and 18th centuries. Certainly by the beginning of the 18th century, the narrow passageway that still exists today below the so-called Wishing Steps is thought to date from around 1707; and has been attributed to Chester's Glover's Company, who were said to have had a meeting house in this immediate area.

It is possible that the building used by the Glover's Company may have been connected with the property known as "Clayton House", which recalled the thoroughfares early name and suggested as being the home of Roger Comberbach, a Recorder of Chester during the same period and for whom the nearby "Recorder's Steps" were first constructed. This house lies on the southern flank of Duke Street, close to the eastern wall and was said to have been owned by members of the Soreton family, who were themselves said to be Glover's and Skinners. From around 1902, Clayton House was reportedly being occupied by a Mr Hyde who hosted a School of Commerce within the building, but in later times the property was reported to have been converted into separate flats and tenements.

A second property in the area that had a general link with the leather trade and therefore the city's Glover's Company was Windsor House, which was said to have been built by a Mr Dodd around 1812, although on the very same site as a much earlier property. Reportedly a Merchant Skinner by trade, Mr Dodd's property was thought to have stood at the bottom of the "Wishing Steps" and so once again might have been the location for the 18th century Glover's meeting house. However, there is a suggestion that this second property, the one built in 1812, may well have been taken down in 1924 and subsequently replaced with a much more modern property once again.

The **Cross Keys Inn** which stands on the south side of the street adjoining Bridge Place is thought to have occupied the site since the 1740's, when it was kept by one John Beavan,

making it one of Chester's oldest licensed establishments. The tavern is one of a few properties that have managed to survive the rigours of modernisation that have regularly swept the streets of Chester, as is testified by the presence of the modern mass of the previously mentioned former Quick's building that occupies the opposing flank of today's Duke Street. However, this generally overlooked city street does still contain a small number of late 18th century properties that relate to the history of this particular section of Chester. The title of Duke Street itself is reported to have been named after one Thomas Duke, a former Alderman and Mayor of Chester who was thought to be a major landowner in this section of the city, its name being altered from Clayton Lane (aka Claverton Lane) to Duke Street sometime around 1795.

Immediately adjoining the old Cross Keys Inn is **Bridge Place** which fronts Lower Bridge Street and lies close to the city's 18th century Bridgegate archway. It is a terrace of private houses built in the second half of the 18th century, although not uniform in construction. No 5 Bridgegate House is thought to pre-date the others by around two decades and unlike the remaining properties is built over four storey's as opposed to three. Most of the properties were renovated during the latter part of the 20th century as part of a local improvement scheme. It has been speculated that during the medieval period, this same area was inhabited by a small number of workshops and tenements, which led to and from the long disappeared "Capel" or "Horse" Gate that used to exist in the city's southern wall.

On the western side of Lower Bridge Street, standing opposite Duke Street and Bridge Place is yet another of Chester's historic thoroughfares, a relatively short and narrow lane called **Shipgate Street**. This street undoubtedly derives its name from the ancient "Ship Gate" which used to form part of the city's southern defences, being a postern gate through which people and goods could be brought into the city by way of a ferry that ran between both banks of the river. However, it has also been suggested that the name "Ship-gate" is actually a corruption of "Sheep-gate" implying that livestock were brought into the city through this old entrance way, having been brought across a fording point in the river, which may have existed since Roman times. Either way, this old archway was finally removed in 1831 and relocated to the Grosvenor Park, where it continues to stand as a simple landscape feature.

According to some sources, the great age of this gate is confirmed by the fact that the portal was first noted in the records of St Werburgh's Abbey as early as 1121 and 1129. Others however, suggest that the ancient Ship-gate actually pre-date's these early records and was in existence during the rule of the Anglo Saxon ruler Aethelflaeda, in the late 9th and early 10th centuries. These same sources also contend that this was the only entrance into the city until the reign of Edward the Confessor (1042-1066), when the first of a series of wooden bridges was reported to have been constructed across the River Dee.

Commonly known by local people as the "hole-in-the-wall" despite its reported Anglo Saxon foundation the Ship-gate that was removed from the southern flank of Chester in 1831 was undoubtedly of 12th century construction, making it contemporary with the

Abbey records. It was also only one of three gateways that existed along this section of the southern defences during the medieval period. Apart from the Ship-gate itself, there was the main Bridge Gate, the successor of which stands today and the "Capel" or Horse Gate which was known to have existed to the east of the main portal, close to the present day Bridge Place. This particular entrance was reported to have been in existence during the reign of King Edward II (1307-1327)

This whole area of Chester, from the bottom of St Mary's Hill to the city's southern wall and incorporating the modern day Ship-gate Street is thought by some to have been the location for the long extinct Troutbeck Palace, which was reported to have existed during the 15th century and possibly well before that. It was also noted during the 16th century, that the ancient Ship-gate was described as being obsolete by 1534 and was simply seen as a feature of the extensive gardens and grounds of the Troutbeck's imposing property. Given that the Old Dee Bridge is thought to have its foundations in the mid 14th century, thereby rendering any previous crossing out-of-date, the idea that the Ship-gate was generally unused by the 16th century seems entirely likely. The actual existence of this early Troutbeck Palace is undoubtedly supported by the fact that much of this historic family's lands and property's later passed into the possession of the Talbot family, the Earls of Shrewsbury, who later owned the nearby Bear and Billet.

Shipgate House is located at No 2 Shipgate Street in Chester and is thought to be 18th century in construction, although earlier elements may form part of the property. The house's undercroft is thought to be medieval, with the rear of the first floors reported to date from around 1670-80 and the façade being 18th century.

Shipgate Cottage which adjoins Shipgate House also has an 18th century façade, but repair work on the property during the 20th century uncovered medieval oak trusses from the end of the 16th century, indicating a much earlier building which has been substantially altered and added to. Both buildings were in such poor condition by the 1960's that they were purchased by the County Council, ostensibly to make way for building extensions to the nearby County Hall. By 1968, the cottage was in a further state of decay, but changes in conservation issues meant that the properties were ultimately to be saved and restored to their current state, which was completed by the mid 1970's. No 3 Shipgate Street is reported to be a 17th century building, while No 5 was a 19th century addition.

The **Old Edgar** which stands on the junction of Lower Bridge Street and Shipgate Street is thought to date from the Elizabethan period and although originally constructed as two separate houses these were later combined to serve as a Public House. The property was first recorded in 1550, when a John Houghton was said to have been the inn-keeper. The Inn is thought to derive its name from the Anglo Saxon monarch King Edgar who visited the city in 973 AD and was rowed up the River Dee by eight Reguli or subordinate kings, from Edgar's Field across the river in Handbridge to St John's Church on the opposite bank of the Dee. Known as the "Royal Oak" in 1782, the building served as a Public House until 1884 and from 1895 was reported to have been converted back into two private dwellings. However, this 19th century conversion had been so badly carried out,

that the work caused a major damp problem within the corner building. The property had become so dilapidated by the mid 1970's that the council were forced to acquire the building so that it could be saved. A 12 month restoration project undertaken by the authorities successfully managed to secure the two buildings, which was completed by June 1978. During the latter part of the 20th century the property was known to have housed a café, but is now private residential accommodations once again.

The **Bear & Billet** at 94 Lower Bridge Street in Chester is a post-civil war building that was historically the home of the Earls of Shrewsbury, the sergeants of the city's Bridge gate. The timber built property, dating from the 17th century was in private hands until the latter half of the 17th century and was then purchased by the Corporation in 1666. In 1670 it became a Public House and by the middle and late 18th century was recorded as the "Lower White Bear". In 1809 it was simply called "The White Bear" and fifty years later was known as the "Bridge Gate Tavern". By 1880 however, the property had been renamed as the "Bear and Billet", the title it has held through to the present day. By the 1970's the building was thought to be exhibiting structural problems, with its front gable being in an unsafe condition, due in large part to its main timbers having become rotten, through both wet rot and insect infestation.

As mentioned earlier, this property almost certainly occupies part of the site of the 15th century Troutbeck Palace which was said to have inhabited much of this general area and which had passed into the hands of the Talbot family, following the earlier demise of the Troutbeck dynasty. The rebuilding of the property in the 17th century, a beam in the house noting 1664, may be accounted for by the great age of its predecessor, or perhaps more likely, by the damage inflicted on the city by the cannons and mortars of the Parliamentarians during the English Civil War siege of Chester. A long since extinct structure, John Tyrer's Water Tower, was known to have stood close to the Talbot's property during this period and was known to have been heavily damaged during the conflict. It seems sensible to conclude therefore, that the predecessor to the modern day building also sustained limited damage and was subsequently rebuilt by its later owners.

The present day **Bridgegate Arch** which stands in Chester today is known to have replaced a much more formidable defensive entrance that dated from the medieval period and which was known to have been flanked by two substantial stone defensive towers.

A defensive gateway has almost certainly existed here since the late 9th or early 10th century when this whole southern section of the city was finally incorporated into the precincts of Anglo Saxon Chester, by King Alfred's renowned daughter, Aethelflaeda. It is probably also true to suggest, that this ancient entrance point has developed in tandem with the Old Dee Bridge, the river crossing that it was fundamentally designed to facilitate and protect. According to some sources, the first permanent timber bridge across the Dee was raised during the reign of the Anglo Saxon monarch, Edgar, in 958 AD and if this is true, then the first of many successive gateways would also date from this period.

Inextricably linked to the city's 4 main gateways is the post of "serjeant" or the keeper of the gate who was held responsible for collecting the relevant tolls and taxes on goods being brought into Chester for sale. At the Bridge-gate, the first reference to these historic post-holders is said to have been reported in the late 12th or early 13th centuries, when the Earl of Chester, Randle Blundeville, is thought to have granted the title to a man called Poynz, a servant of his wife, the Countess of the Earldom. For the next four hundred years or more, this vitally important and financially lucrative post was thought to have been filled by members of some of Chester's most prominent and inter-related families. These have included the Raby's, Holes, Erney's, Troutbeck's and finally the Talbot's who were thought to have surrendered their rights to this particular post in the middle of the 17th century.

In common with much of Chester's earliest architecture, the southern gate of the city, the Bridge-gate, was probably constructed in stone during the reigns of the various Norman Earl's who ruled the region around the 12th century. Certainly, the long disappeared Ship Gate is said to originate from that particular period, so it seems likely that the Bridge-gate would have been contemporary with that ancient portal, although obviously continuing to evolve and develop well beyond this early construction date. Unlike its modern day counterpart, which is fundamentally architectural, rather than practically defensive, the medieval Bridge-gate was reportedly a far narrower and much more imposing structure, which was principally designed to protect the city and its citizens from attack.

The western tower of the medieval portal was also known to have been supplemented by an octagonal water tower or conduit, which was raised in the 16th century by one John Tyrer and distributed fresh water around this part of the city by way of lead piping. Generally completed by around 1616 this eye-catching Water Tower was reported to have been significantly damaged during the English Civil War siege of the city during the mid 17th century and was eventually demolished, having subsequently been replaced by a much newer water conduit at Chester's High Cross.

Although the ancient Bridge-gate was known to have survived the Civil War siege of the city relatively intact, except for the damage to Tyrer's Water Tower, it was the widespread outbreak of peace in England and the Georgian fashion for modernisation that inevitably led to its later destruction. Throughout Chester, during the latter half of the 18th century, rampant redevelopment saw large swathes of its historic fabric swept away, including all four medieval gates, numerous ancient houses and most of its medieval castle complex. Designed by Joseph Turner, the man who also created the Watergate, Pillbox Terrace and the little Bridge of Sighs, the old Bridge-gate was finally demolished in around 1781, as part of the road widening scheme of that year and its successor, the present Bridge-gate, was officially opened in 1782.

As with its long extinct medieval counterpart, Turner's Bridge-gate is fronted by one of Chester's most iconic and historic structures, the **Old Dee Bridge**, which up until 1832 was the only permanent river crossing between England and Wales.

Although the Roman occupiers of Chester undoubtedly constructed a bridge across the River Dee, some sources have described this structure as a viaduct, rather than as a conventional bridge and one that lay along a slightly different alignment than does its present day successor. Although the Roman bridge was thought to have joined the north bank of the River Dee at its modern day point, its southern terminus was reported to have been located slightly to the east of today's bridge, now marked by a piece of open ground.

Although this highly advanced piece of Roman civil engineering probably remained in place well beyond the final withdrawal of the legions in the late 4th or early 5th century, eventually it would have failed to withstand the inevitable stresses and strains imposed on it by the currents of the Dee and would have collapsed into the waters below. However, because the local British population were thought to have lacked both the knowledge and skills to replace their previously permanent crossing, it seems likely that a series of generally poor quality and often temporary timber bridges would have been regularly thrown up across the river, only to be washed away during the next tumultuous tide. In 958 AD, a record made during the reign of the Anglo Saxon monarch, Edgar, was thought to have made mention of the Dee Bridge crossing, but this too was probably just one of a series of timber structures that existed throughout this troublesome period.

It was possibly only after the Norman occupation of Chester, in the latter half of the 11th century (circa 1070 AD) that the first substantial post-Roman bridge was constructed across the River Dee, although this one too was merely a predecessor of today's structure. The fact though, that during the 12th century a great deal of Chester's defensive fabric, its castle, walls, gates, etc were being constructed by the Anglo Norman Earls who held power in Chester would all tend to suggest that they were more than capable of building a permanent crossing over the Dee. By 1237 the last of these related noblemen, John the Scot, was reported to have died and the Earldom of Chester passed into the possession of the Crown, in the person of Henry III. Significantly, a record of 1255/6 reports that the Dee Bridge was being repaired, at the expense of the king's agent, suggesting that a permanent bridge was in place at that time and was seen as being the responsibility of the monarch.

In 1499 the southern end of the bridge was reported to have been rebuilt, with an older tower, dating from the reign of Richard II (1377-1399), being replaced by a new building called the Bridge Gate House. At the same time, a drawbridge which had once formed part of the city's early defences, along with the tower, was removed and according to some accounts was replaced with an extension to the most southerly arch. This newly built Bridge Gate House was thought to have survived until 1784, when as part of the general road widening scheme in this area, it was demolished to make way for the pedestrian walkway that was added to the ancient bridge. Perhaps unusually, this gatehouse property was said to have been sold by auction, with the successful bidder winning the rights to demolish the building, reconstruct the southern end of the bridge and then take away the resulting stonework and rubble, all presumably at their own expense.

A later mention of the Old Dee Bridge, reported in 1574, describes the bridge as being "Edwardian" and stating that it was being mended. Clearly, this Edwardian designation might be accounted for by any one of three related monarchs, Edward I, Edward II or Edward III and starting in 1272 and finishing in 1377. However, given that the generally accepted origin for the present bridge is 14th century, this would seem to exclude Edward Longshanks and point more towards one of the other two similarly named monarchs.

Although the bridge which spans the River Dee today is undeniably an ancient crossing, the changes made by the modernisation of the route in 1782 has almost certainly robbed the historic structure of much of its character and prominence. Formerly, where there were castellated walls, designed to protect defender and traveller alike, there are now modern iron railings and a relatively low cut sandstone wall overlooking the river, both of which are poor substitutes for the original defensive features.

Standing on the northwest flank of the Old Dee Bridge, the former **Hydro-Electric Power Station**, now used as a water plant, on the River Dee stands on the site of the city's old Dee Mills which were reported to have stood in one form or another since the late 11th or early 12th centuries. However, these mills finally became obsolete in the late 19th and early 20th centuries, so in 1910 the corporation purchased the remaining mills from their owners and demolished them, using the site for the much more necessary electricity generating scheme, suggested by S E Britton, the city's chief electrical engineer.

Although corn grinding M**ills** are known to have existed along the banks of the River Dee since the time of the Norman invasion, it was only following the construction of the city's Weir Dam in the 11th century that it became a highly industrialised process and profitable enterprise. The establishment of these vitally important buildings has been largely credited to the second Earl, Hugh D'Avranches who held office from 1070 until 1101 and who was reported to have granted the lease of at least one mill to the city's Norman Abbey of St Werburgh in 1093, suggesting that the weir and mills were both in operation by that time. His son and heir Richard was also reported to have granted the lease of a second mill, said to have stood at the south end of the Dee Bridge in 1119 to the same religious house, implying that a good number of corn grinding mills were in operation and generating substantial incomes by the early 12th century.

However, it has also been suggested that a substantial weir dam and a formidable milling operation only really began in the 13th century when the construction of both was put into the hands of King Edward's master mason Richard L'Enginour who was based in Chester and who was thought to have been granted the lease of the mills, in thanks for his work in helping to secure the Principality of Wales for the Plantagenet monarch. The ownership of the mills was said to have passed to members of his family through a lease, including his daughter who was reported to have later married into the Grosvenor family, through which they later inherited the Eaton estates, including the area of Belgrave in modern day London. By the 16th century, those mills which had previously been granted to the Norman Abbey of St Werbugh's had been transferred to the Cathedral of Christ and the Blessed Virgin by the monarch Henry VIII, who had previously dissolved the Abbey church.

Always regarded by some as the root cause of the River Dee's almost inevitable failure as an ongoing trade route because of its restriction of the waterway's natural flow, the weir dam managed to survive a number of calls for its destruction, as well as bombardment by Parliamentary cannon during the 17th century. In 1647 there was a call by a number of Chester's leading citizens to have the causeway demolished, in order to help the navigation of the River Dee which they claimed was being choked with silt and mud as a direct result of the weir's existence. In the same year, Chester's Lord Mayor, a man called Edwards who had previously been a Colonel in Cromwell's victorious Parliamentary Army, was given permission by the national authorities to tear down the obstacle. Unfortunately for supporters of this particular action, Edwards was reported to have died before his instructions could be carried out and the plans were subsequently abandoned. Four years later in 1651, the Parliamentary authorities were said to have sequestrated the weir and its associated mills, leasing them instead to two local men, John Vernon and John Walton, for a rent of £200 per annum less the cost of taxes and repairs.

During the Civil War siege of Chester, the ancient causeway was reported to have been damaged by Parliamentary cannon fire, which no doubt explained the willingness of the authorities to offset the cost of repairs against the annual lease offered to Vernon and Walton. By the time of the "restoration" of King Charles II however, the milling industry in Chester was thought to have been restored to its former levels, with a total of eleven mills standing along the banks of the River Dee, including six corn grinding mills, two water mills which brought water into the city and three other types of mill.

Throughout their long history and doubtless because of their largely timber construction, the Dee Mills were known to have suffered regular damage through devastating fires or component failure. In 1601 it was reported that the mills had broken down, presumably for a non-fire related reason and in September 1789, when the buildings were then in the possession of a Mr Wrench there was a major inferno which damaged or destroyed a number of the mills. They suffered further damage on March 6th 1819 and less than a year later, at least one of the mills was said to have been destroyed yet again. Because of such events and the modernisation of the industry through technological advances, much of which was taking place elsewhere in purpose built mills, by the early 1900's an industry which had existed in Chester since the 11th century was fundamentally extinct.

At the southern end of the Old Dee Bridge, the mills there were thought to have been employed in the "fulling" of cloth, the process of using water driven wooden hammers to beat the cloth or fabric, thereby releasing the unwanted grease and fats. In later years these same mills were thought to have been given over to the production of paper. Further east along the banks of the River Dee, in the area of modern day Salmon Leap; and at the southern end of the ancient causeway, at least three Tobacco or Snuff mills were said to have existed, although little evidence of their presence remains today.

CHAPTER FIFTEEN

GROSVENOR STREET & PEPPER STREET

As a city thoroughfare, **Grosvenor Street** is a relatively modern construction and marked the first street in the city not to adhere to the strict grid-like layout which had been in place since the fortress at Chester was first laid out nearly 2000 years ago. Built entirely to link the newly emerging Grosvenor Bridge with the centre of the ancient Roman city, this is probably the single most vital and yet damaging development that has ever taken place throughout Chester's long and illustrious history. Although this relatively modern highway and its associated bridge have undoubtedly brought greater prosperity and improved trading opportunities to the city, these have proved to have a high cost, both to Chester's architecture and to its local landscape.

As a matter of interest, further south of the elegant Grosvenor Bridge lies the Overleigh Cemetery and the Overleigh Road, both of which recall the historic Overleigh Hall which used to stand in the area. Reported to have belonged to the noted Chester family, the Cowpers, **Overleigh Hall** was thought to have stood on the site now occupied by the Lodge building which marks the entrance to the Duke of Westminster's woodland drive, linking the city of Chester with this noble family's seat at nearby Eaton Hall.

The impressive **Grosvenor Bridge** which spans the River Dee was designed by architect Thomas Harrison around 1820, but work did not start on the project until 1827 and by the time the bridge was officially opened by the then Princess Victoria in 1831, Harrison had been dead for some two years. The work was said to have been completed by his pupil William Cole Junior, aided by engineers Jesse Hartley and James Trubshaw. More noted designers and engineers, Telford, Rennie and Brunel had all been consulted over the location, structure and design of the new bridge, which at 200 feet was the largest single span bridge in the world at that time. The architect's model for the new bridge was restored and relocated by Chester Civic Trust in 1979 and currently stands on a grassy bank below the city walls on Castle Drive.

Bypassing the previously discussed Chester Castle and the former Militia building site, now occupied by a brand new hotel, the **Trustee's Savings Bank**, originally the Chester Bank Building, now houses the Paparazzi Ristorante at the junction of the modern day Grosvenor and Castle Streets and in earlier times may well have been the site for a medieval Great Hall. In 1847, the local architect James Harrison won a competition to construct a Savings Bank building for the city and six years later the property that stands today had been completed, in what is commonly referred to as a Tudor Gothic style of architecture. The clock turret which graces the top of the building was designed and built by Joyce's of Whitchurch. The property was further extended in the 1970's and now serves as a restaurant. Prior to the completion of their new landmark building in 1853, the proprietors of the Chester Saving Bank were reported to have been situated in Northgate Street during the first half of the 19th century, but by 1846 had relocated their business premises to Goss Street

The **Grosvenor Museum** building which adjoins James Harrison's Chester Bank, was designed by T M Lockwood who began its construction in 1885, with the resulting property being completed in the following year. The Chester Archaeological Society, which had previously been housed at the Albion Hotel in Lower Bridge Street, was reported to have relocated to the new museum building in 1887. The museum's precincts were further extended in 1894 and a second property at No 20 Castle Street was added in the 1950's.

On the opposite side of Grosvenor Street stands **St Francis' Church**, the foundation stone of which was reported to have been laid on 23rd September 1862. Unfortunately, much of the early construction work was undone by a violent storm in 1863 which caused a great deal of destruction throughout the whole of Chester and reduced the new church to a ruin. It was a further 12 years before sufficient funds could be raised to rebuild the structure and it was only in April 1875 that the new church was officially opened by the Archbishop of Westminster and the then Bishop of Chester. A monastery was said to have been built on the northern side of the church, facing the modern day Cuppin Street, on land that had previously been occupied by three shops, including a photographer's shop, a beer sellers business run by a man called Thomas Langford and an as yet unidentified store. Significantly, a city tavern called the Recruiting Sergeant was reported as existing in Cuppin Street around 1809 to 1810 and may account for either the Beer Sellers business or indeed the unidentified store which later made way for the monastery. As a matter of interest, this same "pub sign" was said to have later occupied the site now inhabited by the tavern known as the "George & Dragon" on Liverpool Road.

Prior to the construction of their new church and monastery, Chester's Franciscan Order was reported to have established a mission in Watergate Street around 1858 and remained there until 1862, when their new church was started. As noted earlier though, in 1863 a violent storm destroyed much of the fabric of the generally completed church, eventually leading to a 12 year delay before their new basilica was finally completed. According to local sources, rather than abandon the site completely, the Franciscan community continued to hold services in a temporary structure established on the site, until such time as the new permanent church had been completed. As has been noted in the following notes on Cuppin Street, there is a suggestion that St Francis' church was built on lands which had previously been occupied by a 17th century townhouse owned by a local man called Alban Grey. The building immediately adjoining St Francis' church to the east is thought to have been designed by architect John Douglas as a home and training centre for Chester's midwives, having been commissioned by the first Duke of Westminster in 1898.

The historic thoroughfare, **Cuppin Street**, which was formerly known as Cuppin Lane (aka Cupping's) is said to mark the line of the Roman fortress' long extinct southern wall that ran eastward from this point, along modern day Pepper Street and terminating at the SE angle tower, the base of which still exists today, close to the city's ancient "Wolf Gate". The clearly defined footprint of this great defensive structure still remains undisclosed, but the discovery of the footings for the ancient camps southern gateway, close to the later St Michael's Church, tends to suggest that its path may well lie beneath the buildings now inhabiting the southern flank of modern day Cuppin Street.

In its earliest form, Cuppin (Lane) Street ran westward, from its junction with the then existing Nun's Lane (now the southern end of Nicholas Street) to an easterly meeting with the crossroads formed by Bridge Street, Lower Bridge Street and Pepper Lane (now Pepper Street). As with the equally ancient Bunce Street however, the development of Grosvenor Street in around 1826 saw Cuppin Street dramatically altered and shortened by the new city highway, with much of its south eastern section simply being buried beneath the modern roadway.

Apart from the church of St Martin's, which formerly occupied part of the western end of Cuppin Street (possibly on the site now occupied by a municipal car park), early records for this area are generally scant, save for it being noted in 1418 that a John Ewloe, as farmer of the castle mill, was granted lands in this section of the city. It was also reported that many of these same possessions were later thought to have passed into the hands of the Stanley family, who are generally associated with the Earls of Derby.

By the 18th century however; and prior to the widespread redevelopment of the area in the early 19th century, records suggest that there were any number of buildings inhabiting the thoroughfare, many of which were owned by specific families. A house plate bearing the date 1684 and which was commonly attributed to a Chester bricklayer called Alban Grey and his wife Katherine, was reported to have been placed on the northern wall of the 19th century St Francis' church, suggesting perhaps that this building had been sacrificed to make way for the new religious building, although whether or not this house stood in Cuppin Street is unclear.

During the late 18th century, much of the southern flank of Cuppin Street was reported to be inhabited by a collection of buildings, including private dwellings, a brew-house, a kiln, plus private gardens, many of which were said to be in the ownership of one Margaret Sayer, who was described as a widow. Along with another woman, Rebecca Leadbeater, who was reported to have owned yet another property in Cuppin Street, Sayer was said to have bequeathed her properties to members of the Minshull family, who were presumably related to the two women either through marriage or by blood.

Just prior to the laying out of new Grosvenor Street, another resident of Cuppin Street was thought to be one William Boult, who was unfortunate enough to be fatally injured by a boiler explosion at his tobacco works in the street, although its exact location there is unknown. Around the same time that Boult was conducting his tobacco business in Cuppin Street, a building in the old highway was also known to be inhabited by the offices of Chester's emerging gas company whose headquarters were located there in 1817, although they were said to have relocated themselves to new premises shortly afterwards.

Although much of Cuppin Street was affected by the 19th century modernisation of this section of Chester, most notably through the creation of the new Grosvenor Street, the northern flank of the old highway was known to have suffered significantly less destruction than its southern partner. This was obviously due in no small part to the fact that the new civic roadway of 1826 was located to the south Cuppin Street anyway and that the later construction of St Francis' church also occurred in the same general area.

The northern end of Bunce Street joins Grosvenor Street on its southern flank and offers access to the relatively modern range of buildings known as Grosvenor Place, which was thought to have been built on part of the former gardens of Bridge House that were said to have extended westward from Lower Bridge Street. To the south of the original line of Cuppin Street's junction with Bridge Street and immediately north of Richard Grosvenor's townhouse, later the "Falcon Inn", a tavern called the "Angel Inn" was reported to have existed in 1643, but this too has disappeared over the intervening centuries.

The crossroads which links four of Chester's modern streets, Bridge Street, Lower Bridge Street, Grosvenor Street and Pepper Street is an entirely modern invention, which during the Roman period would have marked a spot just outside of their imposing southern gateway and which in more recent times was said to have been the location for a fountain adorned with a dolphin, gifted to the city by one of its leading citizens. As with many other historic features from this general area however, this particular monument was reported to have been lost as a result of the later modernisation and road widening schemes that have so badly affected this particular section of Chester.

Today's modern **Pepper Street** which forms part of the south east section of Chester's constrictive inner ring road system is thought to be at least twice the width of the original thoroughfare and possibly recalls the presence of Spice Merchants who were thought to have commonly inhabited this area of the city. However, it has also been suggested by some historians that the name "Pepper" is actually a corruption of the word "Pebble" and simply refers to the fact that an early Roman road, which preceded the modern thoroughfare, was topped with a layer of small stones, or pebbles, rather than much larger cobbles or flagstones. Their submission is further underpinned by the fact that there are thought to be a large number of "Pepper Streets" scattered throughout Britain; and that most, if not all of them, are generally located within or close to former Roman settlements.

Nevertheless, this suggested origin for the street's later name seems far from compelling and the idea that these thoroughfares actually owe their designation to the selling; storage or transportation of spices, still remains a credible explanation, especially when one considers that early salt supply routes, were often later recalled in street or road names such as Salter's Way, etc. Even as early as 80 BC the ancient city of Alexandria was said to have had its own "Pepper Gate", indicating the importance and financial value of this and other spices that were often considered to be more precious than gold.

Regardless of such possible origins for its later name however, according to some local historians, the actual geographical position of the modern street precludes it from being a Roman invention, suggesting instead, that it possibly lies immediately adjacent to the line of the long extinct southern wall of the fortress, or directly above the route of the Roman's "fosse" or defensive ditch. Assuming that either of these two possible locations is true, it would seem highly improbable that a Roman road or track would have existed along this particular route anyway and pointing once again to a much later foundation date.

Despite its modern appearance and seeming to be a Chester street with little architectural or historical value, much of its past now lies below the utilitarian mass of the Grosvenor Shopping Precinct, office blocks, department stores and multi-level car parks, all of which owe their foundations to the architects and developers of the 1950's, 60's and 70's, when the city's heritage was thought to be a secondary consideration.

Prior to the building of Sir Walter Tapper's Newgate during the late 1930's and the widening of the street during the 1960's this generally narrow thoroughfare terminated at the historic Wolf Gate and a meeting with the then still existing Fleshmongers Row which ran in a northwest direction towards Chester's Eastgate Street. The fact that this earlier medieval gateway was also known as the "New Gate" prior to the construction of Tapper's modern archway, suggests that the thoroughfare itself has commonly been called both "Newgate Street" and "Pepper Street" for an extended period of time and was determined by each persons choice of title as much as anything else.

On the plot of land that marks the junction of Lower Bridge Street and Pepper Street, currently occupied by a modern office building, in around 1694 there were two buildings of note located there. **The Mitre Inn**, which had previously occupied a site in Eastgate Street, was thought to have been relocated to this site and was said to have occupied this particular location from 1694 all the way through to 1846 when it finally ceased trading. Although it has been suggested that the "Mitre" had disappeared from Pepper Street in 1771, to be replaced by another tavern, the "Red Lion", city records show that the Mitre was being used as a polling station right through to 1810, so the later date of 1846 is almost certainly correct. During the 19th century this particular tavern was said to have been used as temporary quarters for military officers from the nearby Castle, whose own accommodations were being rebuilt at the time.

This city tavern was reported to have stood alongside another much more notable and ancient building called the **Black Hall**. (Confusingly perhaps, a second building with the same name, the Black Hall, was known to have existed in Lower Watergate Street and inhabited the site now occupied by Thomas Harrison's 18th century Watergate House). The Black Hall in Pepper Street however, was said to have existed since the beginning of the 15th century and been constantly developed and altered over subsequent centuries. One of the first records relating to this building is thought to date from 1405, when a "messuage" or building was noted in a grant made to an individual called John Euloe (Ewloe). By 1465, it was reported that the "Black Hall" was in the holding of one Thomas Walley, at the same time that the surrounding lands were said be have been the cause of a dispute between a Richard Winnington and another man called Henry Ravenscroft. As a matter of interest, it is perhaps worth noting that the Winnington's were thought to be related to the Grosvenor family, the later owners of the Falcon Inn, which still occupies a site on the opposite side of Lower Bridge Street and which would have faced the old Black Hall.

Sometime after 1465 the hall was thought to have passed into the possession of a parson called Robert de Crouton, who was said to have owned the house and its cellars, possibly as the result of a bequest made by Thomas Walley or another later owner of the property. By 1553 however, the Black Hall had passed into the hands of a William Whitmore from Thurstaston, although it was thought that the building was actually being occupied by a widow called Joan Ledsham.

In common with many of these early buildings, the Black Hall was thought to have been extensively restored and altered throughout its lifetime, so that even by the 17th century it was said to be "an old timber building with several rooms, including a great hall, that have all been substantially altered". Despite having been heavily modernised by this period, the old house was reported to still contain its medieval cellars or under-croft's, which may help to explain the vaults that continue to exist in one or two of the properties fronting onto modern day Lower Bridge Street. The remaining fabric of the old hall and its later additions was still being occupied as late as 1840, when the building was said to have been inhabited by a firm of solicitors. However, this property and the adjacent Mitre Inn were thought to have finally disappeared during the second half of the 19th century, possibly as a result of another round of modernisation taking place in the city. The site then seems to have been occupied by a range of generally temporary buildings until the whole area was redeveloped sometime around 1968 when the current office building was said to have been erected. As a matter of interest, it is worth noting that the elegant pillared property now occupied by a branch of the "Habitat" group was originally constructed as a Methodist Chapel in around 1833 and was reported to have contained architectural elements taken from the old St Bridget's church that was demolished around the same time.

Despite being able to trace its history back to 1405, it may well be that this building, or at least part of its site, had an even earlier history, possibly as the home of a family called Daresbury (Deresbury), who were prominent citizens of Chester during the 13th and 14th centuries; and who were reported to have occupied a building called Daresbury Hall which was known to have been located in Pepper Street.

Reportedly standing on the southern flank of Pepper Street during the 13th century, clearly this hall might well have occupied any number of places along the route, but this does not preclude the possibility that "Daresbury Hall" did indeed become known as the Black Hall in later years.

The Daresbury's or more properly the Deresbury's, were recorded as being prominent citizens in Chester during the 13th century and specifically between 1250 and 1280, when a number of them were known to have held the offices of city Sheriff and Mayor during that same period. However, it is a Ralph de Daresbury and his wife Margery who are most strongly associated with the hall that bore their family name and which was reported in 1288-9, when Richard the Clerk was granted a right of way past their property. It is a predecessor of Ralph and Margery though, who is generally credited with building the hall and his name was Randle de Daresbury, who was recorded as Mayor of Chester in 1277.

Directly opposite the former home of the Black Hall and the Mitre Inn, the ancient parish church of **St Michael the Archangel** continues to stand, although no longer serving as a place of worship, but as Chester Heritage Centre, a role it has played since the 1970's. The church was thought to have first been recorded in 1218, although other unsubstantiated sources claim that this church, along with its generally unrecorded monastery were first noted in 1155, when both buildings were reportedly destroyed by fire.

Although St Michael's is the only building of any great age to survive the generally recent and highly rigorous modernisation of Pepper Street on its northern flank, early city records do tend to suggest that this area of the city, running eastward from St Michael's to the then still used Wolf Gate was indeed being occupied and utilised. In 1364, a plot of land adjoining Fleshmongers Lane (now thought to be marked by an Office Block and a piece of open ground to the east of the Grosvenor Precinct) was granted by John de Stoke to one Robert de Bredon, the parson of St Peter's Church. Immediately to the west of this plot and now thought to lie below the eastern side of the Grosvenor Precinct entrance, another piece of land was reportedly owned by one Hugh de Byrchelle around the same period.

Although it isn't clear exactly what particular use these individual plots were being put to, it seems entirely likely that each of them were occupied by tenements and/or workshops that generated a regular income for the owner, being inhabited by a number of tenants, all of whom paid rent to their private landlords. Prior to the 16th century and the Dissolution of the Monasteries by Henry VIII, a number of individual properties in Pepper Street were known to have been owned by various monastic houses in Chester, including St John's, St Peter's and the convent of St Mary's. Following the Reformation though, many of these same properties were thought to have passed into private hands, so that by the early 17th century much of Pepper Street was reported to have been inhabited by a growing number of small cottages, tenements, workshops and market gardens, all of which were constantly being leased, rented or occupied by various parties.

Another prominent Chester family that were reported to have held substantial properties in Pepper Street were the Leche's who are more commonly associated with the historic house in Watergate Street which continues to bear their name. Robert Leche, who was the Chancellor of the Chester Diocese up to his death in around 1586/7, is widely thought to be the member of the family who first acquired these properties, although most subsequently passed into the possession of the Gregg family and later still, the Barnston's. Early city records also suggest that ownership of these same properties became a highly disputed affair and a number of cases were known to have been brought before the civil courts to determine exactly who owned the 14 "messuages" (properties), 15 gardens, one orchard and three acres of land that the different parties were arguing over, many of which were thought to have lain on the south side of the ancient street.

Back on the north side of Pepper Street, during the 17th century (1658), the previously mentioned plots of land which stood immediately to the east of St Michael's church was thought to have been the location for a small terrace of Alms Houses which were erected by a city Barrister called William Jones to aid the city's poorest citizens. Just over 100 years later though, in around 1784, these houses were thought to have been demolished to make way for a 40 foot terrace of three late 18th century townhouses, each three storeys high that were all said to have been constructed at the same time. Later on, this relatively small row of properties was thought to have been added to by a number of additional houses, each one built individually, but together forming a terrace measuring some 120 feet in length. All of these properties were subsequently demolished to make way for the construction of the Grosvenor Shopping Precinct in the 1960's, which not only obliterated these buildings, but also resulted in the near total destruction of the Legionary Bath House complex that existed immediately north of Pepper Street.

Across the road from the modern day Shopping Precinct, stands Albion and Volunteer Streets, including the remaining facade of the **Volunteer Drill Hall**, a Welsh Chapel and rows of terraced housing which were raised on the former grounds and gardens of the city's Albion Hotel which still exists in Lower Bridge Street, but today is known as Park House. These private grounds were sold around 1865 and later developed to include the properties noted above. Although the Volunteer Drill Hall is thought to be the place where young men signed up for military service during the First World War, its principle purpose was to house the local volunteer's or militia's that were a regular feature of most 18th and 19th century English towns and cities. The building itself was first raised in 1869 and was paid for by public subscription, with the new property reportedly occupying part of the site of two former housing courts or slums, namely Roberts and Wilkinson's, which had previously existed in this area of the city. The designer of the Drill Hall was the renowned local architect James Harrison, who was largely responsible for restoring a number of Chester's ancient churches, as well as designing the Chester Savings Bank building in nearby Grosvenor Street. In the adjoining Albion Street, the Albion Park Church which stands today is reported to date from 1847 and was said to have been constructed by the local Welsh Congregationalist community who worshipped there at the time.

Around the corner, the **Nine Houses** in Park Street, of which only six remain, are the only examples of pre-19th century alms houses which continue to exist in the city today. They are constructed of brickwork placed upon a sandstone plinth, with the upper floor made of timber frames, masonry and infill brickwork. This terrace of Alms Houses were reported to have been originally founded by a wealthy businessman and landowner, Robert Harvey sometime around 1665, when Park Street was still part of Claverton or Clayton Lane, later Duke Street. By the middle of the 20th century however, the houses were thought to be in such a perilous condition that they had to be rescued by the city council in 1968-9. Two of the missing 3 houses were thought to have been replaced by the generally modern half timbered building which now occupies the northern end of the terrace.

Park Street itself is thought to be named after the extensive parklands and orchards which once formed part of the Albion Hotel complex in Lower Bridge Street and which were said to have been laid out by a Mr Dale, the then tenant of that property between 1809 and 1814. It has also been suggested that this road might have formed part of a scenic carriage route for guests that were arriving to stay at the Albion Hotel during the early 19th century.

Nevertheless, this thoroughfare may well have been in existence since the late 9th or early 10th century when this southern section of the city was first enclosed by the Anglo Saxon leader of Chester, Aethelflaeda. Possibly originating as a military roadway that sat immediately behind the eastern defensive wall, it later formed part of Claverton (Clayton) Lane, before becoming part of an extended Duke Street which was thought to have been adopted in 1795. However, it has also been suggested that by the beginning of the 18th century the northern part of the street was said to have been commonly known as Newgate Street, recalling its direct connection with the city's "New Gate", as the Wolf Gate became known after it's rebuilding in 1608. It also seems likely that the highway must have changed its name once again in 1782, when the title "Newgate Street" was attached to the former "Fleshmongers Lane" lying on the north side of Pepper Street, suggesting too that the modern title Park Street might also originate from this period.

Although modern day Park Street comprises little more than the previously mentioned Alms Houses and their adjoining half timbered successor, in 1964 mention was made of the properties that had previously inhabited this thoroughfare. This record indicated that apart from the terrace of Alms Houses, there appeared to be at least seven separate 18th century houses gracing the western flank of the street, all of which were described as being of three storeys and commonly built of brick, stone and timber. One can only assume therefore that many of these reported properties were subsequently demolished to make way for the outstandingly forgettable mass of concrete and steel that houses the Pepper Street car park and its small number of unremarkable retail units.

Forming part of the western flank of Park Street and fronting onto the main Pepper Street the generally unobtrusive, yet highly unattractive, municipal car park, topped by the stone figure of a lion, recalls the presence of the "**Chester or White Lion Brewery**" which used to occupy the site at some time prior to the road widening scheme which swept away many of the older buildings in this area of the city. Reportedly owned and run by members of the Whittle family from around 1800, by 1846 the business was known as Whittle and Jones and in 1873 the brewery was thought to have been sold to two city partners called Walton and Clare, who continued to own the company until they too sold it. The Chester Lion Brewery Company were said to have owned the business until the beginning of the 20th century, before it finally passed into the hands of Bent's Brewery Company who subsequently closed the site down during the early 1900's. From the early 1930's and right up until the mid 1950's much of this area of Pepper Street was then occupied by the business premises operated by the Anchor Motor Company, but following their relocation to a new home on the northern outskirts of the city, the Pepper Street site later became yet another victim of Chester's inner ring road system.

During the 17th century, this same site was reported to have been occupied by a fairly substantial coach house and stables owned by a member of a local family, the Edwards'. A House Plate which existed during the 1960's displayed a date of 1642 and the initials "E E", which were thought to identify one Evan Edwards, the owner of the property who ordered the coach house and stables built in that particular year. The eldest son of Thomas Edwards of Rhual, near Mold, Evan went on to become a Baron of Chester's Exchequer and was the older brother of city Alderman William Edwards, another of Chester's prominent citizens during the 17th century. Both men were thought to have been fairly successful in their careers and Evan himself was reported to have owned substantial assets in the city, including an interest in the "Globe Tavern", later the Hop-Pole Inn, which stood just outside of Chester's main East Gate.

Unfortunately for the two Edwards brothers, the political and religious divides of the 17th century, brought about by the conflict between Charles I and his Parliament, saw the two siblings suffer entirely different fates in respect of their individual fortunes. Reportedly a Royalist supporter by nature and choice, unlike his brother William, Evan was thought to have been penalised financially for his support of the ill-fated English monarch by the city's new Parliamentarian administration. Significantly perhaps, he was reported to have lived in his Pepper Street / Park Street property only until 1665, when it was then said to have been occupied by Alderman Robert Harvey, the man responsible for building the nearby and previously mentioned "Nine Houses", the terrace of Alms Houses which have also been commonly known as "The Cavalier Houses". Later still, in 1697 the property was reported to have been owned by William Sudlow, an apothecary in the city, who later sold the land and building to one Jonathan Whitley who was reported as an Ironmonger. The building was then said to have passed into the hands of a family called Brerewood, who were relatives of the Whitley's and it may have been this family who ultimately sold the land and buildings to the Whittles, who later established the brewery there. Significantly, during the 16th century, an individual called Brerewood was reported to have owned substantial plots of lands at the lower end of Park Street, lying between modern day Duke Street and the city's southern wall.

To complete the story on this particular area of Chester , around 1260, a citizen of Chester called Ranulph de Adleton, granted to Richard le Corneiser, all of his lands in Pepper Street that were described as "running near the walls of Chester towards the gate at Wolfeld" (Wolf Gate), all of which suggests that these lands stood on the south of the thoroughfare and close to the eastern wall, the same location as the later Albion Street, Park Street, Nine Houses and the Whittle Brewery site. Rather confusingly though, in 1294, yet another grant was made by a man called John de Rosse to his clerk, William le Duyn, for all of his lands and properties lying in Pepper Street. Once again described as lying near to the postern gate (only the Wolf Gate existed at that time), this can only mean that the lands referred to were on the northern side of the street, or that the lands previously mentioned as being granted to Richard le Corneiser had changed hands in the intervening 30 years, but which reason is correct, remains unclear.

On the northern side of today's Pepper Street and close to the old "Wolf Gate" is the remnants of what was once one of Chester's most ancient, colourful and important streets, the long forgotten **Fleshmongers Lane** (or Row). Formerly running in a northwest direction to a meeting with Chester's Eastgate Street, much of its historic route now lies below the imposing bulk of the modern Grosvenor Shopping Centre and has been generally scoured away to be replaced by the underground parking and delivery bays that serve the precincts many shops and stores.

The old Fleshmongers Lane was first mentioned as early as the 12th century and was thought to have retained that name all the way through to the 18th century when it was finally renamed Newgate Street, recalling its connection with the "New Gate" (Wolf Gate) that stood nearby. There are a number of dates given for this change of name, including the relatively early one of 1718, although a map of 1745 still identifies the thoroughfare by its ancient name, so this cannot be correct. The most likely date for its name change appears to be around 1782 when the highway finally became known as Newgate Street, the name having moved from the thoroughfare now known as Park Street, on the south side of Pepper Street.

A number of early records relating to this historic lane still exist; including one which dates from around 1200 and details a grant made by the prioress of St Mary's Convent, to a man called Henry Doggett for the lease of a property in Fleshmongers Lane. Yet another is a grant made by a man called Adam Gyn in 1280 to another individual, called Richard Grund, for lands in Fleshmongers Lane, possibly as part of a marriage settlement made on Gyn's daughter who was called Godusa. In 1340, a William de Shavynton and his wife Margery, who also owned properties in nearby Bridge Street and elsewhere, were reported to have granted a plot of land to a man called Edmund de Waterfall; and in 1368 a Chester landowner called Robert le Calf was recorded to have granted two properties in Fleshmongers Lane to one Robert de Bredon, the parson of St Peter's church. This Robert de Bredon is obviously the same individual that four years earlier had been granted a plot of land in Pepper Street by one John de Stoke, a plot tentatively identified as lying close to the rear entrance of the modern day shopping precinct. This same site was subsequently thought to have been the location for William Jones' 17th century Alms Houses, which were themselves later replaced by the previously mentioned terrace of 18th century houses in Pepper Street, which were demolished to make way for the Grosvenor Precinct in the 1960's.

Back in Fleshmongers Lane, in 1453 a John Layet (or Leyot) of Hale was recorded to have granted a lease on a property in Fleshmongers Lane to one Thomas Ferney of Chester, a building that was said to have previously been occupied by a Hugh Woodcock. This same Layet family were also said to have granted lands and properties in the same area to a chaplain called Edmund Tebbit in 1415, these assets having previously been owned by Joan Layet's former husband, John de Ashton. In 1494, a William Cholle of Chester was reported to have bequeathed his lands and properties in Fleshmongers Lane to his uncle, Richard Gough, although in virtually all of these cases, there is no absolute information as to exactly where these lands or properties were located, other than them being "in" or "around" the ancient Fleshmongers Lane.

In later years the estates of the Layet family were reported to have passed into the hands of the fairly prominent Norris family of Speke, presumably through marriage, although it has been assumed that many of the inherited properties in Fleshmongers Lane were later disposed of, as few city records associate the Norris' with this particular area of Chester. It is also worth recalling that the Norris family are thought to have made marital alliances with a number of Chester's most notable families, through which they became significant landowners within the city.

As has been previously mentioned with regard to many of Chester's streets, the churches of the city, including its great Norman Abbey, were reportedly major landowners from the 11th century onwards and it was only in the 1540's that many of these assets were seized by the Crown and subsequently sold off to a number of private individuals. As to how these sequestrations affected the later ownership or development of Fleshmongers Lane is unclear, although as elsewhere, this highway seems to have been periodically modernised, most notably at its northern junction with Eastgate Street, where a number of the city's leading commercial buildings were said to have existed.

By the beginning of the 20th century though, the old Fleshmongers Lane title had been replaced with its current name, Newgate Street; and a number of private residences were reported to be occupying both sides of its southern limits. To the west side of the street, a site now generally marked by the modern Newgate House and open grassed area, there was said to be at least three separate properties dating from the late 18th century, all of which fronted onto the ancient street. Each was thought to be three storeys high, with one said to date from 1765, another from 1772 and the final property's construction date was unrecorded, other than it being noted that it appeared to be contemporary with the other two.

The eastern flank of the street, now occupied by a modern office building, was reported to have contained a similarly small number of 18th century houses, all of which were said to have been constructed over three storeys. No specific construction dates were noted for any of these properties, although it was reported that at least one of them had been extensively enlarged by merging two adjoining houses into one. The only remaining building of note that remains on the eastern side of the street however is the "Bridgewater Tavern", which has previously been known as the "Three Crowns Inn". Dating from around 1800 the "Three Crowns" was reported to have been transferred here from its previous location in Northgate Street, where it had previously stood on the site of Thomas Harrison's later Commercial Hotel. Today, the site of the "Bridgewater" is thought to be inhabited by the "Plumber's Arms", while the former sign has since been transferred to a public house in the suburb of Newtown.

A noted property of the very early 18th century that formerly existed on the eastern side of Newgate Street, but whose remains now lie below today's modern buildings, was the mansion house of a prominent city barrister, Andrew Kenrick. This property gained some notoriety within Chester because of its builder's seemingly common habit of borrowing money from all quarters to construct the house and then finding that he was unable to repay his debts, leaving his family and client to sort out his finances affairs even after his own death. This particular case has previously been reported on page 12 of this book.

The builder, Thomas Morris, is often described as a speculative bricklayer, who was said to have been admitted as a Freeman of Chester in 1689, his own father being a bricklayer cum linen draper and Freeman of the city. Seemingly a relatively successful businessman who was reported to have had a financial interest in at least one property in Bridge Street, around 1702 he entered into an arrangement with barrister Andrew Kenrick that would ultimately prove to be disastrous for both parties, primarily because of Morris' financial mismanagement.

Having acquired an area of land on the eastern side of Newgate Street adjoining the city walls that was said to contain an old tenement, outbuildings and stables, Morris set about clearing away these old structures in readiness for the mansion house that he was to build for his client Kenrick. Between 1703 and 1704 this work seems to have progressed fairly well, so much so, it was later reported that Morris had managed to construct three new stable blocks, three new coach houses and had managed to build the new mansion up to the second floor level. Unfortunately for Morris and unknown to Kenrick at the time, the builder then seems to have run out of money to complete the project, money that had been largely acquired through loans secured on the property itself. Although it isn't clear whether this financial shortfall was caused by Morris' own ineptitude or greed, ultimately it fell to others to provide him with additional funds to complete the task.

By the time Kenrick's new home was completed in December 1704, allowing the barrister and his new wife to move in, the builder Thomas Morris was reported to be sinking in a sea of debt, although he was thought to have continued in his main profession for some years after 1704. By 1712 however, other reports then have him working as a Cordwainer or Shoemaker in the city, suggesting perhaps that he was unable or had been forbidden from carrying out his main line of work, possibly as a result of the Newgate Street fiasco. Even his death a short time later, did not allow him or his family to escape the outstanding debts and it was only through the efforts of his wife and son; plus the intervention of Kenrick that finally allowed his estate to be settled some 15 years after the mansion had first been built.

Barrister Kenrick went on to become one of Chester's most prominent citizens and in common with the later mentioned Nicholas Newhouse was reported to have leased the nearby Wolf's Tower from the city authorities for use as a laundry. In order for members of his household to access this ancient watch tower Kenrick also sought permission from the city council to construct an entranceway through the city walls directly to his new laundry, which rather surprisingly seems to have been granted. In later years and particularly during the 20th century, this ancient tower was reported to have become a fairly ruinous structure and eventually lost the groined roof that had protected it for centuries, allowing it to become little more than a rubbish bin for those passing along the walls. Fortunately, in more recent years this situation has been remedied with the construction of a new roof, albeit one than looks to be completely artificial and out of place.

The **Wolf's Tower** has gained its name because of its close proximity to and long association with the nearby gateway; although today it is also referred to as the Thimbleby Tower, marking its connection with a Lady of that name who was reported as a parishioner of the nearby church of St Michael's between 1597 and 1615, the year of her death. She was said to be the wife of Sir Richard Thimbleby, who occupied Hilbre Island, just off the Wirral peninsula, in 1575 on behalf of a member of the Stanley family from Hooton. Whether or not Lady Thimbleby actually had any interest in the tower that bears her name is unclear, but her name continues to be linked to the flanking tower nonetheless.

Although he was thought to reside in St Michael's parish, it seems that Kenrick chose to become a member of St John's congregation, being one of its wealthier parishioners that were reported to have paid for the construction of a raised gallery on the north side of the church's north aisle where they and their families could worship. His connection with this particular church and with the city, is possibly best represented by the fact that although he eventually moved with his second wife, to live at the family seat at Woor Hall in Salop around 1747, upon his death he was brought back to St John's in Chester and buried along with members of his first family.

His former home in Newgate Street was later said to have passed into the possession of the Farmer's who were relatives of the Kenrick's and who were thought to be residing there until the 1830's, when it was then inherited by the Boydell family. Finally, at some time during the 19th century the house was said to have been purchased by a Veterinary

Surgeon called Storrar who ran his highly successful business from what was then described as the "ivy covered house" in Newgate Street.

Chester's still standing **Wolf Gate** has successively been known as the Pepper Gate and the New Gate, although nowadays in its present form of a city artefact it is commonly referred to with its original title, the Wolf Gate. Its early predecessor was thought to have existed from the time when Chester's Roman defences were first extended southward towards the River Dee, which has been generally attributed to the Anglo Saxon settlers of the late 9th or early 10th centuries, under their leader, Aethelflaeda.

There are a number of suggestions as to the derivation of its title as the Wolf's Gate; the first being that the name originates from the emblematic Wolfs Head which was carved on the gateway and that was synonymous with Earl Hugh Lupus D'Avranches, the second Norman Earl of Chester. The next suggestion was that the title derives from the numerous hides and fleeces which came from the animals slaughtered in the nearby Fleshmongers Lane and which were hung up or deposited near the "Wool Fell" gate, ready for their collection by the people who were employed in the city's wool and leather industries which were located outside the walls, around the then existing Barker's Lane.

The third suggested origin for the name, is that it was named in honour of a notable member of the local Hiberno-Norse community, which was known to exist in the south east section of the city from the early post Roman period. It has also been suggested that the Viking raiders who temporarily captured the city during the reign of King Alfred, in the late 9th century, may well have gained access to Chester's inner precincts with the help of a fifth columnists who was a member of this local Hiberno-Norse community, adding weight to the idea that in fact this gateway had existed during the late 900's.

Finally, it has also been suggested that the name "Wolf's Gate" was a shortened version of the term "Wolf's Head Gate" and actually identified the place where the severed heads of local outlaws and thieves who had been executed were displayed as a warning to other would be lawbreakers.

In its original form this gateway was designed to allow only foot traffic to pass through its portal, but during the reign of Edward III (1327-1377) the "Wolfeld" Gate was thought to have been widened sufficiently to allow horses and animals through the entrance; and at the same time an open grating in front of the gateway was added. By around 1490, the ancient portal was reported to include a house that has been "bylded" on the Wolf's Gate and which was being leased to one Nicholas Nuhouse (Newhouse) by the city authorities, for a period of 101 years. This property almost certainly stood on the northern side of the gateway, as about the same time, presumably the same Nicholas Newhouse, a Chester Glover, was reportedly renting the nearby Wolf's Tower from the authorities, as well as lands in St John's Lane, which lay outside the city walls. Although no evidence of this house or tenement, which was attached to the Wolf Gate, exists today, it seems likely that it occupied the space now occupied by both a modern office block and a small piece of open land that lie on the western side of the old gateway.

According to some city records, in 1603 a local joiner called John Robinson was reported to have petitioned the local council asking for the lease of this still standing gate house, but his request was denied, as another lease was already in place with a man called Edward Thompson, so quite why Robinson should have asked in the first place is a mystery. However, other records suggest that prior to 1603, a man called Hollinshead was leasing the house at the Wolf's Gate; and that it was only after his death in that same year, a second man called Moyles petitioned the council to have the lease of the property, on condition that he would completely rebuild the by then, generally decayed gateway. It was also around this same time that a number of local traders and inhabitants were said to have lobbied the council to have the gateway widened, so that carts could be brought into the city, rather than them having to traverse the defensive walls to one of the main gates. The authorities subsequently gave their permission for the entrance to be widened, but according to some sources the rebuilding of the gate was so badly planned that within a relatively short time, people were once again complaining that their carts couldn't get through the postern gate and so it had to be reconstructed once again.

In 1608, the ancient Wolf Gate was rebuilt close to the south east corner of the former Roman fortress and renamed as the "New Gate" although even by the 16th century the gate itself had become part of the city's legendary past. It was said to be at the Wolf Gate in 1573 that a local alderman's daughter, who was playing "stool ball" in Pepper Street was reportedly stolen away by a local man, but who in reality had probably eloped with her young lover on horseback.

Ralph Aldersey was a member of the influential Aldersey family who had held the office of Sheriff in Chester around 1541. While serving as a city Alderman in 1573 his daughter, Ellen, was alleged to have eloped with a Draper called Ralph Jaman, without the permission of her family. The young couple was thought to have escaped the city by way of the medieval Wolf Gate and in response her father persuaded the council to have the gate closed at night times, in order that such an event could not reoccur. Two local men, Hugh Rogerson an Alderman and Richard Wright, a draper in the city, were both charged with being accomplices to the event. For his part Rogerson was reported to have been fined 10 shillings and Wright had his business premises in the city closed. However, father and daughter were later reconciled with one another and the gate was said to have been reopened in 1574. This historic event though was said to have spawned the local phrase "when the daughter is stolen, shut the Pepper Gate", although whether this local saying has ever been used in such similar circumstances again is impossible to know.

At the eastern terminus of Pepper Street stands the city's **New Gate**, built between 1937-8 to the designs of Sir Walter Tapper, but substantially completed by his son Michael following his father's unexpected death The archway is said to be built of concrete and steel, but faced with Runcorn stone. This new gateway, adjoins the city's earlier Wolf Gate, which itself has been called the New Gate or Pepper Gate at various times in its history. Tapper's gateway however, is thought by some to be little more than a "folly" and simply a design solution to a modern transport problem, rather than being any sort of landmark structure or architectural masterpiece and is probably best compared to that other replica of Cheshire's medieval history, Peckforton Castle.

CHAPTER SIXTEEN

THE AMPHITHEATRE & ST JOHN'S

Little St John Street continues the route of Chester's Pepper Street eastward, although its original route has been substantially altered by 20th century roadwork developments, both in the 1940's and the 1960's. Prior to the construction of Walter Tapper's "Newgate" arch in the late 1930's, local traffic was forced to negotiate the much narrower and far older "Wolf Gate" which still stands on the northern side of Tapper's creation. In its original form Little St John's was supposed to drive straight across land partially occupied by St John's House, the northern partner of the still standing Dee House, despite the fact that the remains of the hidden Roman amphitheatre had been discovered below it some ten years earlier.

Nevertheless, this highly damaging scheme would undoubtedly have gone ahead, had it not been for the intervention of local archaeological groups and national government who forced the contractors to navigate the new road around this priceless monument, creating the curved thoroughfare that exists today. During the 16th century Little St John Street was said to have been known as Church Lane, a title that it may well have carried for hundreds of years, prior to its current designation. Much of its northern flank, including its junction with the similarly named St John's Street, is lined with relatively modern buildings, the biggest and most obvious is which the Travelodge Hotel, formerly occupied by a telephone exchange. East of this building is a collection of 19th century cottages, constructed and owned by the Grosvenor Estates, which occupy a small city cul-de-sac known as Lumley Place, which may once have formed part of the earlier main route. This small terrace is fronted by the Chester Visitor's Centre, the former St John's School building, which may have once been the home of the Chester Blue Girls School that was established in this area of the city at the beginning of the 19th century.

Just outside the Newgate and before the partially exposed remains of the Roman Amphitheatre lies Souter's Lane, which runs from this point, southward to the banks of the River Dee. The land which lies between this thoroughfare and the city's walls, now houses the city's "**Roman Garden's**" a fairly modern feature which brings together a number of the Roman artefacts that have been discovered in the city over time. Prior to its use as a tourist attraction, parts of this site were known to have been used for producing clay tobacco pipes, one of a number of such places that established themselves in Chester during the 17th and 18th centuries.

Souters Lane is a sharply inclined thoroughfare which at one time ran from Chester's ancient Wolf Gate southward to the banks of the River Dee, but which since the 20th century has had its northern terminus close to Sir Walter Tapper's New Gate archway. In earlier times, its northern end was thought to mark the site of "Cockpit" or "Cockfight Hill" which was said to have existed on or near to the much more ancient Roman Amphitheatre. Formerly known as both "Souters Lode" and "Dee Lane" during its lengthy history, in 1710 this thoroughfare was adapted to accept wheeled traffic and shortly afterwards the Corporation began to receive complaints that citizens were using the lane to deposit their waste and rubbish along the banks of the River Dee, much to the detriment of the general area.

Although now separated by the city's inner ring road system, **Dee House** was primarily identified with Little St John Street in the city, which is now marked by the modern day Lumley Place. Since 1929 the property has found itself at the centre of a huge local controversy, standing as it does on the southern, as yet uncovered half of Chester's Roman amphitheatre. Dee House itself is thought to date from the middle of the 18th century, having been built for James Comberbach, a wealthy merchant and Mayor of Chester, reportedly by the architect Thomas Harrison. The house was further extended in the 1740's; giving an L-shaped look to the property and it was reported to have been owned by the same family until 1860 when it was sold to the Anglican Church. Four years later the building was acquired by the Companions of Jesus who established a convent school on the site and added an east wing to the house, which included a chapel. This work was said to have been carried out by the Liverpool architect Edmund Kirkby, who was also responsible for the nearby St Werburgh RC Church on Grosvenor Park Road. Kirkby was a Liverpool based architect who was said to have worked with the noted Cheshire architect John Douglas prior to establishing his own practice. He and his two sons were reported to have worked extensively in the Liverpool area and in the wider northwest region of England.

Dee House's chapel was built between 1867-9 and the property's west wing was rebuilt around 1900. The Ursuline Order from Crewe took over the school in 1925 and it was during preparations for a new south wing in 1929, that the remains of the amphitheatre were first rediscovered. The convent school finally closed during the 1970's and the building has since been used as a corporate headquarters, but in recent years has stood empty and idle whilst its long term future is decided.

During the years that Dee House was owned by the Comberbach estate, a number of private tenants were thought to have occupied the property, including two sisters by the name of Massey and the much more notable George John Chamberlain. This particular gentleman seems to have been a figure of some local notoriety, although as to exactly why he had some sort of infamous reputation isn't entirely clear. Reportedly a member of a fairly prominent local family who originated in the outlying suburb of Saughall, they seem to have gained much of their local status through marriage and were reported to have had held Hope Hall, as well as extensive properties rights in Tranmere. Chamberlain himself is also reputed to have been involved with the development of the port town of Birkenhead on the Wirral peninsula. Following his death in around 1860, Dee House was said to have passed into the possession of the Reverend James Brown, which perhaps marks the point where the property came into the ownership of the Anglican Church.

Representing one of the greatest archaeological treasures of the city, Chester's as yet only partially excavated **Roman Amphitheatre** is thought to have first been built during the first century of legionary occupation at the fortress and was said to have been completely constructed in stone by the year AD 80. Rediscovered purely by accident in 1929, by a workman who was investigating the cellars of the now extinct St John's House, the presence of huge cut sandstone blocks below this later building finally alerted both the local and national authorities to the archaeological treasure, that but for a stroke of luck may well have been destroyed by a new road scheme associated with the 1930's New Gate which was being considered by the then city council.

Apart from being the centre of civic entertainment and the site of gladiatorial competition, such buildings were often used as "Ludi" or weapons training areas, where new recruits would receive instruction on the latest fighting techniques, as well as learning how to fight as a combined unit when facing a common enemy. Often, these classes or training sessions were reported to have been led by one or more of the gladiators who fought in such arenas, as they were quite rightly regarded as being the leading "experts" in such martial matters.

The general layout and construction of such amphitheatres was of an oval space enclosed by both an inner and outer wall, commonly built of timber or stone. The inner wall which could often be up to 3 ft thick and 12 ft high was said to have surrounded the central compound, providing a barrier between the spectator and those that were participating on the arena floor. The outer wall of the amphitheatre could measure up to 9 ft thick and 35 ft high, with the intervening and angled space filled with row upon row of seats or benches for the thousands of potential spectators to sit on, whilst they watched the events unfold before them.

Lying on a generally north south alignment, the amphitheatre at Chester was thought to be around 315 ft in length and approximately 286 ft wide, with the arena floor alone measuring some 190 ft by 160 ft. At both the north and south ends of the arena, were the main entrances which led to the centre of the amphitheatre, with the northern entry reportedly consisting of a sloping passageway which had a central drain running through its middle and the entry protected by formidable wooden gates. As the southern half of the amphitheatre remains unexcavated through to the present day, it is surmised that the south entrance to the arena would have mirrored its northern counterpart, a conclusion that can only be amended if and when the amphitheatre is ever fully disclosed to the modern world.

Along the east and west sides of the arena, a series of entrances were thought to have existed, providing access to the rows of public seating provided for the local population, rather like the modern stadiums people inhabit today, but on a much more basic level. Additionally, the main entrances on both of these sides were thought to have been uncovered, unlike the far more symbolically important north and south gateways, which were the only two entrances which led to the arena floor itself. During excavations which took place in the early 1960's evidence of the earlier timber amphitheatre was also discovered which suggested that this earlier arena had in fact only been able to accommodate half of the 8000 capacity of the later stone built arena.

The same archaeological program of 1960/1 also uncovered the altar dedicated to the Roman deity "Nemesis" on the west side of the northern entrance and reportedly housed within a shrine ostensibly called a "Nemeseum". The shrine was thought to have been placed there for easy access by the gladiators who would pray to Nemesis, the God of

Revenge, for guidance and perhaps good fortune in their forthcoming battles. This historic altar was later removed to the Grosvenor Museum for conservation and for its protection

On the eastern side of the arena, a small chamber was discovered which archaeologists speculated to be a "holding room" for the gladiators and other participants who were due to take part in events within the amphitheatre. A number of such chambers were thought to have been located around the edges of the arena floor at the time that it was being employed by the resident legionary force.

The floor of the amphitheatre was reported to have been cut deep into the natural sandstone bedrock taking its level to below that of the surrounding ground, explaining the slope from the northern gateway and essentially creating a bowl-like structure. There is also some evidence to suggest that both the central drain, running through the centre of the arena on a north to south alignment and a second drain, abutting the curved inner wall of the amphitheatre were both cut even deeper into the native red stone and the filled in with crushed rock and stone, allowing water to flow through them, yet at the same time preventing the drains from becoming a tripping hazard or littered with floating debris. Initial investigations of the floor area in 1960/1 also indicated that sometime around the end of the 3rd century the arena floor had in fact been resurfaced, a conclusion substantiated by the fact that below this later level there was evidence of the amphitheatre having fallen into an extended period of disuse, due to the presence of a layer of detritus which lay between the first and third century floors.

Above this secondary arena surface, there was some evidence to suggest that following the final abandonment of the fortress sometime in the 4th century, the amphitheatre had been used for a variety of purposes by the local population, including as a cess pit. There was also some indication that the site had been employed in the post Roman period as a site of generally low level civil occupation, which was speculated to include a number of basic huts and cottages which had been established outside of the city's defensive walls. It was possibly as a result of this later occupation, as well as the successive centuries of temporary use and abandonment, that eventually caused the impressive amphitheatre to become lost and forgotten over time, until its accidental rediscovery in 1929.

The most notable victim of the modern excavation of the northern half of the amphitheatre was St John's House, an 18th century property with extensive gardens that was completely demolished to fully reveal the buried Roman antiquity. Previously land that had been in the possession of St John's church, by 1750 the house was reported to have been occupied by a prominent local resident called Thomas Slaughter, who was granted the house and its lands by Sir William Young and Walter Warburton in the same year. Slaughter and his wife were thought to have occupied the property for an extended period, as the couple were still resident there right up until 1790, the year that Thomas finally departed this life.

Following the Slaughter's occupation of St John's House, the property was then thought to have come into the possession of a gentleman called Meadows Frost; and it was said to have remained in that family's possession until its acquisition by the authorities in the 20th century, when it was purchased with monies raised by public subscription.

The historic **St John the Baptist Church**, which is thought to have its first foundations in the 7th century, was at one time Chester's Cathedral Church, having been relocated from Lichfield by Peter, the then Bishop of Mercia in 1075. Only small amounts of the fabric of the early Anglo Saxon and later Norman church continue to exist today following a large scale deconstruction of the property which took place around 1545, as a result of the reforms instigated by Henry VIII. Elements of these earlier phases of continue to exist, but only in small measure and most notably in the remainder of the church's Nave, where examples of Norman, Transitional and Early English architectural stonework are evident. This deliberate destruction was reported to have been added to by the damage caused by a violent storm in 1572, which was reported to have caused the steeple of the church to collapse, as well as much of the west end of St John's.

The remaining substantive parts of St John's was further damaged by the vicious fighting encountered during the Civil War siege of the city during the 17th century, when one of the church's towers was reportedly used as a gun platform by the attacking Parliamentarian forces led by Sir William Brereton. However, much debate still rages, as to whether or not the cannon were placed in the tower itself or at its base, although either way such usage would inevitably have undermined the stability of such ancient structure and was likely to be responsible for the later collapse of the tower and its surrounding fabric.

During the 19th century St John's was fundamentally rebuilt, presenting us with the church that continues to stand today, which is largely the work of R C Hussey and John Douglas. Hussey was reported to have undertaken an extensive rebuilding program at the church between 1859 and 1866 and then again, between 1886 and 1887, whilst Douglas was employed there in both 1881 and 1886 when he oversaw the rebuilding of the north Porch and northeast Belfry respectively. The interior of today's modern church still contains numerous monuments to the many and varied members of its congregation, most notably the Warburton's. It also contains a number of wooden dedication plaques that are thought to be the work of the various Randle Holmes, the related historians and heralds that were resident in Chester between the 16th and 18th centuries. The church is also said to contain the organ which was played at the Coronation of Queen Victoria at Westminster Abbey and which was erected at St John's on 20th October 1838. In 1895, architect Thomas Lockwood was employed to design a case for the instrument, which during its time at St John's has subsequently been converted and relocated to a number of different locations within the church precincts.

An associated religious fraternity with St John's was the Chartulary of St Anne's, comprised of a hospital and convent which were adjoined to the much older and much more renowned religious centre of St John's. The fraternity and hospital of St Anne's had been reported as early as 1360, but ultimately suffered a similar fate to other monasteries, chapels and churches, etc during the purges of Henry VIII. Throughout its relatively short-lived existence however, the fraternity was reported to have been well supported by the well-to-do families of Chester and had been bequeathed extensive property holdings within the city, including land and messuages in St John Street, Eastgate Street, Northgate Street, Parsons Lane (now Princess Street), White Friars Lane and Cuppin Street. The site of the long extinct buildings of St Anne's are thought to be generally marked today by the south western gateway of the 19th century Grosvenor Park complex.

The **Old Bishop's Palace** which stands overlooking The Groves on the River Dee is thought to date from before 1745 and to have been commissioned on behalf of Bishop Peploe who died in 1752, but not officially used as the Bishop's residence until after 1845 when its predecessor at the Cathedral's Abbey Green was demolished. This Bishop's Palace was reported to have been substantially extended during the 18th century and modified once again in the 19th century. Having served as an official residence for the local Diocese for an extended period, it was used as a YMCA hostel from the 1920's onwards, before being converted into commercial offices in the 1980's.

The Anchorites Cell, which is also known as **The Hermitage** is located on a former sandstone cliff, overlooking the River Dee and located close to the site of an early medieval quarry. The building is said to date from the middle of the 14th century when it was thought to have been used as a religious retreat by a monk or local hermit, with the name of John Spicer generally associated with the building. The cell is connected to the Church of St John the Baptist and was restored as a habitable structure during the 19th century. The entrance to the cell was brought from the former Chester church of St Martin's-in-the-field which used to exist around St Martin's Way in the city and which was finally demolished in 1897. The Hermitage was substantially refurbished once again in 1970 and stands in a suburb of Chester formerly called Redcliff, a name undoubtedly connected with its early use as a quarry. In earlier times, the Hermitage was reported to have been used as a meeting place by Chester's Tanners and Cordwainers (Shoemaker's) companies. In 1817, a city lawyer called Price was reported to be residing in this ancient building.

St John's Rectory which lies on Vicars Lane originally served as the vicarage for St John's Church and is reported to date from the middle of the 18th century. Up until 1957 the property continued to fulfil this purpose, but was then employed as the residence for the city's Grosvenor Club, which had previously been accommodated at the HSBC bank building in Eastgate Street, directly below the city's clock.

Chester's main recreation area is still the city's **Grosvenor Park** complex, which lies to the south of historic Foregate Street and the much more modern Union Street and Grosvenor Park Road. Prior to the middle of the 16th century much of these lands, including Billy Hobby's Field and the Headlands Walk had been in the possession of both St John's church and the Fraternity of St Anne's, but along with other religious properties in the city was seized by the monarch Henry VIII in the 1540's. Ultimately, most of these particular lands then passed into the possession of the Cholmondley family, whose great city mansion was known to have been located in the area of the later Grosvenor Park complex. This notable family were thought to have occupied the property until the outbreak of the English Civil War in the mid 17th century, when they removed themselves to a new home in the city, a site now marked by Chester's Public Library on the Market Square.

During the bitter conflict, the Cholmondley mansion, along with virtually every other building outside of the city's walled defences was deliberately razed by Chester's Royalist defenders, to prevent them being used by the besieging Parliamentary forces. Following the surrender of the city though, this great house was not rebuilt, but rather parts of the property seems to have passed into the hands of a man called Mr Darlington and by 1725 was reported to have comprised a large well built house, a large courtyard, orchards, gardens, stables and a large number of miscellaneous conveniences. These details were noted in that year, as the property was being advertised for sale and it is assumed that it was at that time the lands finally came into the possession of the Grosvenor family, who subsequently gifted them to the people of Chester.

Officially presented to the city around 1867 by Richard, the 2nd Marquis of Westminster, the parkland was reportedly laid out by a Mr Kemp of Birkenhead and contains a fine statue dedicated to Richard Grosvenor, which was designed by Thomas Thorneycroft and ceremoniously unveiled in July 1869. The modern park has been further adorned by a number of buildings and structures designed by the renowned local architect John Douglas who was extensively employed by the Duke of Westminster between 1865 and 1867, designing the Park Lodge building, featuring figures of the various Earls of Chester and the canopy for Billy Hobby's well. The southwest section of the park also features three ancient stone-built arches, all of which have been relocated from their original homes in the city, ostensibly to preserve them, but also to create an interesting visitor feature. The three arches include a remnant from the 12th century St Mary's Benedictine Convent, Chester's 13th century Ship-Gate and an archway from the city's St Bridget's church, which no longer exists in the city.

On the corner of Grosvenor Park Road and Union Street adjoining Bath Street are Chester's **City Baths** which were first opened in 1901. Designed by Harold Burgess of Kensington, the interior host's two separate swimming pools, the "Atlantic" and "Pacific" and was reported to have also contained washing facilities for those local residents who did not have ready access to baths in their own homes. The outside of the building was completed by John Douglas, in a combination of brick, timber and stone. No's 1 to 11 **Bath Street** is a terrace of six cottages designed and developed by architect John Douglas, who also built the former Prudential Assurance building at the junction with Foregate Street in 1903. Number 13 Bath Street is commonly known as "The Spinney" and is reported as a relatively small town house built in a similar fairy tale style, to that of the other adjoining properties.

Today's Union Street, linking Grosvenor Park Road and Vicars Lane, may derive its modern title from an association with Chester's Quaker community, of which the builder Thomas Lunt was a part; and that was attached to a number of other Lunt projects and properties in this part of the city, including the Union Hall, Union Walk and the Union Bridge. In earlier times the still existent Vicars Lane ran along the route of today's Union Street, but was then known as Barkers Lane, a name recalling a connection with the city's early and medieval leather tanning industries which were thought to have been located in this area of Chester. During the 16th and early 17th centuries, the northern flank of this thoroughfare was known to have been inhabited by a large number of properties, including 19 cottages, 17 gardens and an orchard, all of which were ultimately razed from the ground to make way for the development of the Barnston family's city mansion, Forest House, which was constructed in nearby Love Lane.

Recent archaeological investigations in and around the Grosvenor Park grounds and Bath Street have revealed evidence of a previously unknown Roman road which was thought to have run on an east west alignment to the city's amphitheatre, close to the present day Union Street. Also within the grounds of the public park, archaeologists have investigated the remains of the medieval Chapel of St Anne, a religious fraternity associated with the nearby ancient church of St John's, whose property later passed into the hands of the Cholmondley family following the Dissolution of the Monasteries by Henry VIII in the 16th century. The Cholmondley's were reported to have built a new brick built mansion on the site, a property which was subsequently destroyed during the English Civil War siege of Chester during the 17th century. After lying derelict for decades the site was said to have been rebuilt during the first half of the 18th century, but was finally demolished forever when the grounds for the new Grosvenor Park were laid out in 1867.

Grosvenor Park Road was primarily laid out following the gift of land, including Billy Hobby's Field, for the purpose of establishing a public park for the citizens of Chester, granted to the Corporation by the Marquis of Westminster. Having designed the Lodge building in the new park complex, John Douglas then set about designing a terrace of almost continental looking houses, as well as a Chapel and a County Police building on land that he personally owned and managed. Located on the eastern flank of the new roadway, this development and the ones in nearby Bath Street soon earned the area the name of "Douglasville" in honour of their designer. This terrace of houses included a Baptist Chapel, which now serves as the Zion Chapel and along with no's 6 to 11 Grosvenor Park Road was built by Douglas between 1879 and 1880.

Standing directly opposite to Douglas' buildings on Grosvenor Park Road is the soaring St Werburgh's Roman Catholic Church designed by the celebrated architect Edmund Kirby, who was also responsible for elements of Chester's Ursuline Convent which continues to stand over the southern end of the Roman Amphitheatre. St Werburgh's was officially opened by the Roman Catholic Bishop of Liverpool on 13th July 1876 and its first phase was constructed of Yorkshire stone and blue Welsh slate. The church was further enlarged and fully completed in 1914, with the later sections built of the much preferred Stourton Quarry stone.

CHAPTER SEVENTEEN

EASTGATE STREET

Representing the eastern section of the Roman's fortress' Via Principalis, which was formally known as the Via Principalis Sinistra, **Eastgate Street** would have been the main thoroughfare in and out of Chester's military fortress, linking the eastern gate with the Legions Headquarters building, the Principia, which lay at the centre of the fortress.

The great Roman gateway, which was reported to have remained virtually intact until the late 18th century was thought to have been a twin double barrel vaulted entrance, which was flanked by guard towers on either side and topped by a patrol walkway that linked the northeast and southeast sections of the fortress' immense defensive walls. Even after the Roman's had abandoned the military base in the 4th century, their great gateways were thought to have remained relatively intact, being adapted and supplemented by the various British, Welsh and Anglo Saxon occupiers who successively held control of the city.

It seems that rather than dismantle the imposing Porta Principalis Sinistra, these later defenders of Chester simply chose to employ one set of these double archways as an entranceway and incorporated the other into their own buildings and structures. Although there are no records to indicate when this transformation was actually first undertaken, most sources believe that the great Anglo Saxon leader Aethelflaeda, may have been responsible, given her noted refortification and rebuilding of Chester in the late 9th and early 10th centuries.

Nevertheless, it seems clear from later records that the underlying presence of the Roman gateway had been largely forgotten by the mid 18th century, when the medieval fabric of the eastern entrance had become so ruinous that the city authorities sought to replace it. Around 1766-1767 work finally began on dismantling the medieval gateway and as the workmen slowly removed the various phases of construction that had been applied to the gateway over the preceding centuries, the great mass of the hidden Roman gateway was slowly revealed. A number of local commentators were compelled to record the discovery of this soon to be demolished Roman structure, with some urging a halt to the planned modernisation of the city's east gate and proposing that the newly discovered historic archways should be left intact. Sadly though, their pleas were left unanswered and along with its medieval successor the Roman's imposing Porta Principia Sinistra was taken down and carted away, leaving only a written record in its place.

According to one of these written reports, the gateway consisted of two sets of twin arches, with one pair facing out, towards what is today, modern day Foregate Street. Some several feet behind this first pair of arches, was the second identical set, which marked the eastern end of the Via Principalis, today's Eastgate Street. It seems likely that these two separate sets of archways were joined at their centre by a massively constructed central pillar, which was set into the middle of the main thoroughfare, helping to create two lanes for the traffic that flowed in and out of the military fortress. The double set of twin arches were also thought to have been further connected by the Patrol Walk which ran on top of them and which helped to link the northeast and southeast sections of the bases massive defensive walls.

Although most illustrations and physical reproductions of this gateway tend to suggest that each pair of these vaulted entrances was made up of two identically sized arches, 15 feet wide, by 16 feet high and 10 feet deep, other historians believe that this is incorrect. Instead, they point to the fact that most existing Roman gateways of this type and from this period, generally consist of two arches, but of completely different sizes. They have argued that a difference in width would generally be attributed to the function that each particular archway served, with smaller ones for foot traffic or horses and larger ones to allow large freight carts in and out of the protected precincts.

The only other feature which was noted about this long extinct gateway, was that on its eastern facing front, that is looking out towards Foregate Street and visible to those coming into the fortress' precincts, was a carved figure of the Roman deity, Mars. It was said to be over this ancient carving that the severed heads of both Piers de Legh (1399) and Henry Hotspur Percy (1403) were publicly exhibited on the orders of the usurper king Henry Bolingbroke during the late 14th and early 15th centuries.

During the Roman occupation much of the northern flank of this military roadway would have been inhabited by the regular troops that lived within the defensive walls of the fortress and in all likelihood would have been occupied with row upon row of wattle and daub timber built barrack blocks. Some of the tracks, paths and ditches which serviced these extensive lines of legionary barrack blocks were thought to have subsequently developed into the medieval side-streets and boundary ditches which eventually evolved into the modern lanes and streets that remain with us today. Godstall Lane, Leen Lane and St Werburgh Street are all thought to have their earliest foundations in the Roman period, albeit with the first two thoroughfares originating in a much different form. According to some historians, both Godstall and Leen Lanes, which now occupy elevated positions on the northern side of modern Eastgate Street, began their lives in a similar form to that of modern day St Werburgh Street, beginning at street level at their southern junctions and being steeply inclined towards the north. However, later civil and commercial development along the northern flank of Eastgate Street have resulted in both of these ancient paths being raised aloft, to form part of the elevated rows for which the city of Chester is famed.

Towards Eastgate Street's northwest junction with Northgate Street, it has been suggested that during the Roman period a building of some importance occupied this particular site, rather than it being inhabited by even more rows of legionary barrack blocks. Although there have been a number of suggestions as to what purpose this long extinct building actually served, possibly as the Legionary Commanders residence (Praetorium), the argument for it being this building are not wholly compelling. Indeed, during the extensive archaeological excavations at the old Market Hall site in Northgate Street during the late 1960's, one of the Roman buildings discovered there was subsequently identified as the Praetorium and is the commonly accepted location for that particular building in Chester.

Rather, it seems far more likely that this "unidentified" legionary building in Eastgate Street may in fact have been the Legionary Hospital or Valetudinarium, which was known to have stood in this general area of the fortress and would have occupied a central position within the camp. The only argument that would go against this site being occupied by the hospital is that typically such a building would have been located in a fairly quiet area of the fortress, so that the patients would not be unduly disturbed by the day to day noise and activities of their healthier comrades. However, it is perhaps worth noting that this particular building may well have adjoined the vast open space that is now largely occupied by the church and precincts of Chester's great Norman Abbey, which would not have existed at the time and does not appear to have been extensively used by the resident 20th Legion, apart from perhaps a later Christian shrine. In either case, the fact that this particular area of the city is now inhabited by a large number of Chester's earliest landmark buildings and structures virtually ensures that in all likelihood the opportunity to fully explore the site of this so far unidentified Roman building will almost never arise.

At this same junction of Eastgate and Northgate Streets is a short flight of steps which allow access to the elevated row on the northern flank of Eastgate Street and which in earlier times were commonly known as the "**Butter Steps**" or "**Milk Stoops**" recalling the sellers of such produce who traded in this particular area. The present first floor elevated row, lying between Leen Lane and Northgate Street was reported to have been known locally as "**Baxter's Row**" owing to the number of associated tradesman who established their businesses there, although throughout its extensive history this particular Row has had a number of different names. Apart from being called Baxter's Row, it has been known as Butter Shops Row, Dirke Lofts which became Loft's Common Passage, Dark Row, Country Bakers Row, Dark Entry and finally Pepper Alley Row. In 1592, it was reported that a property within the "Dark Row" was granted to the Mayor and his Corporation by two of the city's most prominent citizens, William and Richard Leche, presumably members of the same family whose name is recalled in Watergate Street's "Leche House". Although not specifically mentioned in the record, it is assumed that this property was granted to the Corporation as a charitable bequest, with its rents being used to provide for the city's poorest inhabitants.

City records also indicate that the Council subsequently demolished this property along with a number of other tenements and built a block of "**New Buildings**" in the area, which were then leased out to various tenants and shopkeepers, including an Ironmonger called Thomas Cross in 1635. Largely located on the eastern flank of lower Northgate Street, the city's Ironmongers were said to have established their business premises in this area of the city, although prior to settling here, members of this particular company were reported to have congregated around St John's Street, just outside Chester's eastern gate. Around the same time that the Corporation were constructing these "New Buildings", another brand new property was reported to have been constructed nearby. Built on the orders of one Humphrey Haughton from the city of Manchester, this new house was reported to have occupied a site in between the ancient Leen and Godstall Lanes.

At least three of the previously mentioned "Dark Row" properties, which were demolished by the Council along with the Leche's building around 1600, were thought to have been in the Corporation's possession since 1403, when "three messuages" were reportedly granted to the Mayor and his Aldermen by Chester's Franciscan Order, the Grey Friars. Prior to their ownership of the properties, these same sites, which were thought to have occupied the area between Leen Lane and Northgate Street were reportedly in the possession of a number of Chester's leading citizens, including Richard le Bruyn, Roger de Meols, Robert Candelan and John Brychull (or Brickhill). Ultimately though, by 1345, most, if not all of these messuages or tenements ended up in the hands of one particular individual, a man called Matthew the Tanner.

During the 17th century, the townhouse of the often mentioned Aldersey family was reported to have been located in this area of the city, the site of their great city mansion now said to be partially marked by Chester's "**Boot Inn**" tavern, which had formerly occupied a city plot in Northgate Street. The building which exists today is thought to date from the 17th century, which is contemporary with the Aldersey family's home, although its frontage was known to have been extensively renovated during the 19th century and is thought to have included the replacement of the Oriel window feature that graces the front of the present building. Since that time the Boot Inn has been subsequently refurbished and enlarged by a national brewery chain sometime around 1988.

A number of early city records refer to various members of the Aldersey family owning properties in and around this particular section of Chester, so much so, that it can often be difficult to identify with any certainty exactly which plot of land or building is being referred to. In his will of 1555 for example, Rauffe Aldersey was reported to have bequeathed his property in Eastgate Street to his son Hugh, a property that was said to have included extensive gardens, which adjoined St Werburgh's churchyard. In the same will, Rauffe was said to have bequeathed a second property in Eastgate Street to his other son William, a messuage he had previously purchased from Sir William Norris. It is probably worth noting in regard to this particular property, that most records indicate that Norris' building occupied a site on the northwest flank of Leen Lane, in an area that is now generally devoid of historic buildings due to much more recent modernisation.

The family's great mansion which was said to have become such a prominent feature of Chester's Eastgate Street was reportedly constructed around 1650, although elements within it may well have originated from an even earlier property. In a lease of 1662, three gardens lying between Godstall Lane and St Werburgh's Street were noted as having "previously been in the possession of William Aldersey", suggesting that they had formerly been owned or leased by William, but he had then given up his rights to them or simply sold them off. These later gardens may well be the same "void piece of land" that William had first been granted in 1574 and which is now marked by St Werburgh's Mount and the buildings immediately to the rear of the modern day National Westminster Bank building in Eastgate Street.

Possibly first reported during the reign of King Edward III **Leen Lane** is located on this northern side of Eastgate Street at first floor level and like Godstall Lane further east, linked the city's principal thoroughfare with the historic churchyard of St Oswald's in Chester's great Norman Abbey. Its name is thought to derive from the passageway's early form, which was both extremely narrow and steep, existing as it did before the elevated Row in this area was even built and therefore rising from Eastgate Street's ground level to the much higher St Werburgh's Mount and Abbey precincts. In fact, the incline was reported to have been so steep that heavily laden carts were unable to traverse its length and instead had to access the churchyard via another less arduous route.

At the northwest corner of this ancient alleyway, the Vicarage of St Oswald's church used to stand, but this was subsequently replaced by the modern buildings which flank the south side of today's Music Hall Passage, leading from St Werburgh's Street, westward through to Northgate Street. In modern day Chester, Leen Lane's historic thoroughfare only retains a small portion of its original form, the northwest section having been redeveloped into an open courtyard, which is now used for deliveries to the modern shops units which occupy the eastern frontages in Northgate Street.

Connecting Eastgate Street with the site formerly known as St Werburgh's Mount, **Godstall Lane** is thought to have been named in memory of a local hermit called "Godescal", although as with the neighbouring Leen Lane it seems far more likely that this passageway owes its earliest foundation to the Roman occupiers of Chester. As with its contemporary however, prior to the construction of the city's elevated Rows in this area of the city, Godstall Lane was probably a relatively steep and fairly narrow passageway, which reproduced the incline of today's much wider and far more accessible St Werburgh's Street.

Standing almost directly opposite to the two famous Browns buildings, at the junction of Eastgate Street and St Werburgh's Street, sits the **Natwest Bank** building designed by George Williams around 1860. In common with his fellow architects Harrison, Penson and Wyatt, Williams' building was designed in a classical style, with stone pediment and columns. Originally, the property was said to have been built for Dixon and Wardell's Chester Bank as their corporate headquarters in the city; and who were known to have many notable characters as clients, including the world famous railway engineer Thomas Brassey. It was during the construction of this building that the eastern end of Eastgate Street's northern elevated Row was lost forever, as the new structure could not and did not accommodate such a traditional feature. Fortunately perhaps, the remaining early 19th century street frontages which occupy the remainder of the terrace did accommodate an elevated row and helped to preserve the two ancient lanes that lie behind them. Dixon and Wardell's Bank later evolved into Parr's Bank, then the Westminster Bank, before finally becoming the National Westminster Bank, which is now commonly known as the Natwest.

Prior to the construction of the Natwest Bank building, an ancient hostelry called the **Mitre Inn** was reported to have stood on the very same site and was known to have existed there from around 1649, when it said to have been purchased by a man called Robert Leigh. During its lifetime, part of the same property was thought to have been occupied by a Fletcher called Richard Smith who was known to be working there in 1672 and was said to have succeeded a Draper called William Hulton who was reported to have owned or leased the property prior to 1649. Around 1676, the Mitre Inn was thought to have been relocated elsewhere in the city and its former home then became known as the **Black Dragon**.

Around the corner and on the eastern side of **St Werburgh Street**, numbers 2 to 18 are a terrace of generally modern buildings designed and developed entirely by the noted architect John Douglas between 1895 and 1899, but which were said to have been influenced by the Duke of Westminster, who suggested that a half-timbered style would be more pleasing and appropriate for the city's historic thoroughfare. Prior to Douglas' complete redevelopment of the area, the site was thought to have housed a number of notable buildings which had been unfortunate enough to fall into disfavour or disrepair.

At the left-hand bend of this street, **St Werburgh's Mount**, which is now an arcaded parade of shops, designated as No's 15 to 27 was designed by Douglas between 1873-4 for local builder Mr George Hodgkinson and is thought to be one of the architect's first projects in the city. Prior to this development though, the "Mount" was reported to have been occupied by an elegant townhouse, last inhabited by Thomas Hughes, the author of "The Strangers Handbook to Chester". During its long history, this particular section of the thoroughfare has also been known as "Bed Post Row", but in 1574 was reported to have been a void parcel of land granted to William Aldersey the younger.

At the north western end of St Werburgh's Street is **St Werburgh's Row** which adjoins the ancient chapel of St Nicholas and dates from 1935, having been designed by the renowned architect Maxwell Ayrton, the designer of Wembley Stadium and its famous twin towers. Prior to the construction of Ayrton's beautifully crafted arcaded row, much of the site was thought to have been occupied by one of Chester's early Linen Halls, along with the remnants of the historic St Oswald's churchyard. St Werburgh's Street itself was thought to have been formally laid out sometime around 1850 on the instructions of the Dean of Chester's Cathedral and some 20-odd years later the historic King's School Building, which adjoined the Cathedral, was reported to have been rebuilt, the site today housing a branch of Barclays Bank.

Back in Eastgate Street itself, much of the northeast section of the street, running from St Werburgh's Street to the great Eastgate arch, was formerly known as the **Green Dragon Row**, being credited to a tavern of that name which was located there sometime around 1707. Prior to that date the hostelry's sign was said to have been located on the opposite side of the street, on a site that was reported to have stood close to the modern day entrance of the Grosvenor Shopping Precinct. Although the "Green Dragon" was known to have existed on the northern side of the street through to the 19th century, records suggest that it had eventually disappeared or been relocated by around 1817. Two other properties within this row of generally retail premises are worth particular note, the first being the current Barclay's Bank building which is located at the eastern junction of Eastgate Street and St Werburgh's Street and at one time was known to have housed a branch of Martin's Bank, although nothing more is known about this financial institution.

The second property that should be noted now fronts the modern day "Next" building, but which was formerly inhabited by an early Woolworth's store in Chester. The façade of this building appears to be extremely modern, with little evidence of it having been constructed prior to the middle of the 20th century.

However, an early photograph of Eastgate Street, dating from around 1890, features this particular frontage and perhaps suggests that it may in fact be contemporary with many of the half timbered properties that were designed by the likes of Lockwood and Douglas. That having been said though, parts of the street level façade were known to have been altered during the 1970's when the building was taken over by the Next Group who subsequently replaced Woolworth's as the tenants, which might just account for the general brand new look of the property.

Within the same terrace, during the 18th century Chester's Corn Exchange building was reported to have been sited in this same area, occupying a site close to the "Green Dragon Inn". Rebuilt in 1859, this new Corn Exchange was later converted into Chester's first Picture House by a Mr W Hunter who officially opened his new "Picturedrome" on the 8th November 1909 and continued in business until the 29th March 1924 when the picture house was finally closed. These premises were later reported to have housed a second entrance to Chester's large Woolworth's department store, the main body of which lay at the back of the main street frontages, towards the city's Cathedral.

Prior to the construction of the generally modern Woolworth's shopping hall, to the rear of the old Corn Exchange building and reportedly accessed by a passageway facing the Grosvenor Hotel, a property called the Manchester Hall was noted in 1823. This hall was thought to have existed until as late as 1874, although little information as to its actual age or purpose has thus far been found. However, the fact that it was called the "Manchester Hall" would seem to indicate a commercial purpose, suggesting that it was designed to host textile fairs within the city, or served as some sort of permanent trade hall for regional manufacturers and their wares, rather like Chester's Union and Commercial Halls which lay outside of the city walls.

Moving towards the East gate and almost directly adjoining the archway is the HSBC building which was originally designed and constructed as the **Grosvenor Club** by John Douglas between 1881 and 1883. The building was further extended by Douglas in 1908 and it was later used by the Midland Bank, before being taken over by its present tenants. This property is similar in design to Douglas' County Police Headquarters constructed at the junction of Foregate Street and Grosvenor Park Road in 1884.

This specific site is particularly noteworthy, in that its extensive history has been generally well recorded, undoubtedly because of it having been in the possession of a number of prominent citizens, as well as the city authorities. In 1737, the site was known to have been leased to a Tanner called Nathaniel Hall, although it seems unlikely that he conducted his business there, given the generally unpleasant nature of the leather industry.

One of the earliest and most prominent owners of this property was Thomas Green, a Tallow Chandler by trade, who was elected a Sheriff of the city in 1551 and Mayor of Chester in 1565. Upon his death in 1602, his extensive property holdings in Eastgate Street, which were said to include houses, outbuildings, kilns, malt-houses, shops and courts were bequeathed to the Mayor and his Corporation, for the benefit of the city's poor. Chester's city records for this period suggest that the first potential tenant for these new Corporation properties was a man called David Allen who had petitioned for the lease, but for some reason refused to accept the terms of the contract being offered by the Council and was consequently refused the tenancy.

By 1681, much of Thomas Green's former property was reported to be in the possession of one Henry Hall, who was described as an Inn-holder and said to have held the lease on these same properties until 1704. In 1736, a Nathaniel Hall, presumably Henry's son, was thought to have petitioned for a new lease on the property, which by then was said to have included houses, malt-houses, shops and courts. By 1759 however, the lease of these same properties was thought to be in the hands of a city Alderman called Ralph Probert, although by this time many of the individual structures were thought to have been in a fairly ruinous condition and with at least one heavily damaged by fire. Finally, by the beginning of the 19th century, parts of Thomas Green's former estate were said to have been in the possession of a Mrs Dutton, described as a widow of Foregate Street, who may well have been sub-letting the Eastgate Street property to other tenants, although there are no specific details regarding this.

The city's **Eastgate** which dates from 1768-9 was built to the designs of an architect called Mr Hayden, whose plans were first accepted in February 1768 and ordered to replace the heavy medieval gateway demolished in 1766-7, which had itself replaced a double barrel arched gateway raised by the Romans. When the medieval gateway was demolished in 1766-7, the two Roman archways were still in place, some 1700 years after they were first built, but they too were demolished by the Georgian builders of the time. The clock and turret which was officially unveiled in 1899, was originally designed and constructed to celebrate the Diamond Jubilee of Queen Victoria in 1897, but delays and arguments were thought to have delayed the project. Designed by the Chester architect John Douglas, the ornamental turret was produced by Douglas' cousin James Swindley of Handbridge, whilst the clock was manufactured by J B Joyce of Whitchurch.

As with all of Chester's main entrances, the eastern gate was put in the custody of a "gate keeper" or "Serjeant" that was responsible for collecting tolls or taxes on goods being brought into the city for sale. These men were also tasked to maintain the security of their particular gateway and to ensure that they were kept in good order. At the Eastgate, one of the first recorded keepers was Henry de Bradford, who was granted the serjeancy of the gate by King Edward I in 1274, purportedly in exchange for the manor of Delamere, which was held by de Bradord, but which the monarch wanted to grant to the Abbey of St Mary's at Vale Royal.

Possibly de Bradford failed to survive much beyond this date, or simply fell out of favour with Edward Longshanks, for in 1275 Thomas de Ipgrave, was said to have been granted the tolls of the gate by the same monarch. Significantly for the age perhaps, following Thomas' death sometime after 1275, the right to the tolls were then passed to his widow, Joan de Ipgrave, although in 1278 she and her new husband, William Maufee, were said to have surrendered their rights to the royal grant for some unspecified reason.

In 1285, King Edward was reported to have granted the serjeancy of the east gate to a Harvey de Bradford, presumably a relative of Henry, but he was later reported to have sold his rights to a member of the Trussell family, who in turn passed these historic rights on through marriage to the de Vere family, the Earls of Oxford. However, some 350 years later, in 1630, the "serjeancy" of the gateway was thought to have been purchased by Sir Randal Crewe, giving him and his heirs the right to collect the tolls of the Eastgate.

The southern flank of the early Roman Via Principalis was known to have been occupied by one of the most visibly imposing and vitally important buildings within the military fortress, the Praetentura, or **Roman Bath House** complex. However, many of the very earliest archaeological remains in this whole area, lying between Eastgate Street and modern day Pepper Street, were systematically destroyed and swept away during the construction of the Grosvenor Shopping Precinct in the 1960's. Fortunately however, the presence of a number of notable buildings, or at least their inner fabrics, prevented the wholesale destruction of all the Roman artefacts and the current buildings, which line the southern flank of Eastgate Street and the eastern flank of Bridge Street, undoubtedly sit over a great deal of yet generally undiscovered architecture.

The Roman Bath House complex was thought to have occupied almost the entire area lying between Pepper Street and Eastgate Street, with its midway limit generally marked by St Michael's Arcade which lies within the main body of the modern shopping centre. From this point northward, much of what remains from Chester's early history is said to still lie buried beneath the fabric of much later medieval and early modern buildings that have been successively built along the developing Eastgate Street thoroughfare.

Significantly though, it is this northern section of the area that so little is known about, which is almost entirely due to the presence of these historic and untouchable buildings, along with their world famous elevated shopping rows. Although no full-scale excavations were permitted during the construction of the Grosvenor Shopping Precinct in the 1960's, observations by local archaeologists were allowed and from these they were able to calculate the size and actual layout of the complex. Although much of the Bath House, including the Basilica (a large covered hall), the Palaestra (covered Exercise Hall), the Aqueducts along with their central Water Tank and the baths themselves were largely destroyed, certain features, including the Natatio (Swimming Baths) were not specifically identified and along with other features may continue to exist beneath later, still standing buildings.

It is perhaps also worth remembering, that as elsewhere in the historic city centre, the ground levels of today and that which felt the full force of Roman hobnailed sandals are generally quite different, sometimes up to a depth of several feet. Thousands of years of accumulated debris, dust, sand and soil, along with hundreds of years of human detritus have altered street levels, giving us a distorted view of where things were and how they looked. On several occasions during the 17th and 18th centuries, workmen employed on properties on the south side of Eastgate Street and the east side of Bridge Street, both of

which bordered the great Roman Bath House complex, were said to have found artefacts some three feet below the level of Chester's elevated Rows, but 7 or 8 feet above ground level. This might suggest that the original Roman buildings were built on a significantly higher plane than the immediate ground level, possibly to take account of the naturally undulating bedrock or to allow for massive hypocaust system that were needed to heat their Bath House. Alternatively, this increased land height might be accounted for by the later occupants of Chester using the long abandoned Roman buildings as rubbish tips, which inadvertently helped to level off the immediate area. If this particular scenario were true, then the presence of Roman artefacts, such as coins, tiles, etc. might just as easily be explained by their being accidentally transferred during local building work or rubbish removal.

Moving westward from the city's East Gate, the mid 18th century canopied property immediately adjoining the city gate and eastern defensive wall is thought to date from around 1770 and was once the location for a city tavern known as Huxley's Vaults. During the 20th century it has successively been occupied by the **Leeds Building Society**, the Halifax Building Society and has since served as the location for a city centre jewellers and pawnbrokers. However, this is such a fine property it was undoubtedly built as a private residence for a notable citizen of the city, prior to being given over to its more mundane retail purposes, but as yet no information exists as to clearly identify its original tenants.

On the southern side of Eastgate Street stands Chester's **Grosvenor Hotel**, the design of which has been attributed to local architect TM Penson, although it was said to be his brother Richard Kyrke Penson who actually oversaw the construction work. Two earlier hostelries, The "White Talbot" and "Golden Talbot" along with a third property were reported to have been converted into the "Royal Hotel" before becoming today's Grosvenor Hotel. The "Golden Talbot" hotel was reported to have existed on the site since 1751, when it had relocated from its previous home in Northgate Street, on the site now occupied by the city's Art Deco "Odeon" cinema. The "Golden" and "White Talbot" hotels were thought to have been combined in 1782 to become the "Talbot Hotel", which by 1790 had been taken down and rebuilt as the "Royal Hotel". The Talbot Assembly Rooms which were said to have first been constructed in 1777 are thought to have been the only feature that managed to survive the wholesale rebuilding of the site in 1860 to form the Grosvenor Hotel.

However, prior to the establishment of these early hotels, much of this very same site was known to have been occupied by a number of individual properties, owned or inhabited by the great and the good of the city. Some reports have suggested that in 1533 at least one of these houses was in the possession of Sir John Talbot, a prominent citizen and landowner who was associated with the Earls of Shrewsbury, sergeants of Chester's Bridgegate and one-time owners of the Bear and Billet in Lower Bridge Street. A second property on the site was reportedly owned by the Fraternity of St Anne's and the third house or tenement was said to have been in the possession of Sir John Porter.

Earlier still, this southeast section of Eastgate Street was said to have been occupied by a similarly small number of city tenements or messuages which were owned and leased by various city tradesmen. In 1410, the third house immediately east of Fleshmonger's Lane (now generally marked by the modern shopping precinct entrance) was reportedly owned by a man called "Roger the Potter", although its rental income was said to have been donated to the priests of St Anne's Fraternity, which lay close to the ancient church of St John's. Immediately adjoining Roger's Eastgate Street property, the buildings on either side were reported to have been occupied by one Richard de Hogh who was described as a Cartwright and the other by a Richard Heinke, who was described as a Barbour.

Immediately west of the modern day Grosvenor Hotel is the canopied entrance to Chester's 1960's utilitarian Grosvenor Shopping Precinct, which is thought to mark the site of the northern junction of the now extinct Fleshmonger's Lane or Newgate Street. First recorded as early as the mid 12th century, **Fleshmonger's Lane** was thought to be the original site of the city's butcher's shops and flesh-sellers stalls, where animals were slaughtered and their carcasses displayed for the passing shoppers. It was thought to have retained this title right up until the beginning of the 18th century, but by 1718 was also being referred to as "Newgate Street" because of the nearby southeast gateway, which is now more commonly called the "Wolf Gate". On the Lavaux map of 1745 which illustrated Chester's ancient streets, Fleshmonger's Lane still retained its historic title, but by 1782 it was more generally referred to by its later title of Newgate Street, suggesting that the name change had become permanent. More about this ancient thoroughfare has been noted in the section dealing with Grosvenor and Pepper Streets. However, it is worth noting, that in 1673, the two buildings which were reported to stand immediately west of Fleshmonger's Lane were said to have been occupied by an Elizabeth Balferon in the first and the White Horse Inn occupying the second property. This second house was said to have been owned by the prominent local figure, Sir Thomas Smith, but was leased and kept as a tavern by a man called Thomas Heath, who was later succeeded by his son Matthew. Today, the site of these earlier pre-17th century buildings is occupied by an elegant looking property that appears to be 18th century in design and two much more modern buildings that form part of the present shopping precinct. Significantly though, the street level shops which sit below these more recent properties are both located within subterranean cellars that may well have heir origins in the 13th or 14th centuries.

The modern day **Browns Crypt Building** stands upon four vaulted bays which are thought to date from the end of the 13th, or beginning of the 14th century and may be contemporary with a long since vanished medieval Abbot's Hall (aka Stone Hall) which has long since been absorbed into Eastgate Street's elevated Rows. The front of the building which overlies these under-crofts was designed by the local architect TM Penson in 1858 and was designed in an Early English Gothic style in order to best match the ancient cellars on which it stands.

The long extinct "Abbot's Hall" was thought to have disappeared sometime around 1540, undoubtedly a victim of Henry VIII's religious reforms that occurred during that period. However, its presence on the site of the later "Browns" building is not entirely definitive, with at least one or two other Eastgate

Street locations being suggested. A second site, formerly owned by an individual called Beckett has been proffered as a potential home for this early medieval building, as has the 1465 "Stone Hall" owned by a Henry Ravenscroft, both of which were reported to have existed in Eastgate Street. It was also noted in 1557 that two local citizens, Fulk Dutton and Joseph Wiseman, were contesting the ownership of a "Stone Hall" in the city, which Dutton ultimately won, although this particular hall was thought to have stood on the north side of the street, rather than the south. Also, a later record of 1681 reports that two men, Thomas and Robert Ravenscroft, were occupying the "Stone Hall" in Eastgate Street, but as with the other records it does not specifically identify the exact location of the property in question. One of the final references to this particular structure relates to the 18th century, when one John Tilston, a prominent builder and mason in Chester, was reported to be to be residing at the "Stone Hall" in Eastgate Street.

Clearly though, the "Browns" site has much to commend it as the location for the ancient Abbots Hall, not least because its medieval cellars which are thought to date from around 1290. However, the fact that the north side of Eastgate Street was known to have immediately adjoined the walled churchyards and burial grounds of Chester's great Norman Abbey would tend to suggest that any such hall would be closer to the Abbey, rather than further away.

The Brown family were reported to have established their business in Eastgate Street around 1828 and were said to have initially occupied existing shop premises, before moving into their extended "Crypt" building which was designed by Penson in 1858. At the same time the architect was thought to have designed the three buildings immediately adjoining the new Brown's property, two of them in a more traditional half timbered style of decoration; and in doing so started a trend amongst Chester based architects that has helped to create the almost unique "Chester Look".

Standing next door to the Browns "Crypt Building", closer to the modern day Precinct entrance is one of T M Penson's buildings which is thought to have been constructed in 1856. This property was said to have been constructed on the site of Chester's historic "**Honey Steps**" where such products used to be sold, reportedly by local women during the October Fairs. In 1780, the Honey Steps (or Stoop) were reported to be located at the foot of the stairs fronting the city property of a man called Maddocks, but by 1858 this stairwell was said to have been removed and rebuilt, following the enlargement of the Brown business premises in that same year. During the 17th century, the original staircase had been described as "a broad pair of stone stairs with hand rails, on the south side of Eastgate Street, which belonged to the great stone building that is supported at its street front with 5 arches and strong pillars".

Severely Classical in design, Penson's 1856 building, which lies closer to the world famous Clock, is said to be reminiscent of Thomas Harrison's work in the city, incorporating as it does the Greek Revival style columns for which Harrison was noted. On the opposite side of Brown's Gothic Crypt building are two more of the architect's early commissions, both of which were constructed in the Black and White revivalist style. The first of these is a single gable building, which was reportedly renovated by Penson in 1858 and is said to contain a number of internal features from the

17th century, including a Jacobean ceiling, mantelpiece and staircase. The twin gabled property adjoining this first house is also a Penson project, which was undertaken in 1852 and is yet another restoration by the architect. Once again the original building is said to date from the beginning of the 17th century and although there is little information regarding the interior, the right hand gable bearing a date of 1640 seems to give some indication of the buildings great age.

At No 18 Eastgate Row south, a city tavern called the "**Crown and Glove**" was reported in 1826 and was thought to have existed all the way through to 1920. Accessed via a narrow passageway, when work on constructing a parlour for the inn was undertaken in 1826 a quantity of Roman coins and tiles were discovered by the workmen. Undoubtedly artefacts from the then as yet unidentified Legionary Bath Houses, along with this whole terrace of buildings, the "Crown and Glove" was thought to have sat atop the covered Exercise Hall which adjoined the main Bath House Complex and known as the Palaestra. Today, the site of the former city centre tavern is thought to be occupied by a jewellery company called Pykes'.

CHAPTER EIGHTEEN

FOREGATE STREET

Modern day **Foregate Street** was formerly known as Forest Street and during the Roman period was reported to be the site of the "Vicus" or civilian settlement which commonly established themselves outside the defences of legionary fortress' and permanent bases. Stretching from the fortresses main double barrel vaulted gateway through to the area of modern day Boughton, this main access road was thought to have been flanked by stone built shops, timber built booths and an assortment of permanent and semi permanent structures which housed the traders, merchants and artisans who commonly attached themselves, their businesses and their families with the resident legionary force.

Laid out along the length of the street, as in later times buildings were thought to have been built on individual and fairly regularised strips of land, possibly ten metres wide and stretching backwards away from the main thoroughfare, sometimes to a depth of 30 metres. The street facing frontage would have been used as the shop front, with their workshops and storage areas immediately behind this area. The rear section of the building and often the smallest part was given over to the merchants living area, where he and his family would have eaten, slept and brought up their children.

Typically each of these individual plots would have been separated by a narrow passage or open piece of land which may or may not have carried a gutter, helping to carry away the rain from the roofs, liquids or waste from the household or other equally unpleasant materials. As one of the major routes in and out of the military fortress, it seems likely that Foregate Street during the Roman period would have been a well constructed and maintained road, with a slight camber to its centre forcing rainwater into the side gutters where it could be safely and efficiently washed away. Possibly the gutters or drains laid down between the nearby civilian buildings would have helped to carry away much of this waste material, finally depositing it on uninhabited areas which lay far enough away from their homes and businesses so as not to be a nuisance.

It seems entirely likely that these early civilian settlements formed the core of the later Chester, even after the last Roman legionary had finally withdrawn from Britain. Although many of the merchants and traders would undoubtedly have relocated themselves to new sites within the central area of the Roman fortress, their early presence seems to have ensured continuity for the settlement and later archaeological excavations have confirmed that the Foregate Street area has been constantly occupied throughout every period of Chester's extensive history. Significantly, in 1825, workmen digging a trench for new water pipes on the north side of the street, between the Eastgate and Frodsham Street, discovered the remains of 2 Roman pavements, as well as an ancient horseshoe and a stone pillar, at a depth of between 6 and 8 feet below the modern surface.

This thoroughfares one-time designation as Forest Street has been suggested as deriving from its former route towards the ancient forest of Delamere, although most historians now believe this possible origin to be an unlikely foundation. Rather, it seems far more plausible that this name simply originated from the streets actual position in relation to the city's main gate, being "fore" and "east" of the principal gateway and eventually being corrupted from "Fore-east" to "Forest". City records also suggest that it was reported with that particular name in 1698 by a noted historian who was visiting the city in that year. It's more common title of Foregate Street, is thought to have an equally early foundation, possibly being derived from an Anglo Saxon term "Forgeat" or "the street of the main gate".

The **Old Bank Building** which is located below the Eastgate clock on the southern flank of the street was redesigned by TM Lockwood in 1895 and includes a short pier arcade linked to the Eastgate archway. The earlier buildings which had stood on this site prior to the outbreak of the English Civil War were reported to have been demolished during the siege of Chester, but by 1650 the site was once again occupied by city inns, reportedly first by "The Maidenhead" and then by the "Elephant and Castle". In 1792, this tavern was finally demolished to make way for William's Bank which had formerly been housed in the city's main marketplace. The sign of the "Elephant and Castle" however was subsequently transferred to Chester's main market square, where it sat alongside another city hostelry, the Coach and Horses. At the same time that the new William Bank building was being raised in 1793, a strip of land immediately adjoining the ancient and narrow St John's Lane was granted to the city's corporation so that this particular historic thoroughfare could be widened and made much more convenient for resident and traveller alike.

Early city records suggest that prior to 1297 this same area of land in Foregate Street, adjoining the ancient Saint John's Lane (Street), was reportedly in the possession of a man called John the Goldsmith, who in that particular year was said to have granted the property to a notable Chester citizen, William of Doncaster for the princely sum of £10. Also mentioned in the same grant or charter were other former owners and occupiers of the land, including William the Butcher, Thomas the Marshal, Richard of Conway and Henry of Thelwall. It seems particularly ironic that the 13th century owner of the property should have been a goldsmith, given that such tradesmen were quite often regarded or used as bankers during that early medieval period and that 500 years later his former lands became home to a modern bank.

The **Lloyds Bank building** which stands at the junction of Foregate Street and St John Street was reputed to have been designed by architect Lewis Wyatt and is described as an early 19th century stone fronted building designed in the Greek revival style. Wyatt's work was thought to have been heavily influenced by the classical styles of both TM Penson's and Thomas Harrison's work in Chester. In 1895, the two adjoining banks companies, Williams' and Lloyds were said to have been formally amalgamated into one commercial enterprise and two years later, in 1897, architect Thomas Lockwood was employed to further extend the Lloyd's Bank building southward along St John's Street.

On the site of one of the two previously mentioned buildings stood the townhouse of one Richard Tyrer, who was possibly a relative of John Tyrer, the man responsible for erecting the water tower at Chester's Bridgegate. Whilst workmen were excavating a new cellar in this Richard Tyrer's property, which was reported to lie just outside of the city's Eastgate on the southern side of the street, a Roman altar was discovered in 1648. A city tavern known as "The Greyhound" or possibly the "Black Greyhound" was also said to have stood in the same general area as Tyrer's house, perhaps suggesting an entirely separate phase of use for the same property. As the site of the Old Bank Building was thought to have been inhabited from 1650 onwards, by the Maidenhead and then the Elephant and Castle, it seems likely that Tyrer's house and the Black Greyhound would have occupied the site now inhabited by the later 19th century Lloyd's Bank building designed by Wyatt.

Directly opposite the Old Bank building is Chester's **Burtons Menswear Store** which lies on the north side of Foregate Street, directly below the Eastgate Clock and which was designed by the Leeds based architect Harry Wilson. Close by is the property of **W H Smith's** retail premises, which at one time was linked to the now extinct Mercia Square, a 1960's shopping development which has subsequently been replaced by even newer individual retail shopping units that are now primarily located in nearby Frodsham Street.

The histories of both of these sites, Burton's and Smith's, can be traced back to at least the beginning of the 17th century and possibly even earlier than that. Prior to the English Civil War siege of the city in around 1645, the 2nd house on the north side of Foregate Street was reported to have been owned or occupied by a local man called James Hurlston, whilst the 3rd house along was said to have been in the possession of Thomas Massey.

In 1511 James Hurlston was reported to have granted his property to a man called Richard Rogerson, a Barker in the city who leased a messuage, kitchen and stables, all of which were located behind the main street frontage. However, the grant from Hurlston was also thought to have included a number of other outbuildings, including one called the "Bark House" and yet another property described as a "Smoke House". All of these particular buildings were thought to occupy the lands between the back of the main Foregate Street frontage and the southern limits of the vegetable gardens of Chester's Norman Abbey, which are now commonly known as the Kaleyards.

Both Hurlston's and Massey's properties were thought to have been occupied by a number of individual tenants throughout the late 16th and early 17th centuries, before both fell victim to the destruction wrought by the English Civil War in the 1640's. People such as Rafe and Richard Wright, who were mercers in the city, were thought to have inhabited the site and it has even been suggested that they established a tavern called the Hart's Head there. Later on, an individual called Thomas Hatton leased part of the property and was then followed by a John Billingham, who in turn was succeeded by a William Wall, a city Alderman and Ironmonger, who was reputed to have kept a good house.

Although little is known about the history of the site following its rebuilding in the 17th century, in 1874, a Miss Emma Salmon was reported to be holding the licence to a Spirit Vaults at number 7 Foregate Street, whilst at the same time holding yet another licence for a Spirits Vaults at 16 Watergate Street. Thought to have been the daughter of Joseph Salmon, the former proprietor of the "Castle and Falcon" in Watergate Street, Miss Salmon was clearly a very busy and enterprising woman.

In 1945, a company, called J E Brassey was reported to be occupying the site of number 9 Foregate Street and according to local records had done so for the preceding 135 years, being founded by a Benjamin Brassey in 1809. A Grocer and Ironmonger, his business premises were reported as "standing opposite" to the "Bank Building", although whether or not this was the Old Williams Bank, Lloyds Bank or the Westminster Bank is unclear, as any, or all three may well have been appropriate, given the location. According to records, this same building had previously been occupied by a Miss Bingley, who was said to have been the daughter of one William Bingley, another Chester grocer and ironmonger.

Today's No 13 Foregate Street was formerly occupied by a branch of the national footwear company Stead and Simpson. However, the site itself has a far lengthier history, being reported as the site of the **Hop Pole Hotel** up until the early 20th century and before that The Globe which had existed from around 1642. In common with many of the pre-17th century buildings in this area of the city however, the property was thought to have been destroyed during the Civil War siege of the city. Prior to the middle of the 16th century, this plot of land had been granted to the Fraternity of St Anne's in the city, but following the Dissolution of the Monasteries the premises were reported to have passed into the hands of two land agents, Edward Sellers and William Blake, who in turn were said to have sold the plot to a Robert Singleton family in 1605.

When Singleton died in 1612, his properties in Foregate Street, then described as a house, four shops and a barn were subsequently divided equally between his relative, William Singleton; and the city's corporation, with both parties being given half of the rents raised from the buildings use. According to early records, the building and its attendant lands were of a substantial size, measuring some 40 feet in width and some 240 feet in length. In 1623 however, William seems to have surrendered his interest in the properties for a full and final settlement of £110, putting them entirely in the possession of the council. Around 1630, all of these properties were reported to have been leased to a city Alderman called William Edwards, who along with his brother Evan, was thought to have completely rebuilt the site shortly afterwards and establishing The Globe Inn in these new city premises. In 1643 though, William was reported to have been forced to leave the city because of his support for the Parliamentary cause and along with the likes of his compatriot, Sir William Brereton, would only return to Chester once the national conflict had been resolved through force of arms.

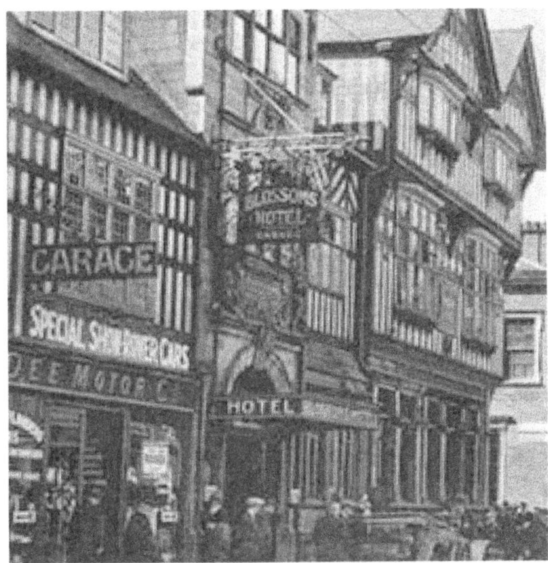

During the Civil War siege of the city and as part of the city's defensive strategy, virtually all of the buildings immediately outside of the city walls were said to have been razed from the ground by the Royalist defenders, to prevent them being used by the Parliamentary forces who were besieging Chester. Following the end of hostilities though and with most of the country settled, Chester along with most major towns and cities began to rebuild its shattered infrastructure. Both Brereton and Edwards returned to Chester as part of the victorious Parliamentary army that had captured the city and by 1657, Edwards was said to have begun rebuilding his Globe Inn property in Foregate Street, as well as continuing his involvement in both local business and politics.

Edwards was reported to have died in 1667 and although little is known about his Globe Inn for the next 60-odd years, it is assumed that as an entirely council owned property, it was successively leased to a number of different tenants. The next mention of the Globe Inn was in 1725, when it was reported to still carry that particular sign, although by 1782 it had changed its name to the Hop Pole Inn and was being kept by two tenants, a John Axon and one William Hassall. In 1795, Axon was still reported as the tenant of a licensed house in Foregate Street, but the name, the Hop Pole Inn, seems to have disappeared from the thoroughfare. Clearly though, this was an oversight, as the Hop Pole Inn was subsequently recorded in 1811 as the site of an auction for a property known as Parry's Yard, so evidently it was still in existence at the time.

Nearly 40 years later, in 1850, the property was thought to have evolved into the Hop Pole Hotel and was reported to be in the keeping of one Elizabeth Bell who was said to have held the licence for well over a decade and was still residing there in 1860. By 1873 however, the hotel had a new occupant, a man called A C Lockwood and it was thought to be during his tenancy that the ancient building was extensively modernised, helping to make it one of the city's most popular hostelry's of its time. Sadly though, within 40 or 50 years of this major renovation the property was reported to have been acquired by the footwear company Stead and Simpson and turned into a retail unit during the 1920's.

The **Blossom's Hotel**, which is now located in St John Street, Chester was rebuilt in its present location in 1895. Prior to that, the hotel had been primarily located on the south side of Foregate Street in Chester, on the site of the later National Westminster Bank Building, but which now houses the "Lush" retail store. This same site was thought to have been reported during the 16th century, when a Sir John Downey was recorded to have owned a tenement at the eastern junction of Foregate Street and St John's Lane that was being occupied by one Margaret Gawyn, probably during the 1530's. Although the Blossom's was reported to have occupied the building from around 1650 through to 1895, a later tenant of the property was said to be the National Provincial Bank of England, who in turn were replaced by the Westminster Bank, which later became the National

Westminster Bank. Thomas Lockwood was thought to have designed elements of this later bank building in 1896 and then again in 1911, although this second phase of work may well have been undertaken by his son W T Lockwood.

Modern day **St John's Street** is thought to be able to trace its foundations all the way back to the time of the Roman legions and is considered to be the main route that linked the fortress with its outlying amphitheatre complex, by way of the bases' main gate, the Porta Principia, which is now marked by Chester's Eastgate. Separated from the fortress' eastern wall only by the "fosse" or defensive ditch that fronted the imposing battlements, it seems likely that parts of this ancient thoroughfare would have been inhabited by elements of Chester's earliest civilian settlement or vicus, which commonly established themselves immediately outside such major Roman garrison bases.

Although it is generally unclear as to what level or type of habitation took place along this route during the Roman period, the foundation of St John's church in the latter part of the 7th century (689 AD) is thought to mark its formal establishment as a recognisable city highway and gaining it the title that it continues to carry today. Despite these early origins though, most publicly available records for buildings and land ownership in this area of the city tend to begin in the 13th century, suggesting that prior to this date most of the land in this south east section of the city were owned, either by the church itself or by the crown through its agents.

Such land ownership was illustrated in a grant of 1253, where Alice de la Hay, the prioress of St Mary's convent in Chester, granted to Thomas Harre (Hare) certain lands in St John's Lane at a rent of 3 shillings per annum. Some 20 or so years later, a local woman called Gunware, the daughter of one Robert Rope, was recorded as having granted her remaining lands in St John's Lane, to one Henry de Aldelym (Audlem), which adjoined the lands she had previously gifted to the church of St John's, proving that such land grants and gifts inevitably worked in favour of the various church bodies.

As elsewhere in the city, these individual grants often applied to a variety of plots, those which contained base tenements, those that were purely agricultural, or those that contained business premises, such as shops, forges or even timber yards. Certainly during the 14th century and the reign of Edward III, St John's Lane was reported to have been the home of Chester's ironmongers and smiths, who were said to have congregated along the length of the street. Although these particular tradesmen are more commonly associated with the "Ironmongers Row" at the southern end of Chester's Northgate Street, St John's Lane was in fact their first home and it was only in later years that they moved into the protective precincts of the city proper.

Prior to the 1540's, great swathes of land throughout the city were known to have been in the possession of Chester's great religious houses, including St John's, St Mary's and of course the Norman Abbey of St Werburgh's. However, the sweeping religious reforms of the monarch, Henry VIII, changed this situation entirely, by dissolving a large number of these wealthy and politically influential houses, seizing their often substantial assets and raising revenue for his own treasury through the sale of these sequestrated assets. This certainly seems to have been the case in St John's Street in Chester, where prior to the Reformation, much of the land was thought to have been in the possession of the nearby

St John's and St Anne's religious communities. Yet by the late 16th century, many of these same holdings were reported to be in the hands of a small number of the city's leading families, including the likes of the Aldersey's, who were known to have owned property in the historic thoroughfare around 1577.

Remarkably perhaps given its extensive history, the modern day St John's Street is almost totally devoid of any notable architectural features, other than the few remaining 18th century street frontages that have somehow managed to avoid the developers eye. This total absence of pre-Civil War buildings though, is easily explained when one considers that virtually every standing property outside of the city walls was deliberately destroyed in the run-up to the siege of Chester. Although some reporters have blamed the forces of Parliament for the loss of these historically significant buildings, most historians and recorders attribute the blame for their loss to the true culprits, the Royalist defenders of Chester. Desperate to avoid giving their Parliamentary adversaries any sort of advantage, the military commanders appointed by Charles I, were said to have ordered the complete devastation of the immediate suburbs, in order to deny Parliaments forces any building that might be put to military use.

It was only after the cessation of hostilities in 1646 that the outlying suburbs of Chester were slowly rebuilt by the inhabitants of the city and even then, the lost properties of the great and the good seem to have taken precedence in terms of rebuilding. This was no doubt due to the fact that the wealthy and influential citizens of the city had both the financial and political means to reconstruct their own shattered buildings, as well as laying claim to the many abandoned building plots that were thought to have existed after the highly destructive siege. It seems clear that following the Parliamentary capture of the city, it was common practice for local merchants and tradesmen to claim compensation from the new authorities for the financial losses that they had suffered during the conflict. Such representations often involved the injured parties requesting permission to usurp a previous property owner's rights to a particular property, especially if the former owner happened to be missing, dead or perhaps a member of the earlier Royalist garrison. Aside from the destruction wrought by the vicious fighting of the two parties themselves, the post war period also witnessed often widespread property seizures and sales, as the new Parliamentary authorities sought to impose severe financial penalties on those leading figures that had led the war against them. A number of Chester's leading families were thought to have lost their fortunes because of their support for King Charles I; not least the Gamul's who were reported to have been stripped of much of their wealth by a highly vindictive pro-Parliamentary corporation in the late 1640's and early 1650's.

By the 18th century, much of St John's Street was reported to have been occupied by a diverse mix of both private and commercial buildings, including tenements, great houses, gardens and timber yards. In 1725, a James Comberbach, presumably a member of the prominent city family of that name, was reported to have owned and operated an extensive timber business in St John's Street. Around the same time and on the opposite western side of the street, a messuage owned by a city plumber called George Griffiths was granted or leased to a widow called Esther Croughton, although they were actually tenanted by yet another person called Isaac Dannatt.

Some half a century later, a number of prominent citizens were reported to be making their homes in St John's Street, not least of which was Thomas Lunt, the city foundry owner and builder who was responsible for building some of Chester's greatest commercial properties. By 1817, there were thought to be even more of the city's leading figures living in the street, including a Doctor Freeman, a celebrated local physician, who was said to have occupied a fine house on the western side of St John's Street. On the opposite side of the road there was said to be the city mansion of Mr Massey, yet another member of one of Chester's most prominent families, although his great house was later thought to have been occupied by a Mr John Walker, a notable Town Clerk of the age. These well known citizens were also joined by the likes of Mr Boden, one of Chester's leading builders, whose predecessors had been helping to build the fabric of the city for several generations. There was Mr Palin and his son who ran Chester's Post Office, along with Thomas Dixon, the brother of the prominent city banker, who was said to be operating a timber yard in St John's Street, possibly the same one that had been owned by James Comberbach around a hundred years earlier. Virtually this entire historic site, including the nearby Brassey storerooms and Dobson's Paper Warehouse are now thought to lie below the mass of the early 20th century telephone exchange that was built in St John's Street around 1908 and which in recent years has itself been reconfigured to accommodate a major city hotel.

Unhappily, only a small number of interesting buildings continue to survive in modern day St John Street, the earliest of which is thought to be the mid 18th century **Royal Insurance Chambers** that occupies a site on the west side of the thoroughfare. Other properties of note are the Calvinist Chapel which sits on the eastern side of the street, facing the city's main Post Office and the Methodist Chapel located close to the southern junction of today's city street. Both of these religious centres though are reported to be 19th century in construction and represent a time in Chester when non-conformism was flourishing in the city, albeit in a variety of forms. The present **Calvinist Chapel** building is reported to date from 1876, although the congregation is thought to have existed in Chester since 1789 when its first meetings were held at a private house in Gorse Stacks. The present chapel is said to stand on the site of the Massey Mansion, which later became the home of John Walker, the former Town Clerk previously mentioned.

The **Methodist Chapel** building on the western side of St John's Street dates from 1811, with the current building reportedly standing on the site of a much earlier building which was inhabited or owned by an individual called Alexander Eaton. Contemporary reports from the time, also suggest that the buildings immediately alongside the site of the new chapel were owned by another local man called Robert Fearnall, who was probably a butcher in Chester who conducted business in the city's Bridge Street area.

Back in the main Foregate Street thoroughfare, the **Royal Bank of Scotland** building on the corner of Foregate and Frodsham Streets was designed by architect Francis Jones of Manchester, originally for the Manchester and Liverpool District

Bank and was constructed sometime around 1921. An earlier tavern, "The Raven", which had previously occupied the site since 1682, was thought to have been demolished sometime between 1904 and 1912, a period when much of Frodsham Street was being widened and redeveloped, resulting in the widespread destruction of much of the south western area of the thoroughfare. Described as a relatively small, but very well regarded establishment, the building which housed the Raven was thought to have been constructed some years after 1645, following the destruction caused by the English Civil war siege of the city.

The site itself though is known to have had a much more extensive history, being the location for an even earlier city tavern, "The Crow", which was reported to have been in existence since the late 16th century, although for most of its life was thought to have been located on the site of the later Royal Oak, further east in Foregate Street. It seems likely therefore that the properties existence as "The Crow", on the site of today's RBS building, can only have extended from the end of the English Civil War siege of the city in 1645 through to the later arrival of "The Raven" in 1682. Notably, the Raven was thought to have existed in one form or another right up until 1904 and it was only the road widening scheme of the early 20th century that finally heralded its final demise, with its final landlord recorded as one Samuel Jennings who held the licence prior to its demolition.

Directly opposite the modern day RBS building, the southeast junction of Frodsham Street and Foregate Street has for many years been occupied by Samuel's Jewellery Store. A record of 1574 however reports that this "void parcel of land" was granted to one Robert Wilding by Chester's Corporation, suggesting that the site had been left by its former owners as a charitable bequest, or had been in the possession of one of the city's dissolved religious houses, before being handed over to the city authorities.

During the medieval period, today's **Frodsham Street** was more commonly known as Cow Lane, a title it was thought to have held right through to modern times, although it has also been referred to as both Coole Lane and Warrington Lane during its lifetime. The lane itself though might well have had a far more extensive history, as it was thought to mark the eastern limit of the Roman parade ground area, or Campus, which was located just outside of the eastern ramparts of the military fortress, in the area of the later monastic Kale Yards which still bear that name. This open area of ground however, now housing a municipal car park has had several titles throughout its history, including the Kaleyards, the Hop Pole Paddock and the Recreation Grounds, but today, is still generally referred to by its earliest title. Despite being outside of the central core of the historic city, the importance of this street seems to have been appreciated during the 16th century, when Frodsham Street was reported to have been paved on behalf of one William Bennett in 1552, making it one of the earliest Chester streets to be resurfaced in this fashion.

Immediately north of Francis Jones' Royal Bank of Scotland building, on the western flank of modern day Frodsham Street, is a terrace of entirely modern retail units which replaced an earlier 20th century development, commonly known as Mercia Square. As previously mentioned, the entire south western section of the main thoroughfare was taken down in around 1904 so that the street could be sufficiently widened at its junction with Foregate

Street. Consequently, the oldest building currently occupying this part of the street is the RBS building which was first erected in 1921, although most of the adjoining modern properties actually occupy the site that was formerly known as the Hop Pole Paddock, a piece of land and formal gardens associated with the Hop Pole Inn which once stood in the city's Foregate Street. These new retail properties are bounded on the north by what was once known as the Recreation Ground entrance, but which today simply serves as the main entranceway to the Kaleyards car park. Although there is little to recommend the roadway itself, at its western limit there is a stone built flight of steps which links Frodsham Street with Chester's east facing defensive wall. Constructed sometime around 1930, this elegant stairwell, which is overlooked by the Cathedral's modern Bell Tower, actually sits above the remains of a medieval flanking drum tower which was thought to have been built during the late 13th century.

St Werburgh's Bell Tower, which is more properly known as a Campanile, was designed by architect George Pace and reported to have been generally completed by 1974. Built mainly of concrete and steel, the outer faces of the tower are covered with Bethesda Slate and it is noteworthy for the fact that it is said to be the first free standing Cathedral Bell Tower constructed in England since the 15th century. The bells contained within the tower are thought to be named after Celtic or Anglo Saxon Saints who have been venerated in Chester or in the surrounding regions.

Directly opposite this stairwell, on the eastern side of Frodsham Street, there is a small side street through which modern day pedestrians can access the British Home Stores building. Lying between the main terrace of shop fronts and a former Quakers Meeting House building this passageway is thought to have once served as an entrance to Thomas Lunt's long since disappeared **Commercial Hall** which was finally demolished around 1950, to be replaced by the BHS and Littlewoods Stores which still exist today.

Built at the beginning of 1815, the Commercial Hall was opened for business in July of the same year and was reported to have been a large building with an open central space surrounded by 56 single and 26 double shop units spread over two floors. The raised first floor or gallery which was supported by ornate cast iron pillars was accessed by wide flights of stairs located in each corner of the hall. Built to house Chester's two main fairs held in both July and October, traders from around the country including those from London, Glasgow, Manchester, Nottingham, Birmingham and Sheffield would attend these events in order to sell their wares to Chester's retailers and citizens alike. The building was constructed in partnership by two local businessmen, one of which was Mr Thomas Lunt a well known builder and foundry owner who was also responsible for the construction of Chester's Union Hall, the still standing Union Bridge and the now much reduced Bold Square in the city. Significantly, Lunt was thought to have been a member of the Society of Friends whose meeting house lay in between the Commercial Hall alley and the more northerly Union Walk. The original Quakers Meeting House which formerly occupied this eastern block of Frodsham Street was thought to have existed from the 18th century and in 1824 was reported to have included its own graveyard, where members of the community might be laid to rest, but this, along with the original buildings have been subsequently lost amidst the various rounds of redevelopment.

Early 18th century records for this site, recall that in 1701 a Richard Lister was said to have conveyed the land to one Nathaniel Badder, a city bricklayer, with the lease noting that the property had previously been owned or held by a Mr Bradshaw, although there are no more details offered about this particular individual. Records also suggest that in the following year, 1702, Nathaniel Badder had leased his newly built premises on the site, to a number of Chester businessmen, including a Cheese Factor, a Smith and a Mercer.

The small alleyway called **Union Walk** which used to lie on the eastern side of the street between the modern day Temple Bar and the former Farm Foods outlet (but now a clothes store) is reported to have marked the northern limit of Chester's early St Werburgh's RC Infant and Junior Schools which had been built on the site of the city's main Roman Catholic Chapel. The title "Union Walk" is commonly associated with Thomas Lunt's Commercial Hall which was located slightly south of the school, on the site of the present day British Home Stores. Up until the late 1960's and early 1970's the Union Walk alleyway ran eastward between Frodsham Street and Queen Street, but is now interrupted by the mass of the modern day Tesco supermarket building.

On the western side of Frodsham Street, the **Kale Yards** and its associated postern gateway both have their early foundations in the vegetable gardens of St Werburgh's medieval Abbey and date from around the 13th or 14th century. Although today, the site of these former Abbey vegetable patches is largely associated with and covered by modern car parking facilities, prior to the cutting of the Chester Canal in the 18th century these Kale Yards were thought to have extended much further north and on towards the still standing Phoenix Tower.

In 1541, the newly founded Cathedral of Christ and the Blessed Virgin was granted the area known as the Kaleyards, by the monarch Henry VIII, who had recently dissolved its predecessor, the Norman Abbey of St Werburgh. In 1601 however, Henry's successor, his daughter Elizabeth I was said to have reassigned these same lands to the Hospital of St John the Baptist, with the grant reportedly including three houses and six gardens on the eastern side of the Cow Lane thoroughfare. Twenty five years later, in 1626, a William Dutton was reported to have petitioned the Corporation for permission to employ these same lands as an Artillery Yard, a place where Chester's young men could be instructed in military discipline, before presumably becoming part of the city's militia. In later years and following the end of the English Civil War, the Kaleyards were thought to have been given over to purely agricultural purposes, with gardens and orchards reported there during the late 17th and early 18th centuries.

Further north and in around 1498 a void parcel of land, adjoining the Abbey's vegetable gardens and now generally marked by the area of land between King Charles' Tower and Cow Lane Bridge, was reportedly granted to an individual called Randle Wirehall, a baker in the city. Much of this same land, during the 18th century was acquired for the emerging Chester and Nantwich canal system, although parts of the site that were unused were later thought to have housed timber yards that employed the new canal system to transport their lumber throughout the wider region. This sort of commercial activity was thought to have continued right through to the middle of the 20th century, when the first of a number of retail premises were built on a large part of the site, represented today by the Slow Dragon Chinese Restaurant and branch of the Iceland retail chain.

Close to this site, in 1543, the land which is now inhabited by a terrace of relatively modern retail shops on the western side of Frodsham Street, bordering the Kaleyards municipal car park, was reported to have been granted to one William Beckington. This may be part of the same lands that some 50-odd years later, in 1601, was granted to a man called Thomas Wall, who was given permission to build a barn and stable on land described as "abutting the Kaleyards, near the Gorse Stacks". Although unlikely to be the same buildings, it is also worth noting that in 1604, a James Hand of Blacon was granted permission to demolish an old stable building in Frodsham Street and then build a new stable block with a hay loft above it. Hand though was not the owner of the land, but merely the tenant, whose landlord was reported to be one William Aldersey, presumably the same individual who had extensive property holdings in Chester's Eastgate Street.

Although most of the eastern flank of Frodsham Street, from Union Walk to Queens Place is thought to be largely modern by comparison, it still retains a number of early properties, although most have been refitted with modern shop fronts and windows. The most obvious of these buildings is the Oddfellows Arms public house which stands to the south of the modern Tesco traffic ramp and was reported to have been built sometime around 1771.

Chester's **Cow Lane Bridge** is a relatively modern construction, having first been built during the 18th century to span the new canal system which was laid down in this section of the city and has subsequently been replaced a number of times since its initial foundation. The largest rebuilding of the bridge was thought to have started in February 1959 and took some 14 months to complete, during which much more modern materials such as concrete and steel were employed in its reconstruction. Since that time the bridge has been added to again, due to the ever increasing levels of modern road traffic, which have been attracted by the multi story car park that is attached to the local Tesco superstore. Deriving its title from the former name for Frodsham Street in Chester which was "Cow Lane" both bridge and street names recollect their association with the expansive and historic beast markets that used to be held in and around the Gorse Stacks area of the city right through to the early 1960's.

Prior to 1773, a long extinct postern gate was known to have existed at the northern end of Cow Lane (Frodsham Street), approximately where the bridge now crosses the canal. On the right-hand side of this ancient portal was a cottage, which in much earlier times was reported to have been employed as a Toll House, although the 18th century gateway was thought to have been rebuilt as a defensive structure during the 17th century and formed part of Chester's English Civil War outlying defences. Ultimately, the gateway and its attendant cottage were both demolished when the Chester and Nantwich canal system was first laid down around 1775.

Although the modern name of Gorse Stacks is thought to have a fairly extensive history in its own right, presumably recalling the growing and storing of dried grasses for both feed and matting, an earlier title for the site was "**Henwold's Lowe**", possibly deriving from an individual's ownership of the land or its use as pasture land for the city. Lanes which were known to have connected with this area of land included; Lowe's Lane, Horn Lane, Barkers Lane and of course the main thoroughfare Cow Lane.

The lands subsequently employed for laying the new Chester Canal were once reported to have been part of Chester's "**Jousting Court**", an area of flat lying land used for military exercises and as the name implies, included Jousting Tournaments, etc. up until the 16th century. By around 1625 however, much of this same land was thought to be in the ownership of the Francis family of Chester and Eastham, the father being a tanner by trade, who was also reported to have owned a "Bark House" in the area of the Abbey Kaleyards. According to city records, in around 1562, parts of these formerly mentioned lands were thought to have been in the possession of Alderman Thomas Smith, a prominent political figure in Chester, as well as an extensive landowner in the city. During the Francis family's tenure of the land however, this same site, now thought to be marked by modern day Queens Place, was reported to have housed a Brickyard, which was noted in the will of John Francis dating from 1625. Interestingly, later illustrations of this same general area appear to show a kiln of some description still existing in the late 18th century, suggesting that this kind of industrial activity had a fairly extensive history in this particular area of the city.

Returning to Chester's Foregate Street, immediately adjoining the eastern side of the modern day "Lush" premises, the site now occupied by a sportswear retailer was once the home of yet another Chester tavern, the **Golden Lion**, which was reported there in the first half of the 19th century. This coaching inn was noted as early as 1700, but may well have existed on the site for many years before that. The Golden Lion was mentioned in that particular year in connection with a Chester "Row" (or Arcade) that obviously existed at the time and was thought to be in the possession of two men, one John Bradshaw and a Nathan Bradburn who was reported as an ironmonger. Eventually evolving into one of the city's principal coaching inns, in 1751 the inn was said to have been in the hands of one John Lamkin, formerly the landlord of the Old Wolf's Head in Watergate Street and in 1781 the Golden Lion was said to have been occupied by a man called Thomas Pinnington. It appears though that by 1900, parts of this property were no longer being used as a tavern, as it was reported that a gentleman called Mr Burton was operating a pawnbrokers business in this area of the street.

Also on the south side of Foregate Street is the building currently occupied by the **Marks and Spencer** store at numbers 22 to 28, a building designed by the Manchester architects Norman Jones and Leonard Rigby in 1932. A hundred years before that, much of this same site was thought to have been occupied by the Union Hall, constructed by local builder and foundry owner Thomas Lunt in 1809. Built principally as a commercial enterprise, the construction of the Union Hall had led to the loss of a number of individual properties, including the Eagle and Child Tavern, nine dwelling houses and three stable blocks, all of which had previously been offered for sale at an auction in 1751. The sign of the Eagle and Child was thought to have been a notable city landmark, having moved from its previous location in Shoemaker's Row around 1721, it was said to have existed there and in the city since the middle of the 16th century (1540).

Although far more is known about Lunt's Commercial Hall, in terms of its construction, history and general use, his Union Hall building was recorded on a city map of 1853, even though some reporters have suggested that the property was extinct by this date. Despite such inconsistencies however, during its lifetime the Hall was reported to have become the central location for Chester's still thriving cloth industry and played host to numerous traders and salesmen, who visited the city for the annual fairs. Its upper floor was said to have been largely occupied by Yorkshire cloth merchants and there is even a suggestion that its precincts occasionally played host to the pupils of a local Sunday school. At some point in its existence, the southern part of the Union Hall was said to have been heavily damaged by fire, although there is no indication that this outbreak proved to be fatal for the building. Notably though, reports of the fire did mention the close proximity of the Mr Dobson's Paper Warehouse, Mr Brassey's storerooms and Mr Dixon's Timber Yard, all of which helps to illustrate the layout and purpose of this particular area of the city, lying between the eastern flank of St John's Street and the modern day Marks and Spencer's building. Interestingly, immediately adjoining the Union Hall in Foregate Street and on its eastern side, a public house called the Union Vaults was reported to have existed during the early 19th century, although this same sign now inhabits a property in modern day Egerton Street, further east of its former home.

Further east again on the south side of Foregate Street, the property currently occupied by Dixon's electrical store was formerly the location of the **Royal Oak**, which was said to have been established there sometime around 1697 when a Chester Tanner called Hugh Moulson was reported as the inn-keeper. The Royal Oak itself was known to have replaced an even earlier tavern, the Sign of the Crow which was thought to have dated from around 1580, when it was in the possession of a former Sheriff and Mayor of Chester, a man called William Cotgreave. Prior to 1540, the site was thought to have been held by the Fraternity of St Anne's, but following the dissolution of the monasteries, this property, along with many of the other church lands in Chester were sold off by the Crown and its appointed agents.

When William died in 1590 he was said to have owned a substantial number of properties in the Foregate Street area many of which were passed on to his son, also called William. It was during his ownership that the tavern was said to have been substantially rebuilt, possibly because of its great age, with a mantle beam being inscribed with the date 1607 and the initials H. E. In 1614 Cotgreave was reported to have claimed a right of way, from the main street to the rear of his own property and sufficient to allow a horse and rider to pass through. It was also noted at the time that the property immediately west of Cotgreaves, in Foregate Street, was occupied by a widow called Jane Wilson.

However, when William died in 1620, without issue, he was reported to have bequeathed all of his properties in Foregate Street, including "Le Crowe" to his sister, Eleanor Gamul, the widow of William Gamul. Unfortunately for Eleanor and the rest of her relatives, the outbreak of the English Civil War and the subsequent siege of Chester saw many of these new possessions destroyed as a direct result of the conflict. As a final note with regard to the Sign of the Crow, early records suggest that this particular area of Foregate Street was once the location for at least five separate taverns, all of which stood alongside one another in the same part of the busy thoroughfare.

Occupying the site of today's modern day Boots Store, the **Saracen's Head Inn** was recorded as a tavern in this street prior to the outbreak of the English Civil War in the 17th century and up until 1557 was thought to have been inhabited by a man called John Hankey, when the property was described as three messuages, including the Saracen's Head. The building was said to have been so severely damaged during the siege of Chester that what little remained of it was subsequently demolished and only largely built on again in the 18th century when it became the home of the Wettenhall family. The land on which both buildings stood had previously been owned by the Fraternity of St Anne's, but following the dissolution of the monasteries the property had passed into the possession of John Dean in 1557. As for the sign of the Saracen's Head, that was thought to have been removed to a site on the city's Market Square, eventually falling victim to the redevelopment of that site in the late 19th century. The Saracen's Head was reported to have been the emblem of the Warburton family, who were thought to have been the previous owners or tenants of the property, prior to it becoming the noted city hostelry.

The **Wettenhall Mansion** which replaced the largely ruinous Saracen's Head Inn is thought to have been built by one Gabriel Wettenhall, a renowned city barrister, sometime around 1730. Having agreed a lease for three lives and 53 years and the power to build with the actual owners of the property, the trustee's of the Witton Grammar School in Northwich, the extensive mansion was subsequently raised on the site and was one of the properties specifically noted by the military engineer Alexander Lavaux in his 1745 map of Chester.

Sadly for Gabriel he did not manage to enjoy his home for an extended period of time, as he was reported to have died in 1735 and was buried in his hometown of Audlem. The great city mansion however, remained in the family's possession and passed into the hands of Gabriel's son, Nathaniel; and his wife Arabella. Unfortunately the couple did not have any surviving children, so when Nathaniel died in 1778 only his widow Arabella was left in the great house, where she remained until her own death in 1798. With her demise, the lease between the Wettenhall's and the trustees of Whitton Grammar School was deemed to have lapsed and so a new tenant was sought by the landlords. In January 1800 a new tenant, a Mrs Anne Vernon, was granted a 31 year lease on the house, which presumably expired at the end of that term or when Mrs Vernon died, but no information has been forthcoming to determine the eventual outcome, or indeed any subsequent inhabitants of the property. It is however worth noting that prior to the rebuilding of the property by Gabriel Wettenhall in 1730; the original Saracen's Head Inn was reported to have included a "row" (noted in 1591), possibly much like those elsewhere in the city, but whether or not this was actually replaced by the Wettenhall's or was subsequently lost during the rebuild is unclear.

Although much has changed over the past 40 years or so, the modern day Boots building in Foregate Street is also thought to mark the former home of the **Old Nags Head**, one of the city's most popular, but sadly now extinct, public houses. Rather confusingly, across the road, on the south side of Foregate Street, a second tavern, which was called the Little Nag's Head, was opened sometime after 1812. Prior to the establishment of this tavern, the site was said to have been occupied by a grocers shop, operated by a man called Joseph Bellis, who was thought to have died some years before his former business premises were converted into this new city hostelry. In 1812, his former shop, along with a messuage and a number of other properties were advertised for sale by auction at the nearby Blossom's Hotel and it was after this date that the Little Nag's Head was first established.

However, some 50-odd years later this city tavern was reported to have been converted yet again, this time into a Temperance House, becoming the Little Nag's Head Cocoa House in 1877. The owner of the property, the Marquis of Westminster, was even thought to have employed the noted architect Chester John Douglas to design the new premises. These "alcohol free" houses primarily owed their foundation to the Society of Friends, the Quakers, who saw beer taverns and public houses as a blight on society and sought to create a non-alcoholic equivalent to the pubs and taverns of the time. The presence of the "Nag's Head", "Little Nag's Head" and the "Horse and Groom" in this particular street were thought to recall the days when Foregate Street was the location for Chester's historic Horse Fairs. Ordered to be held there by the city's Corporation in 1704, later Cestrian's could well remember both sides of this busy thoroughfare being filled with numerous horses, of every size, shape and colour, being traded or haggled over by the various traders.

The presence of the Nag's Head and the Little Nag's Head, coupled with a tendency for both to be simply referred to as the Nag's Head, has often led to confusion as to which of the two premises were actually being reported. A good case in point is when researchers are trying to identify the actual location of two long since disappeared Foregate Street alleyway's, called Crown Alley and Ball's Court. According to some reporters, both of these passageways were located on the north side of Foregate Street and on either side of the formerly mentioned Nag's Head Inn. Others though have suggested that these 2 long extinct alleyways were located on the south side of the street and flanked the Cocoa House known as the Little Nag's Head. However, the fact that Joseph Bellis' grocers shop seems to be closely associated with the passageway that was once known as Crown Alley, would seem to suggest that the south side of the street is a far more likely location for both of these missing thoroughfares.

The name Crown Alley is thought to have derived from the ownership of the site, it having remained as a Crown estate ever since the religious reforms of Henry VIII in the 16th century. In 1812, this narrow passageway was said to have led to a fairly extensive cul-de-sac measuring some 140 feet in length and lined with a number of low quality tenements and buildings and was reported to have stood on the eastern side of the Little Nag's Head. On the western side of the same building, a second alleyway, Ball's Court, was reported to have existed throughout the same period and like its neighbour, Crown Alley, was said to have survived right up until 1904, when widespread redevelopments saw these two alleyway's finally absorbed into the surrounding fabric of today's modern properties.

The name Ball's Court was said to have recalled an 18th century "ball and tennis court" that existed at the rear of Foregate Street and which had been accessed through the narrow alleyway. Prior to the establishment of this tennis court in 1777, the site was reported to have been occupied by a small city theatre, which was thought to have been founded sometime around 1687, but was eventually replaced by a new civic theatre housed in the old St Nicholas' Chapel in Northgate Street. The tennis courts themselves were thought to have survived for a lengthy period, before finally being demolished to make way for a double row of small cottages.

Towards the southern centre of Foregate Street and prior to 1555, the Swan Inn was reported to have stood in the general area of today's modern Woolworth's store, the inn later evolving into the **Swan Hotel**, one of Chester's finest and best known hostelries. By 1839 this hotel was reported to have included extensive gardens and orchards to the rear of the property and contained a fair number of cellars, tenements and shops adjoining the main building.

Records suggest that the site of this tavern had passed into the possession of St John's church sometime prior to their dissolution in 1540 and by 1557 had been purchased from the Crown by a man called John Dean, who was the Rector of St Bartholomew's the Great in Smithfield and a native of Northwich in Cheshire. Eager to leave a lasting legacy for the children of his hometown, Dean was said to have helped found the Witton Grammar School around the same time and donated all of his property holdings in Chester to the new school, so that they might benefit from the rents of such properties. The city site occupied by the "Swan" was thought to be fairly extensive and included a number of shops and cellars which were all rented out to raise money for Dean's newly founded school.

In 1557, the Swan Inn, its outbuildings and extensive gardens were said to have been leased by a man called Peter Nicholas and his wife Alice, who were also reported to have held the lands inhabited by the previously mentioned Saracen's Head Inn, on the north side of Foregate Street. Some 140 years later, in 1716, the trustees of the Witton Grammar School were said to have leased the Swan Inn properties to an individual called Daniel Pickance, an inn-keeper, who also agreed to rent Herkin's Well Field from the same landowners. This extensive piece of land was thought to have occupied the space bounded by Queen Street to the east, Hoole Lane to the west, the General Railway station to the north and Foregate Street to the south. Pickance and his family were reported to have held the tenure of the Swan Inn until at least 1754, when the hostelry was thought to have been in the possession of his son, who was also called Daniel.

The next reported tenant of the inn was a Thomas Bulkeley, who was said to have received the lease in 1782, suggesting perhaps that the Pickance's tenure had lasted well beyond 1754, but there is no definitive evidence to support this. In 1796, it was noted that part of the lands adjoining the Swan were rented or leased to a Mrs Mary Walley, the wife of a John Walley, who was reported as a tanner by trade. Significantly, during the 20th century archaeological excavations in the yard adjoining the then still standing Swan Hotel were said to have uncovered evidence of this particular industry, specifically the discovery of old tanning pits. By 1850, a man called Evan Roberts was noted as the landlord of the Swan, but whether or not he was the actual property's leaseholder is unclear. A decade later, yet another local man was reported as the landlord of the inn, with a Robert Rider noted in 1860. By 1873 however, the Swan Inn was simply being described as a "Spirit Vaults", suggesting that its position and purpose had been much reduced for some reason. At that time the licensee of the house was reported to have been a John Massey.

Although the Swan Hotel continued to operate throughout the remainder of the 19th and well into the 20th century, in 1936, much of the adjoining land, which had formerly been part of the early property was redeveloped to house the Tatler Cinema. For the next 36 years this picture palace and the old Swan Inn were said to have sat alongside one another up until 1972, when further modernisation of the city, saw both buildings demolished to make way for the retail premises of the now similarly defunct C & A company.

Reportedly designed by a J W Barrow in 1936 the Tatler was built in the Art Deco style and retained its name until 1957 when it was said to have been taken over by the Classic cinema group and was subsequently called The Classic. It continued in business up until December 1970 when it showed its final picture and then as previously mentioned was later demolished, along with the historic Swan Hotel, to make way for the modern retail premises which were originally occupied by the C & A group and more recently by a branch of Woolworth's.

Back on the north side of Foregate Street, in 1777 a property lately in the possession of a Mr Edwards was reportedly being auctioned at the "Roe Buck" tavern in the city. The property in question was said to include the house fronting the main street and a number of outbuildings located at the rear of the house, including a coach-house and stables that were thought to be known as **Page's Yard**. The auction appears to have been for the sale of the building's fabric only and did not include the land on which the house stood, as that was intended for the development of the soon-to-be-built Queen Street, with the removal of this particular property creating the new thoroughfare's junction with Foregate Street. The successful bidder was ordered to take down Mr Edwards former home and take away all of the useable materials, but was permitted to leave behind any accrued rubbish. At the time, the building immediately west of this proposed new street, an arcaded property originally dating from the 17th century, was reported to be occupied by a Mr Richards who was a maltster. This particular family were known to be still occupying this same building in 1808, when a Mrs Richards was reported to have some sort of correspondence with acquaintances that were travelling abroad.

Although **Queen Street** was not thought to have existed prior to 1745, the general area was thought to have formed part of Chester's historic Jousting Croft which existed up until the 16th century. From the middle of the 16th century, through to the late 18th and 19th centuries this whole area was thought to have been known locally as Herkin's Well Field, an area of undeveloped land that was thought to have passed into the possession of the Witton Grammar School during the mid 16th century. Much of Queen Street's later development was in fact determined by the cutting of the Chester Canal during the 18th century and with the Queen Street Congregational Chapel being built in 1777. Sadly, only a part of its historic Greek Revival façade remains in place, it having been incorporated into the much more modern Tesco superstore development.

In 1779 a Roman Catholic Chapel or Presbytery was erected in the street to cater for the emerging and increasing Catholic community within the city, the building reportedly being built and paid for by Mr Thomas Penswick. There was a sudden and widespread rebuilding of Roman Catholic churches after the passing of the Catholic Relief Act of 1778 as the English Parliament finally overcame its natural terror of the Roman religion. This brick built chapel was said to have featured a fine Doric portico supported by four light stone coloured pillars, which was reported to have been substantially enlarged in 1854 and seen its first faith school built on the site in 1858. The chapel was also reported to have been used to house the body of Daniel O'Connell as it was carried back from Rome on its way to burial in Dublin. It was only in 1876 that this community relocated themselves to the much grander and much more modern St Werbugh's RC Church which stands on Grosvenor Park Road today. The former Presbytery in Queen Street was subsequently redeveloped and enlarged over time to become St Werbugh's RC School, a role it continued to fill until the late 1960's when the building and many of its neighbours were finally demolished to make way for the current Boots and Tesco superstores, both of which remain there today.

During the 1790's a notable Boy's School was said to have existed in the quiet city street, run by a gentleman called Mr Sellers, although whether or not he was related to the Chester brewing family of the same name is unclear. In later years this school may have become known as the Wood and Pullans School which was reported to have occupied a site in Queen Street, although there appears to be little information to confirm this either way. Yet another educational establishment that located itself in Queen Street around the same time was the Chester Blue Girls School. Reported to have been a contemporary of the city's main Bluecoat School, which catered entirely for boys, the Blue Girls School had originally been housed close to Chester's Royal Infirmary, but due to the expansion of that facility, had been forced to find temporary accommodations in Queen Street in around 1810. The school and its pupils were later reported to have moved to new and more suitable premises in Vicars Lane, possibly known as the Grosvenor School, which stood opposite to St John's Church and on the site now occupied by Chester's Visitor Centre.

At its most northerly point, Queen Street was said to have built over the site of the much earlier Shooting Butts, the place where the local men of Chester were thought to have honed their skills with the English longbow, a habit that no doubt contributed to the fame of the legendary Cheshire Archers, who were employed by a number of English monarchs. There is also a suggestion that a second Shooting Butts was formerly located at the city's Kaleyards, which was known to have been employed as a military training area during the middle of the 16th century. Much of the city's Jousting Courts, which lay close to the Butts, was thought to have been used for the route of the Chester and Nantwich Canal around 1773, with the adjoining areas given over to both warehousing and private residences.

The notable local architect Joseph Turner, the designer of Chester's Bridgegate, Watergate, Bridge of Sighs and parts of Nicholas Street was reported to have become involved in a legal dispute in around 1780, relating to a number of unspecified properties in Queen Street and suggesting that he may have been personally involved in their construction, or at least their design. In 1810, a Protestant Chapel was erected in the street and in the following year an Independent Chapel was also constructed. At its south-east junction with

Foregate Street, No 71 in that main thoroughfare is generally described as a mid 18th century property, arcaded over the main street and standing three storeys high. Its side elevation to Queen Street has been altered and refaced which is no doubt due to the fact that its immediate neighbour, the former No 69, was demolished to create the new Queen Street junction.

The buildings immediately adjoining this arcaded property to the east, represented by No's 73 and 75 Foregate Street are thought to have been built in the 17th century, probably some time after the highly destructive siege of the city. Both properties, which in their original form were thought to have been one building, are described as half timbered black and white, constructed over two storeys and arcaded over the main pavement.

Slightly east of today's junction with Queen Street on the northern side of Foregate Street a tavern called the "**White Lion Inn**" was reported in 1782 when it was held by a city brewer called John Peers. The hostelry was thought to have remained in existence right through to the beginning of the 20th century (1930's) when it was said to have been located at number 79 in the main thoroughfare. Described as a half timbered building, its specific construction date is unknown, but it has been suggested that the sign of the "White Lion" may well have been preceded by that of another city tavern, the "Red Lion" which was known to have existed in Foregate Street from the 1640's and prior to its relocation to another site in the city. A local charity, the Chester Brotherly Society was reported to have held its meetings at the White Lion during the late 18th and early 19th centuries.

Originally known as Love Lane, modern day **Love Street** is thought to have extensive links with the city's early leather industries, possibly because of its relative closeness to the waters of the River Dee, the expanse of open land and its distance from the city's walls. Today, the two most obvious building in the street remains the ABC theatre complex which in recent years has been transformed into a city centre nightclub called Brannigan's and the former Co-operative building which stands on the eastern side of the street. This generally unremarkable, but historic thoroughfare was known to have been called Love Lane from as early as 1397 when it was formally recorded as such in a local document, although the designation appears to be a fairly common one, with Love Lane's existing in Nantwich and Knutsford, as well as numerous other towns and cities.

Preparation work for the new **Regal** cinema in 1937 involved the demolition of a row of old cottages, during which the contractors were reported to have uncovered the remains of an old city well. Said to have been around five feet in diameter and measuring some forty feet deep, little is known about it regarding its age, etc. but given the close proximity of the early Billy Hobby's Well and Herkin's Well, both of which seem to have had an agricultural connection, maybe this one too, was dug to provide a water source for grazing animals. The old Regal Cinema itself was reportedly opened in October 1937 and later renamed the ABC, which was finally closed as a picture house around 1990, before re-opening some years later as Brannigan's Nightclub.

The history of this whole western flank of modern day Love Street can be traced back to the middle of the 16th century, when the land was reported to have been in the possession of the St John's church, when the entire area was said to have been occupied by base tenements, orchards and gardens. There is a suggestion that prior to 1565 these former church lands were in the possession of one Alexander Cotes, a nephew to George Cotes, holder of the Bishopric of Chester. However, sometime between 1560 and 1569, the property was reportedly sold to a man called Lawrence Bold of Upton, who may have been associated with the Bold family whose name is still recalled in the still existent, but much reduced Bold Square which lies further east. Around 1570, Bold was said to have sold his interest in these properties to the prominent local citizen William Aldersey, the same individual who owned extensive properties throughout the city. As a footnote to the earlier history of this particular section of the street, from 1750 to 1765 and prior to the construction of the Octagon Chapel in City Road, one of Chester's early Methodist congregations used to meet in a property on the western side of the street, a building that may have been subsequently demolished to make way for the cinema complex.

Directly opposite this building stands the imposing mass of the old Co-operative building which in recent years has been converted into a number of individual retail units. Reportedly constructed at the beginning of the 20th century, circa 1909, in its original form this was once a large department store, latterly operated by the Birkenhead and District Co-operative Society. Despite its classical look however, the building itself has little to commend it, other than the fact that it marks the site of a much earlier and much more prominent building, the largely long since extinct Forest House.

Forest House which stands at the junction of today's Forest Street and Love Street has been credited to the noted architect Sir Robert Taylor, who designed the Bishop's Palace in Chester, although most architectural students have doubts over this prominent designer's actual involvement with the property. The original building, of which little remains visible today, has a suggested construction date of 1759, but other experts have indicated 1780 as being much more likely.

Prior to the construction of Forest House, the site was said to have been in the ownership of the Cholmondley family, whose great city mansion was reported to have stood slightly south of Love Lane (Street), in an area now marked by the Grosvenor Park. Around 1778 the lands that were passed to the Barnston family, including the site of the later Forest House, were said to have contained forty messuages, five cottages, four tofts, two workshops, fifty gardens, four orchards, three acres of land, one meadow and three acres of pasture, all of which had at one time been in the possession of the Collegiate Church of St John's, but lost during the Reforms of Henry VIII. Although only a small part of the former Cholmondley lands were actually used for the construction of Forest House, clearly the later Barnston holdings in this area of the city were substantial.

When it was first built, the elegant and impressive Forest House was thought to have been far larger than would first appear and faced directly onto the city's main Foregate Street thoroughfare. In its original form, this house, which was paid for by Roger Barnston, a Colonel in the local Militia was described as being fronted by a pair of large iron gates that led to an open cobbled courtyard, leading to the main entrance of the property. On either side of the imposing gateway were Coach Houses constructed of both brick and stone, which were said to have resembled individual lodges and that were encircled by the properties sweeping boundary walls which ran southward to join the main body of the house itself.

According to local legend, the builders of the property were reported to have used more bricks for the construction of the buildings underground vaults and cellars, than they used for all of the property which was built above ground. Sadly though, within a relatively short space of time much of the property and its extensive grounds had been redeveloped and rebuilt, effectively causing the old property to disappear within the mass of later buildings. By 1856 the house was reportedly housing Churton's Auction Mart and when that business relocated itself, Forest House was said to have been used as a private school for a period. It subsequently served as a furniture warehouse and during the first half of the 20th century was inhabited by a NAAFI Club, before being altered somewhat to serve as a city dancehall and today as the venue for a Chester nightclub.

The remainder of the Forest House site, including its impressive front entrance with its twin coach houses and extensive rear gardens are now thought to lie below the generally modern buildings which occupy much of this area. At the beginning of the 20th century, much of the street frontage of the old Barnston's house was thought to have been replaced by the heavy mass of the Co-operative Society building, itself now sub-divided into the likes of a clothing shop, an office supplies company and the almost compulsory fun pub. The extensive rear gardens of the house though have fared a little better, with a part of them now inhabited by the former Love Street School, which may well have been designed by the talented County Architect Harry Beswick in the first half of the 20th century. The remainder of the Forest House gardens, from the school, southward to what was once known as the "Headland Walk" now form part of the

Grosvenor Park complex, so in a sense have managed to fulfil their original purpose, albeit with little help from the city planners.

Designed by architect Harry Beswick, **Love Street School** was built in the early part of the 20th century for Chester City Council, to educate local children. The two entrances in Forest Street still show the separate doorways for girls and boys and during the 1960's the school was used to house pupils from St Werburgh's RC Junior School who had previously been accommodated at the 19th century building located nearby in Union Walk, just off Queen Street in Chester. The school was finally closed in the late 70's early 1980's and since then has been used as commercial offices. It is also sad to note, that much of the former school's playground area, where generations of children have played their games, has in the past couple of years been given over to even more high priced city apartments, of which Chester already has a surplus.

Back on the south side of the main Foregate Street again, in 1911, two individuals by the name of Glynn Hill obtained the leases of the properties standing at 110-112 Foregate Street, which were then occupied by Cook's Photographers Studio and Avery Weighing Machine Company and demolished them both. They then replaced these earlier buildings with a new Picture Palace, called "**The Glynn**", which was designed by local architects Minshull and Muspratt, constructed by McLellan's building contractors and officially opened to the public on the 19th June 1911. However, despite its apparent initial success "The Glynn" was said to have been officially ended its life as a Picture House on the 5th December 1931 when it showed its final film. The building has subsequently had a fairly diverse history, playing host to a car showroom, numerous retail outlets and today serves as the premises for one of Chester's countless drinking establishments, the Revolution.

An often overlooked passageway on the northern flank of Foregate Street, **Parry's Entry** was originally a lane, leading to a coach yard owned by a Mr Parry who also owned a nearby coaching inn on the main city street. Around 1900 this entry was reported to have been lined with a number of small cottages and the area was thought to have had a fairly unsavoury reputation.

Parkers Buildings which stand at the northeast corner of today's Foregate Street were designed by architect John Douglas, but owe their name to C T Parker who was land agent to the Grosvenor Estate from 1881 and 1911 and said to be a meticulous and demanding individual. The area was previously thought to have been occupied by crowded courtyards and narrow passages, which were damaging to both their residents health and the reputation of the city. Parkers Buildings were originally built as accommodation for retired workers from the Grosvenor Estates. On or near this same site, the extensive brewery owned by the Seller's family was reported to have stood, with this local family still recalled in the title of Seller Street which stands to the east of Parker's Buildings, but is now separated from them by the modern inner ring road system.

Virtually opposite the site of Parkers Buildings, the modern day Asia Tandoori restaurant, which is located on the southern flank of the street, is reported to mark the site of an early Chester inn, **The Shakespeare**, which was reported in the city in 1898. It has also been suggested that this same site was the location for the former Belgrave Hotel which used to stand in this particular street and that adjoined the impressive townhouse of the Werden family, who made their fortune from brewing in Chester. However, other records suggest that in fact the Belgrave used to stand on the eastern side of the Werden's grand city mansion, placing it alongside the generally modern Bath Street, which was first laid out around 1900.

Reportedly brewers in Chester since the 16th century, members of the Werden family were thought to have been so successful in their field of enterprise that they were able to invest heavily in both land and property in the city and surrounding area. Their family home in Foregate Street, **Werden House**, was said to have been a substantial property which was fronted with a covered arcade and extensive gardens to the rear, much of which now lies below Chester's old Public Baths and the precincts of the Grosvenor Park. Following the end of the Werden family's connection with the city, the house was reported to have been occupied by a local surgeon called Mr Watson.

Modern day **Bath Street** in Chester derives its name from the city's public baths which were first constructed in around 1900 to the designs of Chester's John Douglas, although that other notable architect T M Lockwood was also said to have been involved with the complex. This whole area was once thought to have formed part of the extensive and formal gardens of the previously mentioned Werden mansion, but with that family's final demise, the land was inevitably broken up and sold off for other purposes. Virtually the entire eastern flank of this narrow city street is inhabited by the fantasy-type buildings of the architect John Douglas and forming part of the Chester area that has often been referred to as Douglasville. Along with this same architect's city baths, the remainder of the western flank is inhabited by a small number of relatively modern buildings, as well as the almost compulsory car park-cum-delivery bay that sadly, is becoming a repetitive feature of the city's urban landscape.

Back on the opposite, northern side of Foregate Street at this point, there is nothing left of the old street, with virtually all of the early buildings having been expunged from the landscape by the mass of concrete, steel and tarmac that is Chester's Inner Ring Road system. On this northern side of the thoroughfare there is little to investigate or recount, save for a much reduced terrace of buildings which still carries the title, **Bold Square**, but now displays little of its original size or indeed history.

Constructed by the now largely forgotten but highly industrious Thomas Lunt, the man who gave Chester its now extinct Union and Commercial Halls, as well as its still surviving Union Bridge and Egerton Street, Bold Square was thought to be named after a lady called Eleanor Bold at the beginning of the 19th century. Although it is difficult to visualise the property now, given the level of modernisation and associated destruction that has taken place over the past 200 years, at one time this whole area, stretching southward from these three remaining houses to the main Foregate Street would have been private gardens. A prominent local physician, Dr John Haygarth, whose name is still recalled on one of the modern high rise flats in the area, was reported to have owned a substantial city property on this same site during the 18th century. Comprising his main house, formal gardens, numerous outbuildings, coach houses and stables, the property was thought to have been acquired by Mrs Bold following Haygarth's death. Although it's unclear whether or not Lunt redeveloped the site on behalf of Eleanor Bold or purchased part of the extensive lands off her for his own commercial purposes, either way she is still recalled some two centuries later through the remaining section of the square that continues to bear her name. Perhaps typically for Lunt, who seemed to specialise in building large commercial halls, the northern section of the site, almost adjoining the banks of the Chester and Nantwich canal, was said to have contained a large industrial building which later housed Churton's Auction Mart, the same company who were also associated with the nearby Forest House in Love street.

Chester's **City Road** was originally laid out following the construction of Chester General Railway Station and was designed to offer a direct passenger link from the rail terminus to the centre of the city either by carriage or by foot. Prior to the cutting of the Chester Canal and the laying out of City Road with its handful of brand new hotels and guesthouses, the land in this part of the city suburbs was reported to have formed part of the city's fields, where cattle were grazed and crops grown. Cutting through the historic Horn Lane (Milton Street & Lead Works Lane) City Road later became the site for the Presbyterian Octagon Chapel and the Royalty Theatre dating from 1869 which was initially known as the Oxford Music Hall. A number of other hotels were constructed to serve the growing numbers of rail passengers who visited the ancient city of Chester, including the Albion Hotel, formerly the Queens Commercial Hotel and later the Town Crier which is reported to date from 1867 and said to have been linked to the Queens Hotel which stood on the opposite side of the road by an underground passage. The road and foot bridge that carries traffic across City Road today displays a construction date of 1863, which confirms that prior to this date rail passengers completed their journey into the city centre via Brook Street or Egerton Street, both of which had pre-existing access across the Chester and Nantwich Canal.

The site of the **General Railway Station** itself was said to have formerly been occupied by kitchen gardens and fields which were fed by the nearby Flookers Brook which in earlier times had marked the limits of the city's boundary in that area. The engineering contractor for the station was Thomas Brassey, the famed railway engineer, who was reported to have begun work on the new project on the 1st August 1847, with the station being opened to the public exactly 12 months later, in August 1848. By reputation Chester's new rail terminus was thought to be one of the most extensive railway buildings in the country, measuring over a quarter of a mile in length, consisting of both departure and arrival sheds and incorporating waiting and refreshment rooms, booking offices, lavatories and sheds for both cabs and buses. The station complex was also reported to include a private waterworks and a gasworks which was capable of producing six and a half million feet of gas per annum. The first floor of the station building included offices for the various railway companies and attendant staff.

The building was reported to have been designed by Francis Thompson, who was a partner in the architectural firm of Wild and Thompson, although much of the construction work, both building and engineering was undertaken by Brassey himself, who was born at Aldford, but went on to become the most noted railway builder in the world during the 19th century. The stations original iron train sheds were thought to have been designed by C H Wild with some help offered by the famous Robert Stephenson who was at the time, engineer for the Chester & Holyhead Railway Company. The cost of building the general station was reported to have been borne by a number of individual railway companies, including: London & North Western; Shrewsbury & Chester; Chester & Holyhead and the Birkenhead, Lancashire and Cheshire Railway Co. Stephenson was reportedly called in to help organise the linking of the six separate railway routes which were said to have converged at Chester, such was the number of railway companies and the popularity of rail travel during the Victorian period. This rapid expansion of the Chester station complex was also reported to have caused the loss of further land around the Flookersbrook area, including the historic properties and market gardens which had inhabited the area for hundreds of years.

Officially opened on the 26th April 1860, the **Queens Railway Hotel** was ravaged by fire on the 25th November 1861, just 19 months after it had first begun operating and forcing a large-scale rebuilding of the property which was then simply renamed as the Queens Hotel. The local architect Thomas M Penson along with Mr Cornelius Sherlock, a Liverpool based architect worked together to redesign the replacement building, which was completed by the following year. The statue of Queen Victoria which stands above the main entrance to the hotel dates from 1963 and was made by a Mr T Murphy, replacing an earlier figure which had been fashioned by a Mr Bossiter, but presented to the new hotel by its company chairman Mr Tetherington when the new premises were first opened. Across the road, at the north-eastern junction of City Road, the Queens Commercial Hotel was erected sometime after the rebuilding of the main Queen's Hotel and was originally linked to its contemporary by an underground passageway that ran below the main street. The title of this later hotel, identifying it as a commercial hostelry, would appear to suggest that it was designed to cater for less affluent clients, those that could not afford or would not be welcomed at the main Queen's Hotel. However, the Commercial Hotel does not appear to have thrived like its partner, but was said to have been rebuilt and renamed as the Albion Hotel in 1867, marking a move for that particular sign from Chester's Lower Bridge Street area.

The **Leadworks Shot Tower** which dates from around 1800 is reported to be the only such shot tower surviving in Britain since the 1950's and was said to have been constructed by Walkers Maltby and Company. The tower was designed to produce lead shot by means of gravity, with the shot produced in the tower initially being intended for use during the Napoleonic Wars. Throughout much of its lifetime the Lead work's was a significant employer within the city, but changes in fashions, price and attitudes ultimately saw a serious decline in the widespread use of Lead based materials, apart from in highly specialised industrial applications. Consequently, in later years the company was heavily dependant on producing a much smaller range of products, which were almost inevitably affected by imports of far cheaper foreign made substitutes. Today, the site of Chester's historic Lead Works is almost entirely occupied by blocks of modern apartments, which are undoubtedly far cleaner than their industrial predecessor, but add little to the colour or history of the site that they now occupy.

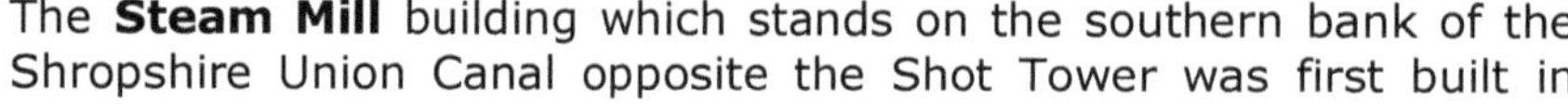

The **Steam Mill** building which stands on the southern bank of the Shropshire Union Canal opposite the Shot Tower was first built in

1834 and was thought to have been commissioned by Frances A Frost a successful flour miller who had purchased the land, following the establishment of the city's canal system in the 1770's. The first building was reported to have been seriously damaged by fire in the 1860's and then had to be rebuilt, but business was resumed and continued successfully until the mill was sold to Miln's Seeds in the late 19th century. Between the site of this former Seed Mill, which is now inhabited by a number of disparate commercial tenants and the main City Road is a large, apparently 19th century building that was said to have housed an unsuccessful shoe factory from 1864 to 1866. Later used for many years as an electrical retailer's store, then an antiques emporium, the site now appears to be occupied by a rather lavish restaurant.

The **Royalty Theatre** which once occupied a site on the eastern flank of City Road, to the south of the 1863 bridge which carries the roadway over the Shropshire Union Canal, has in recent years become yet another victim of the headlong dash to redevelop the historic fabric of Chester. Initially constructed as little more than a timber building dating from around 1869, when it was known as the Oxford Music Hall, within 12 months this building was reported to have been replaced by a much larger wooden structure, erected by a local builder called Farrimond. Ostensibly built for an Italian circus entrepreneur called Quaglieni the new theatre only appears to have hosted the circus for a single season, before the site passed into the hands of a Mr Barnes, a local cab proprietor, who subsequently leased out parts of the new building for entertainment.

By June 1870 it was being advertised as the Theatre Royal, even though another site of that name had previously existed in Northgate Street and a Mr Hengler was reported to have leased the City Road location to host a series of equine exhibitions. When that show finished in the same year, Mr Hengler was thought to have been replaced by a dancing company at the theatre and by the end of 1871 a number of circuses and shows were known to have appeared at the venue, including Cook's Royal Circus. For the next five a resident waxworks show was said to have occupied the property, although by 1876 the building was once again being used for live entertainment, only by this time it had been renamed as the Prince of Wales theatre. Presumably leased from the previously mentioned Mr Barnes, the new theatre was reportedly operated by a Mr Sheridan, but still seems to have been a largely unsuccessful enterprise and by 1882 the premises were closed once again.

Later on, the theatre site was again leased from its owner, only this time by two relatively successful city businessmen, Mr Walker from the city's Lead Works and Mr Carter, the proprietor of the Cestrian Hotel which lay on the opposite side of City Road. These two gentlemen arranged for the generally ruinous wooden building to be taken down and then replaced by a permanent brick built theatre, which was said to have been designed by a Mr B E Entwistle from Southport. Begun in April 1882, this new property was thought to have been completed by December of the same year and in the meantime it seems that Mr Carter had become the sole owner of the building, although quite why Mr Walker had withdrawn from the venture isn't entirely clear.

Nevertheless, Mr Carter and his family were reported to have held ownership of the theatre from 1882 until 1909, when they finally sold their interests in the property to a Mr Bode, who also acquired Mr Barnes' holdings immediately to the south of the theatre site. This property was said to have comprised a carriage building factory and extensive stables, from where Mr Barnes had previously operated his cab business, all of which were taken down by their new owner Mr Bode. According to contemporary reports, Mr Bode's intention was to erect a 4,000 seat Hippodrome on the two adjoining City Road sites and he even went as far as commissioning the noted local architect W T Lockwood, the son of renowned city architect Thomas Lockwood, to prepare plans for his new entertainment palace. Sadly for Mr Bode though, there was such a strong public reaction against his new Hippodrome that the city Council rejected his application for planning permission and he was forced to abandon his scheme.

By 1932 Mr Bode was reported to have sold the Theatre site to a gentleman called Keyes, whose family were thought to have retained possession of it right through to 1966 when it was closed once again. Although the theatre was a generally popular venue, the age of live entertainment had long been supplanted, first by the cinema, then by television and an apparent lack of investment in the theatres fabric by the family, were all thought to have contributed to its almost certain failure. In later years the property was known to have hosted a succession of various events, being employed as a bingo hall, wrestling arena and a place for occasional cabaret shows, but with little if any serious investment made to modernise the premises and virtually guaranteeing its later fate. By the latter years of the 20th century, parts of the building were being used to host a variety of city nightclubs, but ultimately such limited use and lack of financial investment simply helped to hasten its end. Finally, in 2001, property developers who had purchased the site were given planning permission to redevelop the site and by February of that year the contractors began demolishing the theatre for the last time. As elsewhere in the city, another little piece of Chester's long and colourful history was finally consigned to the builders skip and replaced with a highly functional, generally out-of-place modern building, which in this case hosts a brand new Premier Travel Inn.

At the southern end of today's City Road where it meets the new inner ring road system, on the western flank of the street stands the City Road Presbyterian Chapel which was raised sometime after the main thoroughfare was first laid out. Prior to the construction of this later Chapel the site was reported to have housed the notable **Octagon Chapel** which was first built in 1764 and where John Wesley preached in 1776, 1786 and 1790. Prior to the building of the Octagon Chapel the site was said to have been occupied by a temporary structure, known as the Barn Sanctuary, but that was demolished to make way for its more famous successor. However, it was reported that the congregation of the Octagon had moved to a new Chapel in St John Street by 1812 and their former place of worship continued to stand only until 1864 when it was finally demolished to make way for the new City Road.

The final building of note, in what remains of the original City Road, is the bank building occupying no's 4 to 10 at the thoroughfare's eastern junction with the area formerly known as "The Bars". Designed by Thomas Lockwood in 1900, exactly who commissioned the building is unclear, but it seems to have functioned as a bank or finance house throughout its life, a role that it continues to fulfil today.

www.ingramcontent.com/pod-product-compliance
Ingram Content Group UK Ltd.
Pitfield, Milton Keynes, MK11 3LW, UK
UKHW050615260726
13967UKWH00008B/2874